Demographic Perspective of China's Economic Development

China is historically famous for its high demographic dividend and its huge working population, and this has driven tremendous economic growth over the past few decades. However, that population has begun to shrink and the Lewis turning point whereby surplus rural population has been absorbed into manufacturing is also approaching, leading to great change in the Chinese labor market. Will this negatively affect China's economic growth? Can the "Middle-Income Trap" be avoided? What reforms should be made on the labor supply side? This book tackles these key questions.

This book is a collection of 14 papers presenting the author's observations, analysis, and opinions of China's long-term economic development from the demographic perspective, while analyzing real economic problems from the past and including policy recommendations. It provides a critical reference for scholars and students interested in Chinese economic development and demographic perspectives on economic development.

Cai Fang is Professor, Vice President, Party Group Member, and Academician at the Chinese Academy of Social Sciences. Professor Cai's research interests include labor economics, China's economic growth, and income distribution. His recent publications include *Demystifying the Economic Growth in Transition China*, *China's Economic Growth Prospects: From Demographic Dividend to Reform Dividend*, and *Perceiving Truth and Ceasing Doubts*: *What Can We Learn from 40 Years of China's Reform and Opening-Up?*

China Perspectives

The *China Perspectives* series focuses on translating and publishing works by leading Chinese scholars, writing about both global topics and China-related themes. It covers Humanities & Social Sciences, Education, Media and Psychology, as well as many interdisciplinary themes.

This is the first time any of these books have been published in English for international readers. The series aims to put forward a Chinese perspective, give insights into cutting-edge academic thinking in China, and inspire researchers globally.

Titles in economics partly include:

Chinese Macroeconomic Operation
Liu Shucheng

The Chinese Path to Economic Dual Transformation
Li Yining

Hyperinflation
A World History
Liping He

Game Theory and Society
Weiying Zhang

China's Fiscal Policy
Theoretical and Situation Analysis
Gao Peiyong

Trade Openness and China's Economic Development
Miaojie YU

Perceiving Truth and Ceasing Doubts
What Can We Learn from 40 Years of China's Reform and Opening-Up?
Cai Fang

Demographic Perspective of China's Economic Development
Cai Fang

For more information, please visit https://www.routledge.com/series/CPH

Demographic Perspective of China's Economic Development

Cai Fang

Routledge
Taylor & Francis Group
LONDON AND NEW YORK

中国社会科学出版社
CHINA SOCIAL SCIENCES PRESS

This book is published with financial support from the Chinese Fund for the Humanities and Social Sciences.

First published in English 2020
by Routledge
2 Park Square, Milton Park, Abingdon, Oxon OX14 4RN

and by Routledge
605 Third Avenue, New York, NY 10017

First issued in paperback 2021

Routledge is an imprint of the Taylor & Francis Group, an Informa business

Translated by Cai Fang

Publisher's Note
The publisher has gone to great lengths to ensure the quality of this reprint but points out that some imperfections in the original copies may be apparent.

English Version by permission of China Social Sciences Press.

British Library Cataloguing-in-Publication Data
A catalogue record for this book is available from the British Library

Library of Congress Cataloging-in-Publication Data
A catalog record has been requested for this book

ISBN 13: 978-1-03-223590-5 (pbk)
ISBN 13: 978-0-367-47103-3 (hbk)

Typeset in Times New Roman
by Newgen Publishing UK

Demographic Perspective of China's Economic Development

Cai Fang

Routledge
Taylor & Francis Group
LONDON AND NEW YORK

中国社会科学出版社
CHINA SOCIAL SCIENCES PRESS

This book is published with financial support from the Chinese Fund for the Humanities and Social Sciences.

First published in English 2020
by Routledge
2 Park Square, Milton Park, Abingdon, Oxon OX14 4RN

and by Routledge
605 Third Avenue, New York, NY 10017

First issued in paperback 2021

Routledge is an imprint of the Taylor & Francis Group, an Informa business

Translated by Cai Fang

Publisher's Note
The publisher has gone to great lengths to ensure the quality of this reprint but points out that some imperfections in the original copies may be apparent.

English Version by permission of China Social Sciences Press.

British Library Cataloguing-in-Publication Data
A catalogue record for this book is available from the British Library

Library of Congress Cataloging-in-Publication Data
A catalog record has been requested for this book

ISBN 13: 978-1-03-223590-5 (pbk)
ISBN 13: 978-0-367-47103-3 (hbk)

Typeset in Times New Roman
by Newgen Publishing UK

Contents

Figures

Tables

Part 1

New stage of demographic transition

1 Demographic transition, demographic dividend, and the Lewis turning point in China

1.1 Introduction

One of the hot topics that inspire debates among scholars, policy researchers, and even policy-makers is whether Chinese economic growth is losing its source and momentum from demographic dividends. Another related topic is whether China will reach its Lewis turning point—namely, labor supply will no longer be unlimited. In a research paper, Cai and Wang (2005) estimated that the decline in the population dependence ratio, as a proxy for demographic dividend, contributed 26.8 percent to per capita GDP growth during 1982 to 2000, and warned that such a demographic dividend would disappear after 2013 when the dependence ratio would stop decreasing and begin increasing. By examining changes in population age structure, labor demand trends, widespread labor shortages, and wage rises of ordinary workers, Cai (2008a, 2008b) asserts that the Lewis turning point has indeed come, and points out its policy implications in terms of growth pattern transformation, income distribution trends, labor market institutional construction, and human capital accumulation.

While some researchers and even some policy documents support and cite the conclusion about the arrival of the Lewis turning point, others strongly disagree. In previous replies, Cai (2008a) tried to provide a wide range of evidence to defend his arguments. It turns out that people come out with conflicting opinions about economic reality, and explain the same phenomenon in different ways. Many still firmly hold to the conventional wisdom that there is a massive and increasing working-age population and thus endless surplus labor force in rural areas, and that this is an unchangeable characteristic of China. Propositions which assert the possibility of labor shortage or disappearance of the surplus labor force in agriculture—namely that the Lewis turning point is arriving—are not widely agreed.[1] Specifically, all skeptical and critical comments on the judgment about an ongoing Lewis turning point, which result from a static understanding of population and labor force in China, are generally puzzled by the Chinese statistics. In what follows, I unveil some aspects of such statistical puzzles.

First, given that the official survey on utilization of the agricultural workforce is unable to reflect the fast-changing reality of agricultural production, some scholars are unaware of the changed situation, while others who have tried to understand the statistics are actually trapped in "the tyranny of numbers", as was Young (1994) when he tried to challenge the "East Asian miracle". Either case makes any endeavor of econometric analysis hostage to the data. The point is that economic reform in China has been too fast for the statistical system to catch up (Ravallion and Chen, 1999). One of the many examples that cause confusion concerns the accurate numbers of the agricultural workforce actually used. In 2008, the reported total labor force engaged in agriculture was 307 million, accounting for 39.6 percent of the country's total employment, and the figure provided by the 2008 Agricultural Census was even higher. However, the actual input of labor in agricultural production, calculated based on agricultural costs survey data, turns out to be much less than any published aggregated figures (Cai and Wang, 2008). Taking into consideration the changing trend of working-age population in rural areas, the updated situation of labor migration from rural to urban sectors, and the extent to which agriculture is mechanized, one must conclude that the actually used workforce in agricultural production is much less than what official statistical publications declare. Therefore, the declaration that there is large amount of surplus labor to be shifted from agriculture (e.g., Lau, 2010a) and the econometric estimation of marginal productivity of labor in agriculture (e.g., Minami and Ma, 2009), which are both based on the aggregated dataset, tend to overestimate the degree of labor surplus in agriculture and conclude that the Lewis turning point has not come to China.

Second, scholars have difficulties in interpreting statistics on the labor market and rural and urban employment, and thus they often elicit conclusions that deviate from reality. As the result of sectoral changes and increasing diversification of ownership, especially after the labor market shock in the late 1990s, multifaceted sectors have appeared to absorb labor into urban areas, contrary to the pre-reform period when state and collective sectors dominated employment absorption. Among those sectors of employment, large-scale informal employment, as the byproduct of reemployment of the laid-off and of diversity of employment, is new to China. Meanwhile, massive numbers of rural laborers have transformed their jobs from agricultural to non-agricultural sectors, amounting to 240 million, of which 145 million migrated into cities. In routine statistics, neither informal employment of urban residents nor employment of migrant workers in urban sectors has been authoritatively reported, except for estimated figures of migrant workers based on sampling surveys and aggregated estimates of informally employed urban residents under certain assumptions (Cai, 2004). We can view the difference between the number of total employment based on the unit reporting system and the number of employment based on the household survey as a proxy for urban informal employment, which amounts to 95.1 million and accounts for 31.5 percent of total urban employment in 2008. It is, however, useless if one wants to do any statistical analysis on structural characteristics of total employment, because of lack of disaggregated data on it. Moreover, the statistical authority has so far not promulgated an alternative surveyed unemployment rate data series to the discredited registered unemployment rate, and that leads scholars to do various guesstimates on the unemployment rate. Based on incomplete employment data and unfounded guesstimates, Chinese and international scholars have often educed conclusions such as zero growth of employment and a high and increasing unemployment rate (Rawski, 2001; Solinger, 2001; Ru et al., 2008, p. 22) and doubt the authenticity of the widespread labor shortage.

Third, there is no officially published systematic data and up to date information on the status of demographic change and population dynamics. While various rounds of national population censuses provide information about population changes, due to lack of consensus on some important parameters of China's demographics such as the actual total fertility rate (TFR),[2] no authoritative projections of population change, including predictions of magnitude and the age structure of the population, have been periodically publicized. The public and academia therefore do not have updated information about population development trends, and many conceive that the peak of population growth will be reached in or after 2040 and then the total population in China will be as many as 1.6 billion (e.g., Lau, 2010b). More specifically, most scholars ignore the fact that the growth of China's working-age population has been slowing and thus the demographic foundation of unlimited labor supply has been shrinking, and therefore they are unwilling to accept the assertion of an ongoing Lewis turning point associated with a diminishing demographic dividend.

It is obvious that an undistorted understanding of the status and trends of demographic transition will help scholars and policy researchers better understand the state of the labor market and will serve as a foundation for policy decisions on how China can sustain its economic growth. The following sections of the paper argue that demographic transition and dual economy development have a common starting point, related and similar characteristics of development stages, as well as overlapping processes to a large extent, so that the demographic window of opportunity in which a demographic dividend is obtained is one of the stages of dual economy development. Accordingly, the theoretical and empirical work and reasoning about a diminishing demographic dividend and incoming Lewis turning point kill two birds with one stone. The rest of the paper is organized as follows. Section 1.2 reveals a stylized fact about relationship between demographic transition and dual economy development based on international experiences. Section 1.3 depicts China's process of demographic transition and its impact on economic growth. Section 1.4 tries to answer the question of how the "aging before affluence" gap can be narrowed. Section 1.5 concludes by drawing policy implications of the issues discussed in the paper.

1.2 Stages of demographic transition and development of dual economy

The theory of dual economy coined by Lewis (1954) divides a typical developing economy into two sectors: the agricultural and modern sectors. Because labor force is superfluous relative to capital and land in agriculture, its marginal productivity in the sector is very low, even as low as zero or below. As the modern sector expands, surplus labor in agriculture is transferred to the modern sector without substantial rise of wages, and the whole process is typically called the development of dual economy. Such a process continues until it reaches a point at which the growth of labor demand exceeds growth of labor supply and further labor transfer requires increase in unskilled workers' wage rate. That point is generally called the Lewis turning point. In spite of its ups and downs in economics history (Ranis, 2004), the Lewisian theory of the dual economy has always remained an important theoretical model of development economics.

Even before Lewis's prominent paper first appeared, the mature form of demographic transition theory had been published already.[3] Corresponding to pre- and post-industrialization periods, demographic transition is categorized into three stages, which are respectively characterized by (1) high birth rate, high death rate, and low natural growth rate of population, (2) high birth rate, low death rate, and high natural growth rate of population, and (3) low birth rate, low death rate, and low natural growth rate of population. Although we cannot judge whether Lewis noticed those literatures in demography, there is no lack of demographic assumptions related to the theory of demographic transition in his description of development of dual economy. While defining unlimited supply of labor, the key concept of the theory of dual economy, he explains:

> unlimited supply of labor may be said to exist in those countries where population is so large relatively to capital and natural resources, that there are large sectors of the economy where the marginal productivity of labor is negligible, zero, or even negative.

The connotative assumption of this statement is that a typical dual economy characterized by unlimited supply of labor is at the second stage of demographic transition—that is, natural growth rate of population is high as the result of declined mortality and inertial high birth rate. Since agriculture is the primary sector in the sectoral chain, it is the first place where the abundant population and surplus labor force roost.

The key to comprehending the logical and empirical relationship between demographic transition and development of dual economy is to explore how demographic dividend is engendered and obtained. In early literature on demography and economics, the population–development nexus was discussed by focusing on the relationship between economic growth rate and population growth rate or population quantum, while the discussion on demographic transition was mainly about demographic contents such as population quantity, birth rate, and death rate, but not closely related to economic growth. Besides, mainstream growth theory, while incorporating population into endogenous growth, usually neglects characteristics of demographic transition of dual economy. After long neglect of economic development and structural characteristics of population, particularly the relation between population age structure and labor supply, as all developed countries and many newly industrialized economies successively completed their demographic transition process, demographers became conscious of population-aging and its consequences. Economists farther unveil the change in working-age population going with fertility decline and its effect on sources of economic growth (Williamson, 1997). That is, in the interval between a sooner decline of death rate and later decline of birth rate, natural growth rate of population is usually rising at its fastest, and the youth dependence ratio is also increasing. After a certain period of time, as fertility decreases and the baby boomers grow up, the proportion of working-age population is accordingly enhanced. The further decline in fertility as a result of economic and social developments causes slowdown of the natural growth rate of population, and the structural consequence of such a dynamic is population-aging. In short, following a reversed U-shape pattern—namely, the natural growth rate of population first increases and then declines after a turning point, with an interval of about one generation, the growth rate of working-age population presents a similar pattern of changes.

During the period in which the population age structure is most productive, adequate supply of labor and a high savings rate afford an extra source of economic growth and thus form a demographic dividend. Consequently, once demographic transition exceeds this stage—namely, the population age structure becomes less and less productive, because of the rapid aging—such conventionally defined demographic dividend gradually disappears. Since the stages in demographic transition can be sufficiently characterized by changes in total fertility rate (TFR), one can theoretically expect the following relation between demographic transition and economic growth (Figure 1.1): the stage of high TFR coincides with a steady state of low growth rate; as TFR falls and as a result a more productive population age structure comes into being, the demographic dividend promotes economic growth to a higher rate; when TFR further drops to a low level and the population ages, the economic growth rate again shrinks to a low steady state. Correspondingly, at a certain stage of demographic transition when TFR declines rapidly and the population age structure becomes more and more productive, there forms a demographic window of opportunity.

It is worth noting that factors impacting the performance of economic growth are multifold, not just population. This is also true in explaining both the steady state of the growth rate of low-income economies, known for the poverty trap, and the steady state of the growth rate of high-income

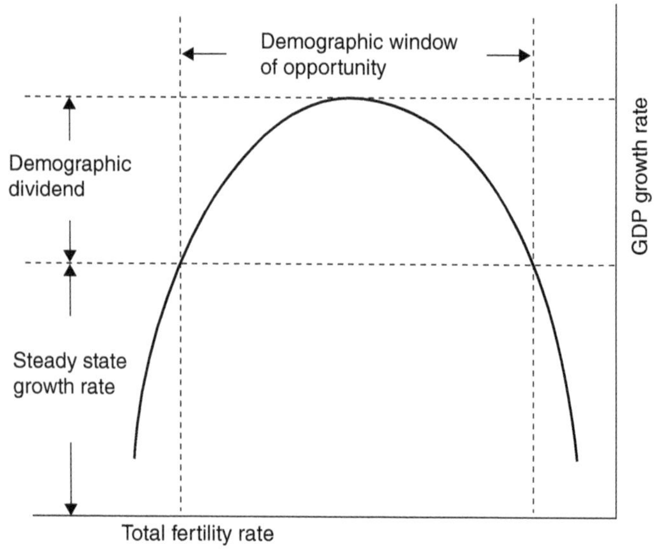

Figure 1.1 Relationship between fertility and economic growth.

economies struggling at the technological innovation frontier. For example, in empirical works defending neoclassical growth theory, economists have found more than one hundred explanatory variables, which are statistically significant in unveiling determinants of growth performances, but none is sufficient and exclusive (Sala-i-Martin, 1997). For simplicity, we also put aside the retroaction effect of economic growth on demographic transition[4] and focus on the straightforward relationship between fertility and economic growth. Under the assumption made above, this fertility–growth nexus can be deduced from the theory of demographic dividend and confirmed empirically.

The panel data from World Development Indicators enable us to picture a descriptive relationship between annual GDP growth rates and TFR levels among countries in the period from 1960 to recent years. For those countries and years for which data are available, annual GDP growth rates ranged from –51 to 106 percent. To avoid the complication of explaining the outliers, we ignore those extreme numbers and only investigate those between 0 and 10 percent, which are assumed to be the normal span of annual GDP growth rate. According to the foregoing discussion, the relationship between economic growth rate and fertility is not a simple linear one but follows an algebraic relationship of a quadratic function. That is, as TFR declines, the economic growth rate increases first and then declines. In Figure 1.2, according to the function relations between GDP growth rate and TFR and the square term of TFR, we present the fitted value of the annual growth rate of GDP with a 95 percent confidence interval.

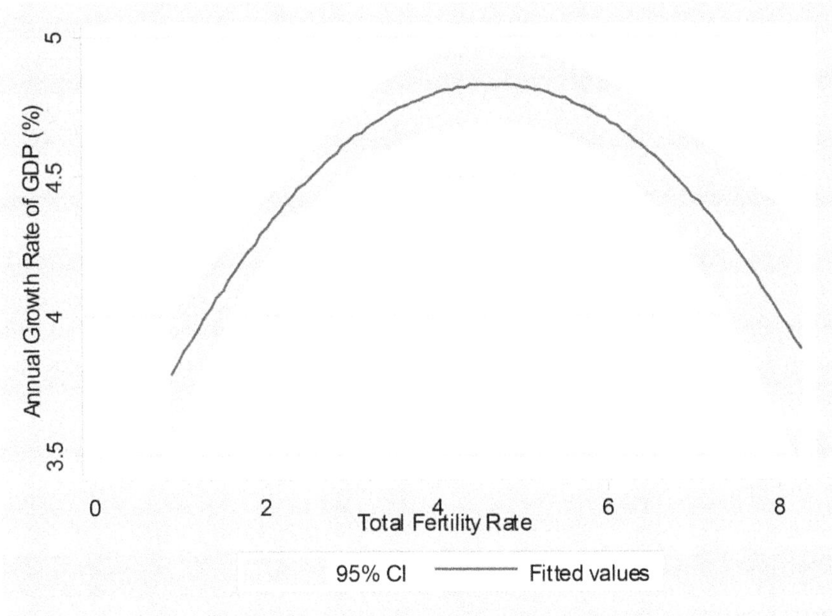

Figure 1.2 Empirical relationship between TFR and GDP growth.
Source: Calculation based on dataset of World Development Indicators.

Figure 1.2 intuitively pictures a reversed U-shape pattern of GDP growth rate against decline in TFR: countries at the earlier stage of demographic transition characterized by high TFR usually suffer poor economic performance; as their TFR levels fall, economic growth speeds up; after a certain point, as TFR further declines and demographic transition enters a later stage characterized by very low TFR, economic growth tends to slow down. Such a simplified empirical curve is perfectly consistent with the theoretical prediction described previously. To further examine the statistical significance of the relationship between TFR and economic growth, by assuming nonlinear correlation and using foregoing data, we regress GDP growth rate on TFR and the squared term of TFR (Table 1.1). The regression results show the reverse U-shape relation between GDP growth and TFR by revealing the significantly positive sign of the TFR coefficient and negative sign of the squared term of TFR.

While the more precise explanation based on both economics theory and empirical evidence requires much more work, the plain fertility–growth nexus here is a sufficient framework, with which we are now in the position of being able to investigate actual relations between demographic transition perceived in demography, demographic dividend coined by demographic economists,

Table 1.1 Regression results: the relation between TFR and growth

	Coefficient	*Standard error*	*t value*	*P* > | *t* |
TFR	0.6852	0.1133	6.05	0.000
TFR square	–0.0736	0.0137	–5.38	0.000
Constant term	3.2359	0.1909	16.95	0.000
Observations	3380			

and the Lewis turning point deduced from development economics, based on China's experiences. In the next section, we will analyze the formation and anticipated disappearance of demographic dividend, and declare the advent of the Lewis turning point in the process of China's economic development.

1.3 The economic impacts of Chinese demographic transition

In the first two decades after the establishment of the People's Republic of China in 1949, the economy rapidly recovered and people's living standard improved well, which pushed China's demographic transition into the second stage. That is, eliminating the abnormal years between the late 1950s and early 1960s, mortality substantially fell, the birth rate kept at a chronic height, and as a result the natural growth rate was constantly high. TFR kept as high as 6 until the 1970s and afterwards it declined dramatically. However, the fastest decline of TFR happened before the one-child policy was formally implemented. TFR dropped by 3.5 percentage points, from 5.8 to 2.3, in the decade of 1970 to 1980, while it dropped by 0.5 to 0.7 percentage points in the entire period between 1980, in which the central government announced a compulsory population control policy, and the present day, when TFR is agreed to be 1.6 to 1.8, which are both well below replacement level. Such a fact shows that the orderly switch-over of major stages of demographic transition is primarily the result of economic growth and social development. In the period of demographic transition from the second to third stage, population at working age grows faster than dependent population and therefore the proportion of working-age population becomes larger and larger, which has released the demographic dividend and upgraded the economic growth rate to a level above steady state.

Although the population dependence ratio—namely, the ratio of dependent population aged 14 and younger or 65 and older to working-age population aged 15 to 64—declined as early as in the middle of the 1960s, and the substantial increase of working-age population and its share in total population, associated with a dramatic fall of the population dependence ratio, started in the middle of the 1970s (Figure 1.3). Such a favorable age structure of population has been translated into demographic dividend that spurred unprecedented performance of economic growth. A series of publications (e.g., Cai, 2008a, 2008b; Cai and Wang, 2005) explain the rationale, process, and empirics of the demographic dividend in the development of China's dual

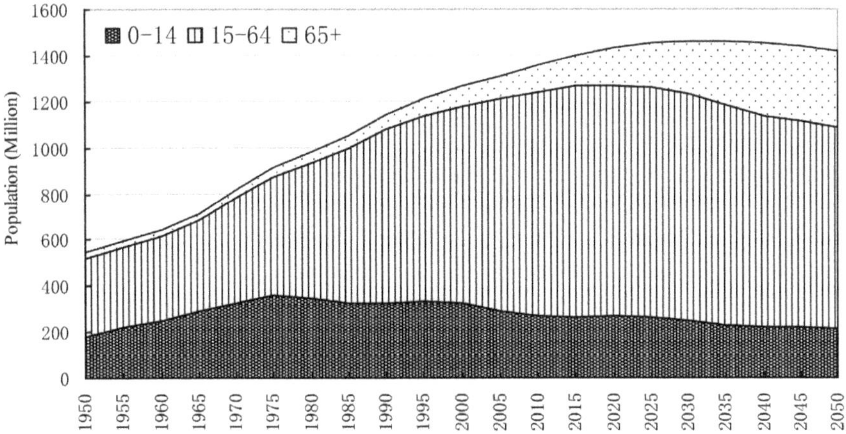

Figure 1.3 Changing trends of age structure of population.
Source: United Nations, 2009.

economy. Those studies also argue that as such a dividend begins diminishing at the stage of demographic transition characterized by low birth rate, low mortality, and low growth rate of population, the development of the Chinese dual economy has reached its critical period of time, the Lewis turning point. This paper is an endeavor to synthesize demographic transition, demographic dividend, and the Lewis turning point, accounting for the logical and historical relations between the three concepts and revealing the challenges facing the Chinese economy in a changing era.

The prediction of China's population and its age composition by the United Nations (2009), shown in Figure 1.3, is a scenario of medium variant and consistent with the 2000 census, the 2005 sample census, and updated (to 2008) estimates of the subsequent trends in fertility, mortality, and international migration. This prospect is by and large identical to those anticipated by various Chinese units. According to this prediction, the total population of China is going to reach its peak in 2030 and amount to 1.46 billion. Much sooner than that, the working-age population aged 15 to 64 will reach its peak, 998 million, in 2015. Although such prospects can in time be obtained from public sources, it is obvious that they are unknown information not only for the public but also for many economists. To acquaint themselves with the changing trends of Chinese population should definitely be required for the scholars who are studying and speaking of the future of Chinese economic development, and are influencing the public.

Further examining the predicted results shown in Figure 1.3, one can see that the growth speed of working-age population has been faster than that of total population in the period from 1970 to 2010, and the trend will turn the other way round—namely, the age structure of the Chinese population will no longer be productive. As the agricultural share of the labor force declines over time, the current demand of urban sectors for labor has been sufficiently met by rural-to-urban migration. As an important part of reform's opening-up and growth in the past 30 years, the massive migration has drawn worldwide attention and been recognized as the largest peacetime movement of population in human history (Roberts et al., 2004). In recent years, as a result of long-standing adjustment corresponding to migration, there have occurred two new phenomena to the labor relocation. On the one hand, the migrant workers become further unwanted as mechanization of agricultural production has increasingly accelerated. On the other hand, the demand of urban sectors for migrant workers becomes more and more rigid and indispensable, as a result of shrinkage of the urban local labor force (Cai, 2010).

According to another prediction, which takes into account the impacts of rural-to-urban migration (Hu, 2009), by 2015, the amount of incremental working-age population in urban areas will be less than that of reduced working-age population in rural areas (Figure 1.4), the same conclusion drawn by the above-cited prediction. This implies that without substantial enhancement of wages and other incentives the migrant workers will not fill up the gap vacated by rapid reduction of the urban labor force. In the course of urbanization, those migrant workers and their accompanying family members who live an urban area for more than six months are already counted as urban residents, so the number of statistically recognized rural residents has been rapidly reduced. The labor market has gradually responded to this situation, which is embodied in tremendous enhancement of the wages of ordinary workers, on the one hand, and nationwide labor shortage, on

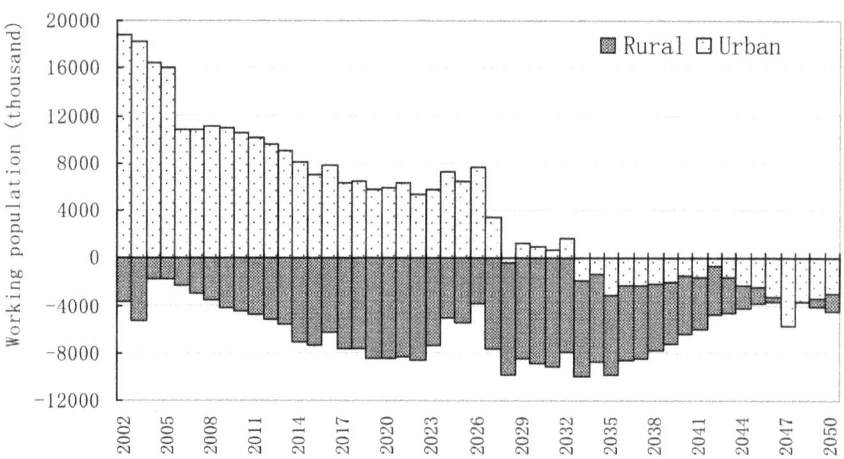

Figure 1.4 Changes of working-age population of rural and urban China.
Source: Hu, 2009.

the other. According to the definition in development economics, those phenomena are signals of the Lewis turning point.

1.4 How to close the "aging before affluence" gap?

Worldwide experiences show that economic growth and social development are major driving forces of demographic transition, while the implementation of population policy plays a relatively minor role additional to the former. Like China, the Asian economies such as Korea, Singapore, Thailand, and Taiwan where no compulsory fertility policy has been enforced have experienced dramatic decline in fertility, from high TFR similar to China in the 1950s to as low as below replacement level in the 1990s. Even in India, where economic growth and social development have not performed as well as in China and those other Asian economies, and where demographic transition has therefore been relatively lagging behind, fertility has also been declining by following a similar path (Lin, 2006).

In spite of its unprecedented economic growth in the past 30 years, due to its late outset compared to the Asian economies above-mentioned, China entered into the new stage of demographic transition at relatively low income per capita, which is characterized by "aging before affluence". In 2000, the proportion of people aged 65 and over in China's total population was 6.8 percent, identical to the world average, whereas China's per capita GNI was only 17.3 percent of the world average based on the official exchange rate, and 56.3 percent of the world average based on purchasing power parity. While one must admit that the strict implementation of the one-child policy is an accelerator pushing down fertility, the demographic transition, in the final analysis, is the result of outstanding economic growth and social development (Du, 2004). The difference of income level between China and developed countries is therefore the root cause of the existing "aging before affluence" gap.

Most developed countries are facing the challenges an aging population poses to sustainable economic growth and pension insurance schemes, and the efforts and effects vary from country to country. However, the developed countries, being at high-income level and on the technological innovation frontier, and therefore with increasing productivity, have dealt well with the challenges and averted the old age crisis so far. Based on their experiences, one can be confident that the key for China to tackle the challenges of shrinking working-age population and growing older-age population is to sustain its fast economic growth and quick increase in per capita income. In other words, demographic transition, thus population-aging, is an irreversible process, which cannot be stopped even if the one-child policy is abolished. The already formed "aging before affluence" gap can only be narrowed and eventually closed through catching up with the developed countries, which will put China in the ranks of high income.

As the Chinese economy ascends in the world's economic pecking order and is expected to become the second largest economy after the United States in 2010, given its slowed-down growth rate of population, the per capita GDP level of China will rapidly step up. One long-term prediction on China's economic size and per capita GDP conducted by the Japanese Center for Economic Research (JCER, 2007) shows that based on PPP and the constant US dollar of 2000, China's GDP volume will reach $17.3 trillion in 2020, $25.2 trillion in 2030, and $30.4 trillion in 2040. The predicted per capita GDP in the three reference years are $12,000, $18,000, and $22,000, respectively. An even more optimistic prediction by Fogel (2007) expects that China's total GDP will reach $123.7 trillion in 2040, and based on the predicted population of 1.46 billion, per capita GDP will be as high as $85,000 then. Those two prospects are widely divergent in terms of methodology, data used, assumptions, and therefore the predicted results. Given the debatable usage of the purchasing power parity GDP term by both researches, their prospects are unlikely to be accepted by Chinese scholars and officials.

The above-mentioned controversial prospects on China's economic volume and per capita income, however, reveal the same facts: beginning from the second decade of the twenty-first century, in the position of second-largest economy in the world, China will speed its transformation from middle-income country to high-income country. Supposing China can maintain the same (or even an appreciably lower) pace of growth rates of both total and per capita GDP realized in the past 30 years, a significant convergence of wealth between China and developed countries will be realized. In this regard, the predictions made by foreign economists reflect the correct direction and vision of the near future, and as the result of the trends, under the assumption of unchanged demographic transition, the gap between economic development level and population-aging will be eventually closed.

In Figure 1.5, we compare the age structure of China's population with less-developed countries in the years of 2000 and 2010 to show the characteristic of "aging before affluence", whereas we compare the age structure of China's population with more-developed countries in the years of 2020 to 2030 to show how the "aging before affluence" gap can be narrowed and finally closed. This shows that the fundamental avenues to dealing with population-aging in the post Lewis turning point era are threefold: (1) tap the potential of remaining demographic dividend, (2) create second demographic dividend, and (3) find new sources sustaining long-run economic growth.

1.5 Conclusion and policy implications

The analysis of China's demographic transition and its economic impacts convinces us of the close relation between demographic transition and economic development, and thus the conclusion of diminishing demographic dividend and ongoing Lewis turning point is commensurate with both economic theory and empirical evidence. Even the scorching debates around

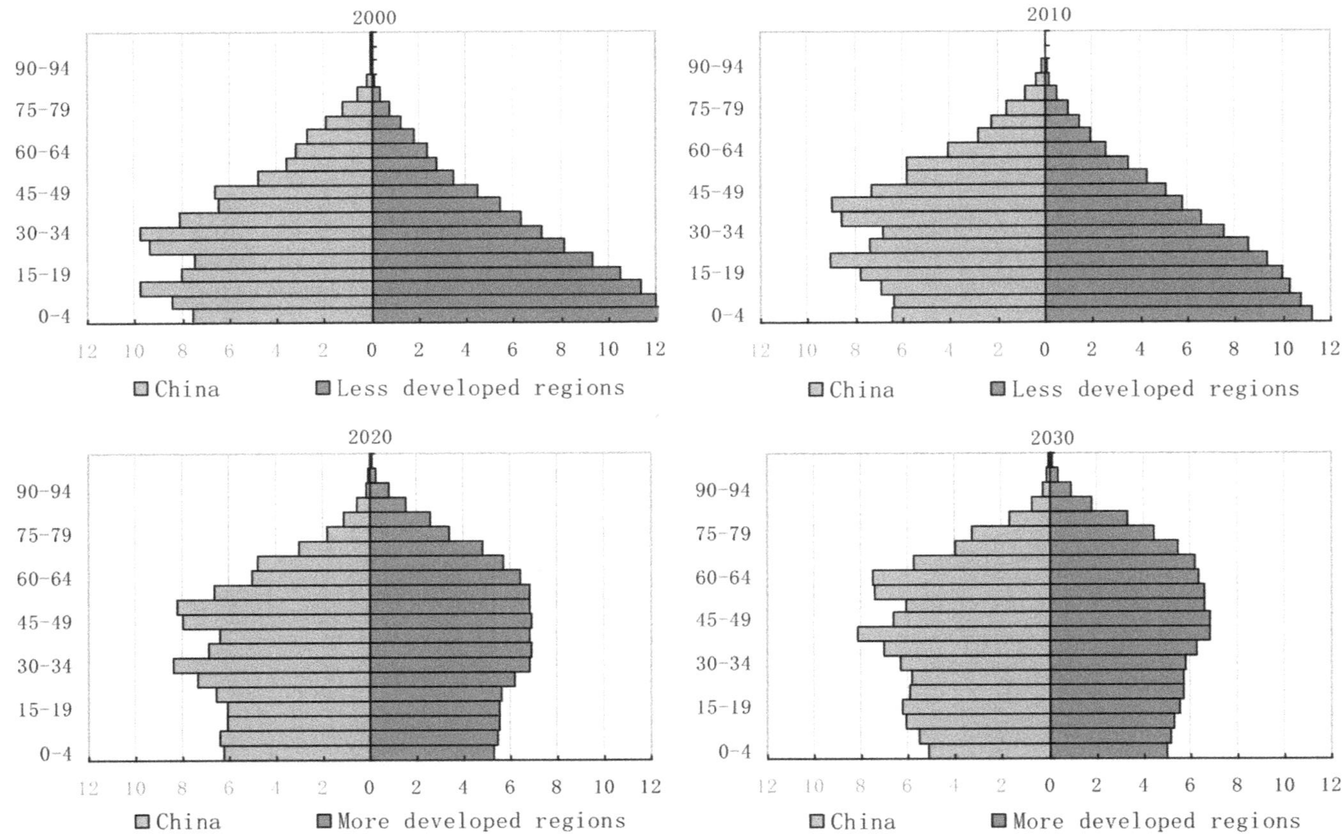

Figure 1.5 Narrowing the "aging before affluence" gap by economic catching-up.

Source: United Nations, 2009.

those judgments are, to some extent, a clue that they are not solely academic discussions, that they also have important implications for policy decisions.

The arrival of the Lewis turning point is a vital milestone for a developing economy, because only when it passes through this point does the marginal productivity of labor in the traditional (agricultural) sector begin to converge with that in modern (non-agricultural) sectors. When eventually the productivity gap among sectors disappears, the economy as a whole reaches its commercial point and the long-standing dual economy terminates. Therefore, the advent of the Lewis turning point is not dismal news at all. In contrast, being cognizant of this turning point has not only theoretical meaning but also practical significance. That is, it has important implications for governments in development policy formation, for enterprises in decision-making, and for individuals in adjustment in the face of labor market changes. In short, the sustainability of economic growth relies heavily on a sound response to the challenges brought forward by the new stage of development. In what follows we examine the potential sources of China's sustained economic growth in the post Lewis turning point period, based on experiences of forerunner economies.

First, there is still potential to exploit the existing demographic dividend in the short run. Let us first divide demographic dividend into two types: first demographic dividend and second demographic dividend. While the first demographic dividend can be defined as the scenario where labor supply is adequate and the savings rate is high, thanks to the increasing magnitude and proportion of working-age population, the second demographic dividend can be seen as the new motivation for savings resulting from precautions for the rainy day of aging and new supply of human capital supposedly brought about by postponing retirement age and extending education and training (Cai, 2009). The exploitation of the first demographic dividend has been manifested in labor transformation from agricultural to secondary and tertiary sectors, accompanied by speedy urbanization. By 2009, urban residents who lived in cities for six months or longer reached more than 600 million, accounting for 46 percent of the Chinese population. While according to the definition, some longer staying rural-to-urban migrants are counted as urbanites, because they do not legitimately have urban *hukou* and lack access to public services, with which urban residents with local *hukou* are inherently privileged, they are not fully urbanized.

More specifically, because migrant workers and their accompanying families still expect to return home to their rural area, periodically during the Chinese New Year period, and permanently after they are not needed by the urban labor market, (1) their supply of labor is not durative, (2) their consumption behavior is still rural, (3) they are not planned for in urban infrastructure policy, and (4) they have no incentives to contribute to the social security scheme, particularly to the fully funded pension system. In 2007, the proportion of urban residents in the total Chinese population, which includes those migrant workers who live in cities for more than six months, was 45 percent, whereas the proportion of population who have formal urban *hukou* was only 33 percent, which leaves an ullage of 12 percentage points between nominal and actual urbanization rates. By transforming farmers-turned-workers into migrants-turned-citizens through deepening *hukou* reform and equalizing public services to all citizens, a more complete urbanization can make full use of the first demographic dividend (Cai, 2010).

Second, there is potential to tap into a second demographic dividend in the medium run. An aging society can also possess population advantages—namely a second demographic dividend—as long as necessary institutional conditions are met (Lee and Mason, 2006; Cai, 2009). As one of the important causes of population aging, the increase in life expectancy—people living longer and more healthily—is the foundation for generating the second demographic dividend. This kind of demographic dividend includes three major sources. A first source comes from the need for old-age support and a supply of pension institutions. As long as there is a fully funded pension scheme instead of a pay-as-you-go or family support system, the older and longer-working workforce will have a larger incentive to accumulate assets, and then high savings rates can be maintained by investing in the capital market (Lee and Mason, 2006). A second source comes from the expansion of education resources. As the quantity of youth population reduces and its proportion in total population declines, the capacity of the working-age population to maintain the youth population at school relatively increases, which is a window of opportunity for extending education and training and hence accumulating human capital. A third source comes from expansion of labor force participation. Extension of retirement age is a major measure to enlarge the workforce and alleviate the burden of old-age support, which is widely employed in developed countries. For China, the obstacle to extending retirement age is that the working elderly are usually less educated and thus unwanted by employers. Until this situation is changed, extension of retirement age may put them in a vulnerable circumstance. Therefore, the exploitation of such a dividend should take a gradual approach through expanding education, especially at the levels of senior high school liberal education, occupational education, and on-job training, particularly for migrant workers.

Third, there is a great need to obtain a brand new driving force for sustainable economic growth through growth pattern transformation in the long run. Assuming scarcity of labor and thus diminishing return to capital, the neoclassical theory of growth developed based on Western experiences argues that the only way to maintain sustained economic growth is to enhance the contributive share of total factor productivity (TFP) to it (e.g., Solow, 1956). Based on this basic assumption, a handful of studies doubted the existence of the East Asian miracle and, if there is one, its sustainability (e.g., Young, 1994; Krugman, 1994). In reality, thanks partially to the characteristics of unlimited supply of labor and partially to felicitous economic policies favorable for exploiting demographic dividend, the East Asian economies had long averted the crisis of diminishing return of capital. As some major economies passed through their Lewis turning points,[5] and the newly entered stage of demographic transition no longer provided first demographic dividend, those economies represented by Japan and the Four Tigers transformed their economic growth pattern from capital- and labor-driven to more TFP-driven. Those experiences indicate that as first demographic dividend diminishes and the Lewis turning point is passed through, the driving forces of Chinese economic growth will be eventually transformed to a reliance on technological advancement and productivity enhancement. The assurance of a changed stage of development requires speeding up the pace of growth pattern transformation.

Notes

1 This paper does not intend to discuss the divarication that is caused by different definitions of the Lewis turning point. According to Lewis (1972) and Ranis and Fei (1961), the Lewis turning point can be referred to as the period of time at which labor demand exceeds labor supply while wages in the agricultural sector are not yet determined by its marginal productivity of labor, and the difference of marginal productivity of labor between agricultural and non-agricultural sectors remains. And the time when the wage rates in agricultural and non-agricultural sectors are both determined by their marginal productivity of labor and the gap in productivities disappears can be called the commercial point. Only at this time does the dual economy end.

2 The 5th National Population Census conducted in 2000 shows that China's TFR was 1.32, which is even lower than the policy-allowable level of 1.51. Many doubt such a result (e.g., Yu, 2002). Since then, debates on what is the actual TFR of China have existed among scholars and policy researchers. Generally speaking, the government departments responsible for implementing the population control policy tend to believe a higher TFR, whereas scholars believe a lower TFR. In spite of the disagreement, the estimates mostly fall in the range of 1.6 to 1.8, which are all significantly lower than the replacement level of 2.1.

3 Whereas Thompson (1929) first identified the three stages of demographic transition and another scholar added two more later stages, neither of them was considered as the father of theory of demographic transition, because they did not provide a standard theoretical explanation of the decline of fertility. The honor was later awarded to Notestein (1945). See Caldwell (1976) for a brief history of this field.

4 In an econometric study, Du (2004) found that population policy, per capita GDP, and level of human capital are decisive factors driving down China's fertility and empirically identified the different effects of the three factors.

5 It is commonly believed that the Japanese economy reached its Lewis turning point in 1960, followed by the Korean and Taiwanese economies, respectively (for example Minami, 1968; Bai, 1982).

References

Bai, M. (1982). The Turning Point in the Korean Economy, *Developing Economies*, 20(2), pp. 117–140.

Cai, F. (2004). The Consistency of China's Statistics on Employment: Stylized Facts and Implications for Public Policies, *Chinese Economy*, 37(5), pp. 74–89.

Cai, F. (2008a). *Lewis Turning Point: A Coming New Stage of China's Economic Development*, Beijing: Social Sciences Academic Press.
Cai, F. (2008b). Approaching a Triumphal Span: How Far Is China towards Its Lewisian Turning Point? UNU-WIDER Research Paper No. 2008/09.
Cai, F. (2009). Future Demographic Dividend – Tapping the Source of China's Economic Growth, *China Economist*, 21 (July–August).
Cai, F. (2010). From Farmers-turned Workers to Migrants-turned Residents: Urbanization in Next Decades, Chinese Style, *International Economic Review*, 2, pp. 40–53.
Cai, F., and Wang, D. (2005). China's Demographic Transition: Implications for Growth, in Ross Garnaut and Ligang Song (eds.), *The China Boom and Its Discontents*, Canberra: Asia Pacific Press.
Cai, F., and Wang, M. (2008). A Counterfactual Analysis on Unlimited Surplus Labor in Rural China, *China & World Economy*, 16(1), pp. 51–65.
Caldwell, J. C. (1976). Toward a Restatement of Demographic Transition Theory, *Population and Development Review*, 2, pp. 321–366.
Du, Y. (2004). The Formation of Low Fertility and Its Impacts on Long term Economic Growth in China, *World Economy*, 12, pp. 14–23.
Fogel, R. W. (2007). Capitalism and Democracy in 2040: Forecasts and Speculations, NBER Working Paper *No. 13184*, Cambridge, MA: National Bureau of Economic Research.
Hu, Y. (2009). *Predictions on Working Age Population of Rural and Urban China*, unpublished memo.
JCER (Japanese Center for Economic Research) (2007). *Demographic Change and the Asian Economy*, Tokyo: Japanese Center for Economic Research.
Krugman, P. (1994). The Myth of Asia's Miracle, *Foreign Affairs*, 73(6), pp. 62–78.
Lau, L. J. (2010a). Expansion of Domestic Demand is Fourfold, *China News*, 21 January, www.chinanews.com.cn/cj/cj-ylgd/news/2010/01-18/2077952.shtml.
Lau, L. J. (2010b). The Chinese Economy: The Next Thirty Years, paper presented at the Institute of Quantitative and Technical Economics, Chinese Academy of Social Sciences, Beijing, 16 January.
Lee, R., and Mason, A. (2006). What Is the Demographic Dividend? *Finance and Development*, 43(3), www.imf.org/external/pubs/ft/fandd/2006/09/basics.htm.
Lewis, A. (1958). Unlimited Labour: Further Notes, *Manchester School of Economic and Social Studies*, 26(1), pp. 1–32.
Lewis, A. (1972). Reflections on Unlimited Labour, in L. Di Marco, (ed.), *International Economics and Development*, New York, Academic Press, pp. 75–96.
Lin, J. Y. (2006). Development Strategy, Population and Population Policies, in Yi Zeng, Ling Li, Baochang Gu, and Yifu Lin (eds.), *China's Population and Economic Development in the 21st Century*, Beijing: Social Sciences Academic Press.
Minami, R. (1968). The Turning Point in the Japanese Economy, *Quarterly Journal of Economics*, 82(3), pp. 380–402.
Minami, R. and Ma, X. (2009). The Turning Point of Chinese Economy: Compared with Japanese Experience, *Asian Economics*, 50(12), pp. 2–20 (in Japanese).
Notestein, F. W. (1945). Population – the Long View, in Theodore W. Schultz (ed.), *Food for the World*, Chicago: University of Chicago Press.
Ranis, G. (2004). Arthur Lewis' Contribution to Development Thinking and Policy, Yale University Economic Growth Center Discussion Paper No. 891 (August).

Ranis, G., and Fei, J. C. H. (1961). A Theory of Economic Development, *American Economic Review*, 51(4), pp. 533–565.

Ravallion, M., and Chen, S. (1999). When Economic Reform Is Faster than Statistical Reform: Measuring and Explaining Income Inequality in Rural China, *Oxford Bulletin of Economics and Statistics*, 61(1), pp. 33–56.

Rawski, T. G. (2001). What's Happening to China's GDP Statistics? *China Economic Review*, 12(4), pp. 298–302.

Roberts, K., Connelly, R., Xie, Z., and Zheng, Z. (2004). Patterns of Temporary Labor Migration of Rural Women from Anhui and Sichuan, *China Journal*, 52, pp. 49–70.

Ru, X., Lu, X., and Li, P. (2008). *Analysis and Prospects on China's Social Situation*, Beijing: Social Sciences Academic Press.

Sala-i-Martin, X. X. (1997). "I Just Ran Two Million Regressions", *American Economic Review*, 87(2), pp.178–183.

Solinger, D. J. (2001). Why We Cannot Count the Unemployed? *China Quarterly*, 167 (August), pp. 671–688.

Solow, R. M. (1956). A Contribution to the Theory of Economic Growth, *Quarterly Journal of Economics*, 70(1), pp. 65–94.

Thompson, W. S. (1929). Population, *American Journal of Sociology*, 34(6), 959–975.

United Nations (2009). *The World Population Prospects: The 2008 Revision*, http://esa.un.org/unpp.

Williamson, J. (1997). Growth, Distribution and Demography: Some Lessons from History, NBER Working Paper *No. 6244*, Cambridge, MA: National Bureau of Economic Research.

Young, A. (1994). The Tyranny of Numbers: Confronting the Statistical Realities of the East Asian Growth Experience, NBER Working Paper *No. 4680*, Cambridge, MA: National Bureau of Economic Research.

Yu, X. (2002). Estimation on Magnitude and Structure of 5th National Population Census, *Population Research*, 26(3), pp. 9–15.

2 The end of China's demographic dividend

The perspective of potential GDP growth*

2.1 Introduction

The unprecedented economic growth in China over the past 30 years can be attributed largely to the demographic dividend. That is, growth of the working-age population guarantees an adequate supply of labor; a decline in the dependence ratio (the ratio of the dependent population to the working-age population) helps to maintain a high savings rate, which is the condition for capital formation; and an unlimited supply of labor prevents return on capital from diminishing, which allows heavy investment to be the main source of GDP growth (Cai and Zhao, 2012).

As is well documented in the economics literature (e.g., Bloom and Williamson, 1998; Williamson, 1998), the demographic dividend is not derived from population size or the growth rate of the population, but from a specific feature of the population age structure. Simply put, an increase in the proportion of the working-age population in the total population and a decline in the dependence ratio provide a country an opportunity to situate itself so that a high savings rate, heavy investment, and rapid economic growth can be obtained; the country thus benefits from the demographic dividend. Over the period of fast growth, few would consider the population age structure as a constraint of economic growth in China.

However, the population age structure is ever-changing. As a result of population aging, the working-age population stops growing and the dependence ratio no longer decreases; eventually, the demographic dividend will cease to exist. While debating the Lewis turning point, Garnaut (2010) suggests using the phrase "Lewis turning period" instead of "Lewis turning point" so that China's regional heterogeneity can be captured. Accepting this advice, we consider the year 2004, in which labor shortage first appeared and migrants' wages started to increase, as the starting time, and 2010, in which working-age population between 15 and 59 peaked, as the ending time of the Chinese Lewis turning period (Figure 2.1). Since China has now passed such a period, all that can be expected according to economics theories is becoming a reality. That is, labor shortage, diminishing return on capital, and a decline in the savings rate will lead to a slowdown in economic growth. This is what has occurred in China in recent years, particularly since 2004.

The potential GDP growth rate is determined by supply-side factors, including labor, capital, and total factor productivity (TFP). In a growth accounting equation, holding constant the labor force participation rate and the natural unemployment rate (i.e., the non-accelerated inflation rate of unemployment, or NAIRU), a reduction in the working-age population will directly reduce the potential GDP growth rate. In addition, the reduced supply of labor, which causes diminishing returns to capital, and the increase in the dependence ratio, which causes a decline in the savings rate, do not support the fast growth of capital formation. Therefore, holding the other factors constant, a reversal of the growth trend of the working-age population in China will inevitably slow its economic growth.

In fact, the process of demographic transition has taken place in China much more rapidly than anyone could have expected, and the number of people from ages 15 to 59 years has already decreased.[1] Based on the data of the Sixth National Census, the China Development Research Foundation (CDRF, 2012) predicts the trend of the population age structure to change, and shows that the working-age population, when assumed to be aged 15 to 59 years, started to decline in size in 2011, while the population dependence ratio calculated based on the working-age population (aged between 15 and 59 years) began shrinking in the same year. This trend will not be reversed even if there is a moderate relaxation of the one-child policy. Given that the population factor has had such far-reaching impacts on the determinants of China's economic growth, including labor supply, the savings rate, the

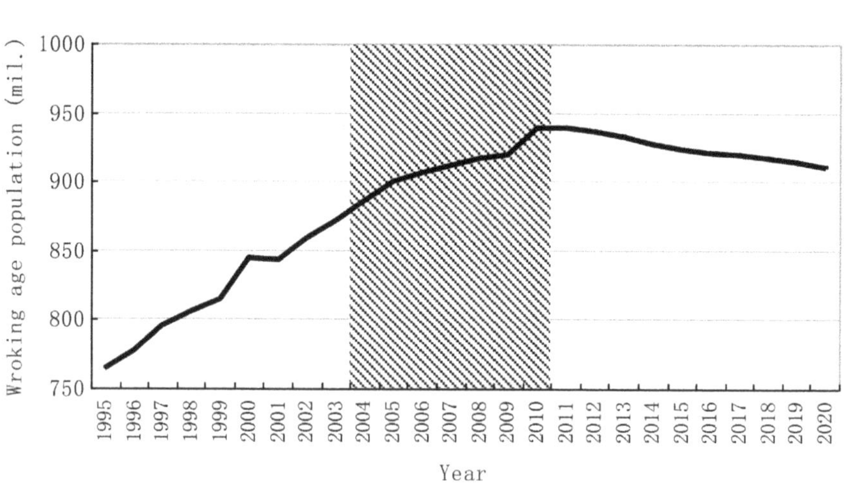

Figure 2.1 The Chinese Lewis turning period.
Source: CDRF, 2012.

marginal return on capital, and total factor productivity, such a change in the population age structure is bound to reduce the potential GDP growth rate in China.

Based on the latest population data, the present paper simulates a decline in the average potential GDP growth rate from 9.8 percent over the period from 1995 to 2009 to 7.2 percent during the Twelfth Five-year Plan period (2011–2015) and 6.1 percent over the Thirteenth Five-year Plan period (2016–2020). Therefore, determining how to sustain economic growth is an important challenge facing China. In light of the properties of the potential growth rate and the experiences of China and the rest of the world, we make the following two suggestions.

First, the government should not seek an actual growth rate exceeding the potential growth rate. Because the potential growth rate is fixed by assuming full employment of existing factors of production, artificial stimulus aimed at lifting the actual economic growth rate above the potential rate would have unhealthy consequences. For example, frequently implemented stimulus plans could cause inflation; overactive industrial policies might result in overcapacity by inappropriately protecting inefficient enterprises and backward production capacity; and regional and industrial policies using heavy subsidies could lead to distortion of prices of production factors, and affect regional industrial structure by impacting comparative advantage.

Second, the potential growth rate can be enhanced through the application of measures to enlarge the supply of labor and capital, and to improve productivity. This requires deepening reforms in various areas, such as household registration system reform and institutional reform. That is, economic reform is the key to sustaining China's economic growth. Kharas (2011) points out that it would take ten years or more for China to see any obvious effects of such reforms, which implies that the Chinese government should waste no time in initiating urgent reforms, while being ready to accept lower growth rates. However, there exist reform opportunities that could enhance China's potential growth rate fairly swiftly, which we discuss in the present paper.

While suggesting the slowdown of the potential rate of China's future economic growth in accordance with the trend of population structure changes, the present paper recommends that policy measures to stimulate economic growth so that it exceeds the potential growth rate should not be taken. Instead, two scenarios are simulated and the results suggest that an increase in the labor force participation rate and improvements in TFP can significantly expand the potential growth rate in the future.

2.2 Estimation of the potential growth rate in China

We use a standard Cobb-Douglas production function to project potential GDP growth rate. This method was applied both by Kuijs and Wang (2006) and Kuijs (2009).

$$Y = AL^{\alpha}K^{1-\alpha} \tag{1}$$

Where Y is real GDP, A is total factor productivity (TFP), L is employment, and K stands for capital stock (in constant price).[2] We deduce the labor productivity by dividing L on both sides of the equation (1).

$$Y / L = A(K / L)^{1-\alpha} \tag{2}$$

In equation (2), labor productivity Y / L (represented by y) is a function of the TFP and capital–labor ratio K / L (represented by k). That is $y = Ak^{1-\alpha}$. With some manipulation, labor productivity growth rate can then be rewritten and estimated from model (3):

$$\frac{\Delta y_t}{y_{t-1}} = \frac{\Delta A_t}{A_{t-1}} + (1-\hat{\alpha})\frac{\Delta k_t}{k_{t-1}} + \varepsilon_t \tag{3}$$

Based on equation (3) we can get the estimated value of return to capital $(1-\hat{\alpha})$ and return to labor $\hat{\alpha}$ by using $\Delta y_t / y_{t-1}$ as the dependent variable and $\Delta k_t / k_{t-1}$ as the independent variable.

From time series of $\Delta y_t / y_{t-1}, 1-\hat{\alpha}$, $\Delta k_t / k_{t-1}$, the growth rate of total factor productivity $\Delta A_t / A_{t-1} + \varepsilon_t = \Delta y_t / y_{t-1} - (1-\hat{\alpha})\Delta k_t / k_{t-1}$ could be calculated by using equation (3). And then, $\Delta A_t / A_{t-1}$ can be estimated by applying the Hodrick–Prescott filter method to diminish error term ε_t.

All steps above are identical with the method which calculates the growth rate of total factor productivity. We need to use potential employment L_t^* to calculate the potential GDP growth rate. Where $L_t^* = Population_{15-59,t} \times Tr_{pt} \times (1 - NAIRU_t)$, $Population_{15-59,t}$ is the working-age population aged 15 to 59 years, Tr_{pt} is the trends of the labor participation rate which can be estimated by the Hodrick–Prescott filter method, and $NAIRU_t$ is the natural rate of unemployment. In this paper, $NAIRU_t = 4.13\%$ (Du and Lu, 2011).

Building on $\Delta \hat{A}_t / A_{t-1}$, $1-\hat{\alpha}$, L_t^* and capital stock K_t, the potential labor productivity growth rate $\Delta y_t^* / y_{t-1}^*$ could be calculated as follows:

$$\Delta y_t^* / y_{t-1}^* = \Delta \hat{A}_t / A_{t-1} + (1-\hat{\alpha})\Delta k_t^* / k_{t-1}^* \tag{4}$$

Where $k_t^* = K_t / L_t^*$, $y_t^* = Y_t^* / L_t^*$, and Y_t^* is just the potential GDP in year t. Building on $\Delta y_t^* / y_{t-1}^*$ and L_t^*, we could deduce an equation as follows:

$$\Delta Y_t^* / Y_{t-1}^* = (\Delta y_t^* / y_{t-1}^* + 1) \times (L_t^* / L_{t-1}^*) - 1 \tag{5}$$

$\Delta Y_t^* / Y_{t-1}^*$ is the potential GDP growth rate in year *t*. where $\Delta y_t^* / y_{t-1}^*$ is the growth rate of potential labor productivity, a function of the growth rate of *TFP* and the potential capital–labor ratio, and L_t^* / L_{t-1}^* is potential employment growth. From equations (4) and (5), three factors would influence the potential GDP growth rate, that is, potential growth rate of the capital–labor ratio, potential growth rate of employment, and potential TFP growth rate. We note that the working-age population will affect the first two factors directly.

Before estimating the potential growth rate, we also need to make some assumptions regarding the capital formation and TFP growth rates in the period to come. The predicted employment growth, the assumed growth rates of capital formation and TFP, and the estimated potential GDP growth rate are presented in Figure 2.2. In what follows, we explain the reasons for such assumptions and present detailed results from the estimation.

Assumption I: capital formation growth will slow down in the next 10 years

Examining the historical data, we find that the annual growth rate of fixed asset investment deflated by the price index of fixed assets was 13.43 percent

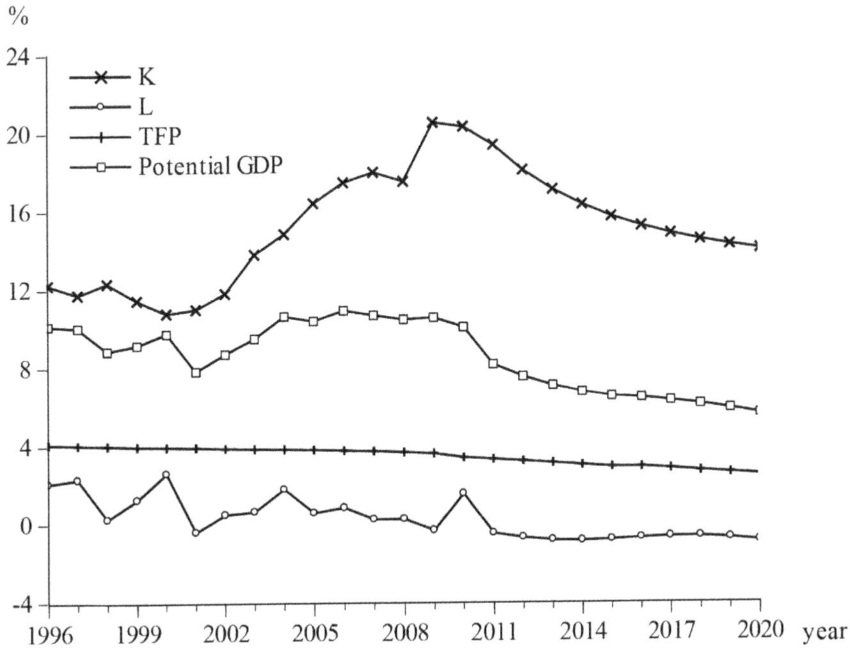

Figure 2.2 Trends of potential growth rate and of its factors in China, 1996–2020.
Notes: K = assumed growth rate of fixed assets investment (capital formation); L = potential growth rate of employment; TFP = growth rate of total factor productivity.

in 1978–1994 and 16.89 percent in 1995–2009. In the latter period, the annual growth rate of fixed assets investment reached 20 percent between 2003 and 2007. In tackling the global financial crisis, the growth rate of fixed assets investment rose to 33.15 percent in 2009. Even if we eliminate the outlier of 2009, the rate was still as high as 15.64 percent in the period from 1995 to 2008.

Such rapid growth of fixed assets would not be sustained in the years to come for three reasons. First, as a result of widespread labor shortages, marginal return to capital is declining at an accelerating pace (Cai and Zhao, 2012), which will impede such a high speed of investment growth. Second, as the population dependence ratio increases, the savings rate tends to fall, resulting in a slowdown of investment growth. Last but not least, relatively slower growth of capital formation will help China transform its growth pattern that overwhelmingly relies on domestic investment and move to a more balanced and sustained pattern of growth.

In an equation based on least squares regression, we incorporate return to capital (wK) as an independent variable to regress the dependent variable of the growth rate of total investment in fixed assets in the whole country (excluding state budgetary investment). Data used in the regression cover the years from 1982 to 2005. The estimated results are as follows:

$$I = -6.1395 + 0.9459 * wK$$

$$(19.7312)\ (0.8422)$$

$$R^2 = 0.0542\ \text{D.W.} = 0.9765$$

We put the average return to capital of 20.22 percent in 1996–2005 estimated by Bai et al. (2006) into the estimated equation and obtain an annual growth rate of investment of 12.99 percent. Therefore, we preset the annual growth rate of investment in fixed assets in China as 13 percent in the period from 2012 to 2020.

It is worth noting that the assumption is not actually made as a result of the above simulation but in light of theory and China's economic reality. That is, a rational response to the substantial fall in marginal return on capital with an absence of government intervention should be slower growth of capital investment. In fact, such a predetermined annual growth rate of 13 percent is still higher than the actual growth rate in the period from 1996 to 2005.

2.1.1 Assumption II: labor force will decrease in the future

The demographic and economic trends have led to a changed relationship between labor supply and demand. Take the annual increase in the number of people between the ages of 15 and 59 on the supply side and the annual increase in the number of urban workers on the demand side. When the two trends are examined together, the changing dynamics of the labor market become obvious. Since the number of agricultural workers has been falling while that of non-agricultural workers in rural areas is not expected to expand, we may treat the increases in the number of urban workers, migrant workers included, as representative of the magnitude of the overall labor demand of the Chinese economy.

In what follows, we take a closer look at the general employment situation in China by comparing the demand and the supply of labor for urban sectors. There are two parts to the statistical data on urban employment in China. The first includes the total number of urban employees, which is published by the National Bureau of Statistics (NBS). This number does not, however, cover most migrant workers in urban areas. According to estimation on the basis of micro data from 2009, only 12.5 percent of the total of 310 million urban employees were migrant workers. The second part includes the total number of people classifiable as migrant workers according to the NBS official definition. According to that definition, an individual qualifies as a "migrant worker" if s/he has been away from the town or township of their household registration for six months or more. Surveys have shown that of all migrant workers, 95.6 percent work and live in cities of varying sizes. Factoring in the overlap between these two numbers, we can calculate the actual number of urban workers inclusive of both registered urban residents and migrant workers. We can then compare this number with the total number of people of working age in the country (Table 2.1).

Table 2.1 Increases in demand for and supply of labor force (million, %)

	Urban resident workers		*Migrant workers*		*Working-age population*	
	Numbers	*Growth rate*	*Numbers*	*Growth rate*	*Numbers*	*Growth rate*
2001	236	-	80	-	844	-
2002	241	2.1	100	24.7	859	1.8
2003	246	2.0	109	8.8	872	1.6
2004	250	1.8	113	3.8	886	1.5
2005	254	1.7	120	6.4	900	1.6
2006	259	2.0	126	5.0	907	0.8
2007	265	2.1	131	3.7	912	0.6
2008	268	1.3	134	2.5	917	0.5
2009	272	1.4	139	3.5	920	0.3
2010	277	1.6	146	5.3	939	2.1
2011	280	1.0	152	3.7	939	-0.1

Source: Authors' own calculation based on *China Statistical Yearbook* (various years), *China Yearbook of Rural Household Survey* (various years), *China Population Yearbook* (various years), and Du and Lu, 2011.

Between 2001 and 2011, the labor demand of urban sectors, which encompasses employment among both urban residents and the migrants, grew at an annual rate of 3.2 percent. During the same period, labor supply, measured by the number of people of working age, grew by an annual rate of only 1.1 percent. For the purpose of this study, we have excluded people older than 60 from the working-age population because, given China's retirement age—60 for men and 55 for women—they by default stand little chance of finding a job in the present labor market. A look at people between the ages of 15 and 59 shows that this population had begun to shrink by 2010. This suggests, among other things, that the problem of high rates of underemployment in both the rural and the urban labor markets was finally easing. As such, constant surplus of supply relative to demand no longer accurately describes China's labor market after the passage of the Lewis turning period.

Having observed that the working-age population aged between 15 and 59 years declines, we assume that the natural unemployment rate will remain the same as it was in 2009, namely, NAIRU = 4.132% (Du and Lu, 2011), and that the labor force participation rate will follow its existing trend, which was calculated using the Hodrick–Prescott filter method. As the population aged between 15 and 59 years peaked in 2010, its annual growth rate will be –0.33 percent in 2011–2015 and –0.31 percent in 2016–2020. This means that the annual growth rate of employment will be –0.76 percent during the Twelfth Five-year Plan period and –0.74 percent in the Thirteenth Five-year Plan period. If the natural unemployment rate and the labor force participation rate remain unchanged in the following two Five-year Plan periods, the reduction in the size of the working-age population will lead to a fall in the potential GDP growth rate.

2.1.2 Assumption III: total factor productivity growth will be reduced but remain relatively high

Kuijs (2009) attributes the impressive increase in TFP during the period from 1994 to 2009 to the state sector restructuring, the entry to the WTO, and the successful integration of manufacturing into the world economy. Those forces, however, will diminish in the years to come. Hence, he expects a reduction of 0.5–2.3 percentage points in TFP per year in the period from 2010 to 2020. Using a Hodrick–Prescott filter decomposition, we assume the trend of annual TFP growth rate to be 3.10 percent in 2011–2015 and 2.70 percent in 2016–2020.

Based on the assumptions made above on the decline in the labor force and TFP growth and the slower growth of investment, we can estimate the potential growth rate of the Chinese economy for the period of 2011 to 2020. Our finding that the potential growth rate will decline and the trend will continue is not surprising, because many others have reached the same conclusion (e.g., Kuijs, 2009; World Bank, 2012). However, our predicted potential growth rate is much lower than that estimated by others (e.g., see Kuijs, 2009). The

Table 2.2 Estimated results for potential inputs and outputs in China, 1978–2020

Growth rate (%)	*1978–1994*	*1995–2009*	*2011–2015*	*2016–2020*
Actual output	10.06	9.90		
Potential output	10.29	9.83	7.19	6.08
Actual employment	2.45	0.97		
Potential employment	3.23	0.90	−0.76	−0.74
Actual labor productivity	6.55	8.84		
Potential labor productivity	6.85	8.86	8.02	6.87
TFP	0.78	3.89	3.10	2.70
K/L	10.38	13.29	18.21	15.43

Notes: TFP = total factor productivity; K = assumed growth rate of fixed assets investment (capital formation); L = potential growth rate of employment.

potential GDP growth rate we estimate is 7.2 percent for the Twelfth Five-year Plan period and 6.1 percent for the Thirteenth Five-year Plan period (Table 2.2). We do not consider our conclusion as any exaggeration, given that we have not taken into account the inevitable slowdown of mass labor migration from agricultural to non-agricultural sectors, which has been the main source of TFP growth.

We do not propose that policy-makers pursue achieving actual GDP growth exceeding the potential rate, but in what follows we recommend ways to enhance the potential growth rate through increasing the labor force participation rate and the TFP growth rate, which require a deepening of economic reforms.

2.3 Increasing the labor force participation rate

Data from the Sixth National Census show that the labor force participation rate was 70.80 percent for population aged 16 years and above and 77.26 percent for population aged between 16 and 64 years in 2010. A further look at geographic distribution shows that the labor force participation rate for population aged 16 years and above was 62.20 percent in cities, 67.32 percent in towns and 77.62 percent in rural areas. For population aged between 16 and 64 years, the labor force participation rate was 68.18 percent in cities, 73.27 percent in towns and 84.92 percent in rural areas. The labor force participation rate at present is lower than in the 1990s, and it is likely to be even lower if we consider the following two factors.

First, the exclusion of the agricultural labor force from the calculation would result in a lower labor force participation rate. Because there is no retirement age in agriculture, when the number of workers engaged in agriculture is counted, as is the common practice in statistics, the labor force participation rate tends to be overestimated. At the present stage of economic development in China, economic growth is accompanied by a constant decline in the

Table 2.3 Labor force participation rates in China by age group and by sex (%)

Age groups	*Total LFPR (including agriculture)*			*LFPR of non-agriculture*		
	Total	*Male*	*Female*	*Total*	*Male*	*Female*
16–20	32.44	33.06	30.72	21.78	22.53	21.31
20–25	72.55	76.66	69.70	62.76	68.91	58.95
25–30	88.88	95.73	82.10	84.33	94.01	74.61
30–35	90.30	97.01	83.47	85.98	95.73	75.79
35–40	90.62	96.92	84.18	85.53	95.36	75.02
40–45	90.73	96.63	84.74	84.43	94.50	73.41
45–50	87.73	95.06	79.58	78.49	91.64	62.87
50–55	76.31	89.90	62.62	56.99	81.62	32.19
55–60	67.29	80.41	53.71	37.57	60.88	15.04
60–65	49.59	58.14	40.11	13.80	22.41	5.89

Source: Authors' calculation based on 1% sampling data of Sixth Census.

Note: LFPR = labor force participation rate.

agricultural share in terms of both output value and employment. Thus, the participation rate of the non-agricultural labor force is a better indicator of the real situation of the labor market.

Based on data of the Sixth Census, we recalculate the labor force participation rate by excluding agricultural sectors and find it to be much lower than that calculated by including agriculture (Table 2.3). For example, for the 20–25 year age group, the participation rate of the non-agricultural labor force is 72.55 percent, which is 9.79 percentage points lower than the participation rate of the total labor force. This implies that as the agricultural share of the labor force further declines in the future, the labor force participation rate will drop much faster than what previous statistics would suggest.

Second, the extension of years of schooling would lower the labor force participation rate. As is shown in Figure 2.3, the labor force participation rate distribution by age can be characterized by a reverse U-shaped curve. That is, for lower age groups, more people are still in school, which makes labor force participation low; labor force participation substantially increases when people enter their thirties and forties; and labor force participation declines as workers get older, because they have either a stronger desire to retire or less sought-after skills to meet the demands of the labor market. For all age groups, the labor force participation rate for men is higher than that of women and the non-agricultural labor force participation rate is lower than the total labor force participation rate.

It is worth noting that although the present labor force participation rate in China is still high, it will change dramatically as population aging accelerates. As the size of the working-age population is no longer increasing, labor force participation determines the labor supply and, therefore, constrains the potential growth rate.

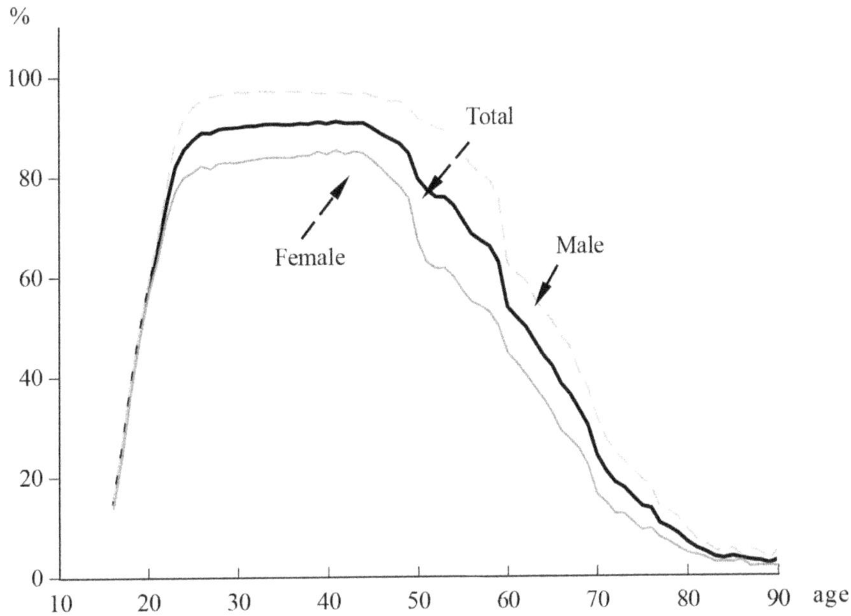

Figure 2.3 Labor force participation rate in China, 2010.
Source: Authors' calculation based on the Sixth Census.

After 2011, the potential employment growth rate will become negative: –0.76 percent in the Twelfth Five-year Plan period and –0.74 percent in the Thirteenth Five-year Plan period. Because the root cause of this negative growth of employment, namely, the reduction of the total population aged 15 to 59 years in 2010 and the population aged 15 to 64 years in 2013, cannot be altered, the enhancement of labor force participation is the only way to increase potential labor supply and, in turn, to expand the potential output.

To test such a hypothesis, we simulate the impact of an increase in the labor force participation rate on the potential GDP growth rate. Based on the above-described growth-accounting equation, we assume a scenario in which the labor force participation rate increases 1 percentage point every year in the period from 2011 to 2020. It results in an average potential growth rate increase from 7.19 to 8.09 percent during 2011–2015 and an average potential growth rate increase from 6.08 to 6.94 percent during 2016–2020. As a result, the potential GDP growth rate will increase by an extra 0.88 percentage points per annum in the period from 2011 to 2022 (Figure 2.4).

There are three potential ways for China to increase labor force participation. The first is to postpone the retirement age so that the labor force participation rate of workers at older ages can be increased. Although this measure is widely used in developed countries, it is not equally relevant for China,

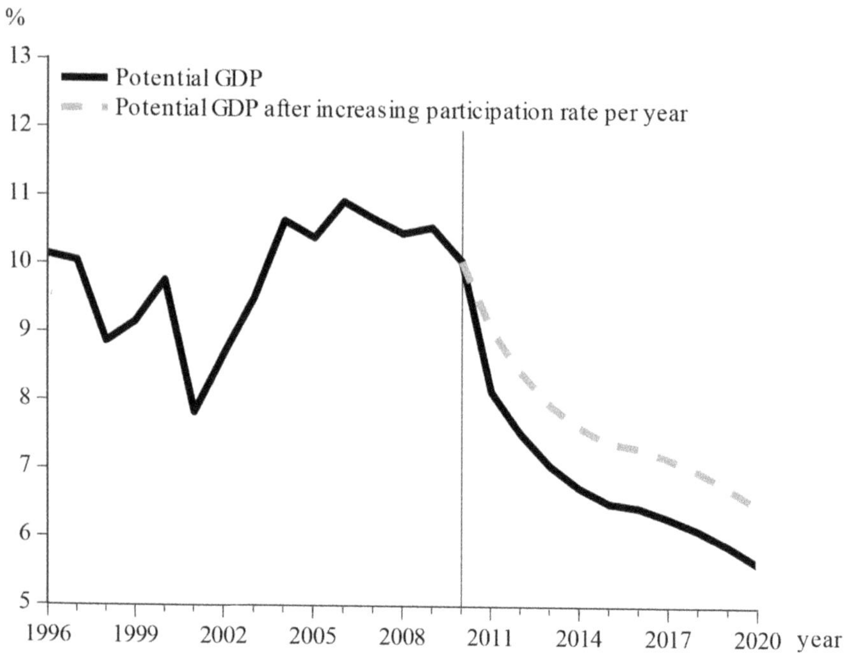

Figure 2.4 Effect of 1 percentage point increase in labor force participation rate on potential GDP growth rate.

Source: Authors' simulation.

because older Chinese workers are often not sufficiently educated to meet the labor market demand for skills and are likely to be in a vulnerable position if they postpone retiring. Therefore, this policy option should not be chosen in the short run.

The second method is to further promote labor migration from rural to urban areas. Compared to countries with similar per capita income, China has a relatively larger share of labor in agriculture. The possibility exists for labor migration to occur so that labor force participation can be increased in non-agricultural sectors. The existing household registration or *hukou* system that segregates the labor market between rural and urban areas still prevents rural-to-urban migrant workers from settling down in urban areas legitimately and permanently. Therefore, *hukou* reform aimed at legalizing migrant workers' citizenship in cities will significantly stabilize supply of labor, tap into the potential labor force, and, therefore, increase potential output.

The third approach is to raise the employment rate or to lower the unemployment rate. As China is moving away from possessing an unlimited supply of labor and toward a neoclassical labor market framework, today's employment problems show both neoclassical and dual economy characteristics. That is, while there is still surplus labor in agriculture, the more frequent emergence of cyclical unemployment, structural unemployment, and frictional unemployment raises new challenges in regard to China's macroeconomic and employment policies. The manner in which such challenges are responded to can reshape potential GDP growth in the future.

2.4 Improving total factor productivity

In the face of a declining potential growth rate, the central and local governments would tend to adopt industrial policies, regional strategies, and stimulus plans to pursue a growth rate exceeding the potential rate. The temptation is great because those policy measures are simple for governments to implement and they generate immediate effects. However, the lessons from China's economic growth per se and from its forerunners in economic development (e.g., Japan) show that those policies are very likely to become distortionary and eventually impact on the sustainability of economic growth.

In contrast, deepening economic reform in various areas to expand the potential growth rate would require considerable long-term effort. As the returns to capital diminish, the old pattern of China's economic growth cannot continue, and the challenge to seek new sources of economic growth intensifies. According to the neoclassical theory of growth, such new sources must come from improvements in TFP.

The residual output that cannot be explained by inputs of production factors comes from TFP growth, which includes technological advancement, resource allocative efficiency, technical efficiency, and institutional and managerial innovation. In a neoclassical model of economic growth, TFP growth is the dominant, if not the only, driver of potential growth of output.

Based on the existing model, we assume a scenario in which TFP grows at a rate 1 percentage point higher per year in the period from 2011 to 2020. That is, the annual TFP growth rate would increase to 4.01 percent from the current 3.01 percent. Our simulation shows that such a higher TFP growth rate would lift the annual growth rate of potential output to 8.19 percent in 2011–2015 and 7.07 percent in 2016–2020 (Figure 2.4). Overall, if China could manage to accomplish an extra percentage point of TFP growth, its potential annual growth rate would increase by 0.99 percentage points in the period from 2011 to 2020.

Over the past 30 years of rapid economic growth in China, the impressive performance in TFP has been largely attributed to resource allocative efficiency through labor mobility from agricultural to non-agricultural sectors. In the course of the dual economy development with an unlimited supply of labor, such productivity gains have been like *low-hanging fruit*. As the surplus labor force has become gradually absorbed by the unprecedented expansion of secondary and tertiary sectors, the mass labor migration has slowed down, and the opportunity to gain resource allocative efficiency has decreased.

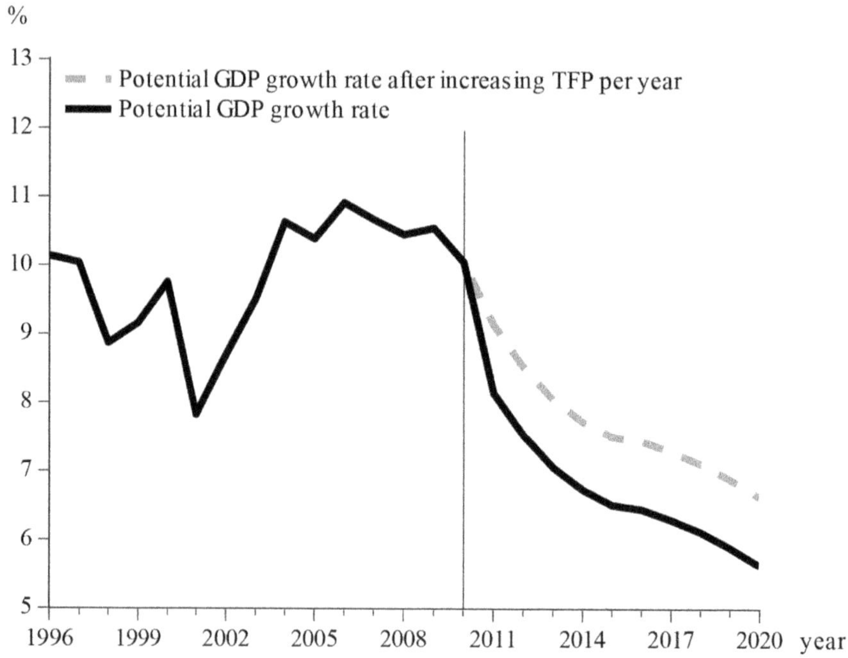

Figure 2.5 Effects of 1 extra percentage point of TFP growth on potential growth rate.
Source: Authors' simulation.

Furthermore, the arrival of the Chinese economy at a higher phase of development means that the gap in technology between China and developed countries has narrowed, which makes it relatively harder for China to increase TFP through technological advancement.

Therefore, China should search for new ways to improve TFP to expand its potential growth. In fact, as China's economic growth follows more of a neoclassical framework, it will be difficult for China to add even 1 additional percentage point to its TFP growth rate. It is extremely important that the government is determined to complete the task and is aware of where the extra productivity should come from. For China, apart from the traditional sources of TFP improvement, such as technological catching-up with the developed countries and labor migration from rural to urban sectors, there is tremendous opportunity to gain allocative efficiency in the following areas.

First, given the large disparities in productivity among subsectors within, say, the secondary sector, the mobility of factors of production from the low productivity subsector to the high productivity subsector can improve the overall productivity of the economy as a whole. Second, the flow of factors of production among enterprises can also provide allocative efficiency because there are huge disparities in productivity performance among enterprises within narrowly defined sectors. A so-called *creative destruction* mechanism could be created, which allows for more efficient enterprises to survive, expand, and develop, and causes long-term inefficient enterprises to be eliminated. This mechanism could generate the third resources allocative efficiency.

As is well documented in the economics literature, in a mature market economy like the USA, allocative efficiency relating to entry versus exit and expansion versus contraction of firms within narrowly defined sectors contributes one-third to a half of the productivity growth (e.g., Foster et al., 2008). Based on an empirical and comparative study, Hsieh and Klenow (2007) find that by reallocating capital and labor to equalize marginal products among plants to the extent observed in the USA, China's manufacturing sector could gain a 30 to 50 percent increase in its TFP.

To gain resource allocative efficiencies in the areas described above requires a policy environment within which factors of productivity can freely flow among regions, sectors and enterprises. There still exist institutional barriers preventing investors from freely entering certain sectors where state-owned enterprises dominate, resulting in a great loss of allocative efficiency. The Chinese government should redefine the role and function of the state enterprises to keep them within necessary and limited arenas of economic activity, while creating equal competition opportunities for all sectors and enterprises.

2.5 Conclusion and policy implications

As a result of the changes in the population age structure, the working-age population (aged 15 to 59 years) stopped growing in 2010. Meanwhile, economic growth continues to generate a large demand for labor, thus absorbing the surplus labor force in agriculture. As the surplus labor force in agriculture is substantially decreasing, the Chinese economy is entering a phase of transition from dual economy development to neoclassical growth.

According to the neoclassical theory of growth, it is unlikely that developed economies can realize growth rates comparable to their developing counterparts, still in the process of catching up. Accordingly, fast growth will eventually slow down as an economy moves to a certain turning point, as experiences worldwide suggest (Eichengreen et al., 2011).

There is no need to fear the slowdown of the potential growth rate. However, the new stage of development requires China to accomplish a fundamental transformation of its economic growth pattern from sole reliance on inputs of capital and labor to greater improvements in TFP. Therefore, the key to sustaining economic growth through expanding the potential growth rate lies in supply-side factors. If government policies wrongly focus on stimulating demand-side factors to reach a growth rate exceeding the potential capacity of production, long-term economic growth will not be healthy and will cause distortions. Instead, sound policies should be implemented bearing the following in mind.

First, the central and local governments should accept slower economic growth. Policy decisions should be made by adjusting supply-side factors rather than demand-side factors. Even an undesirable fall in the growth rate caused by shocks from demand-side factors should not be a reason for policy-makers to introduce expansionary macroeconomic policy measures. Instead, policy-makers need to determine whether growth rates have been reduced to below-potential levels. If this is not the case, a situation where export demand and investment demand are weak could be taken as a chance for the economy to accelerate its transition toward a consumption-driven pattern and to grow in a more balanced manner.

Second, economic reforms should modify the traditional growth pattern. Reforms have been a major driving force of the unprecedented economic growth over the past 30 years. A competitive environment is vital for enhancing the potential growth rate in China over the next decade or so.

Third, there is an important role for the government to play in helping improve TFP. Krugman (1994) was critical of Singapore's growth model. The Singaporean government responded to such criticism by introducing a national goal of 2 percent annual TFP growth (Felipe, 1997). It is worth noting that improving TFP will also depend on China's reform measures.

Notes

* Coauthored with Lu Yang.

1 In this study, we assume that people aged 15 to 59 years make up the working-age population, instead of people aged 15 to 64 years. The reason is twofold. First, the official retirement ages are 60 years for male workers and 55 years for female workers. Second, for China's working-age population, the older the person, the lower the educational level. For example, the average years of schooling drop from 9 years for people aged 20 years to 6 years for people who are 60 years old (Wang and Niu, 2010). Both reasons indicate that, at present, there is little chance for people older than 60 years to successfully remain in the labor force.

2 Capital stock is almost always constructed by the "perpetual inventory method". The well-known equation is $K_t = I_t/p_t + (1-\delta_t)K_{t-1}$, where K_t is the measure of the real capital stock at time t, K_{t-1} is the measure of the real capital stock at time t-1, I_t is the normal investment in time t, P_t is the price index of investment in fixed assets in time t, and δ_t (=5%) is the rate of depreciation. The K_{1978} is calculated by Wang and Guo (2004). Note that K_t is a weighted sum of all past levels of investment and depreciated value of the initial real capital stock.

References

Bai, C., Chang, T. and Qian, Y. (2006). The Return to Capital in China, NBER Working Paper *No. 12755*, Cambridge, MA: National Bureau of Economic Research.

Bloom, D. E., and Williamson, J. G. (1998). Demographic Transitions and Economic Miracles in Emerging Asia, *World Bank Economic Review*, 12(3), pp. 419–55.

Cai, F., and Zhao, W. (2012). When Demographic Dividend Disappears: Growth Sustainability of China, in Masahiko Aoki and Jinglian Wu (eds.), *The Chinese Economy: A New Transition*, Basingstoke: Palgrave Macmillan.

CDRF (China Development Research Foundation) (2012). *China Development Report*, 2012, Beijing: China Development Publishing House.

Du, Y., and Lu, Y. (2011). The Natural Rate of Unemployment in China and Its Implications, *Journal of World Economy*, 34(4), pp. 3–21.

Eichengreen, B., Donghyun P., and Kwanho, S. (2011). When Fast Growing Economies Slow Down: International Evidence and Implications for China, NBER Working Paper *No. 16919*, Cambridge, MA: National Bureau of Economic Research.

Felipe, J. (1997). Total Factor Productivity Growth in East Asia: A Critical Survey, EDRC Report Series, *No. 65*.

Foster, L., Haltiwanger, J., and Syverson, C. (2008). Reallocation, Firm Turnover, and Efficiency: Selection on Productivity or Profitability? *American Economic Review*, 98(1), pp. 394–425.

Garnaut, R (2010). Macro-economic Implications of the Turning Point, *China Economic Journal*, 3(2), pp.181–190.

Hsieh, C., and Klenow, P. (2007). Misallocation and Manufacturing TFP in China and India, NBER Working Paper *No. 13290*, Cambridge, MA: National Bureau of Economic Research.

Kharas, H. (2011). China's Transitions to a High-income Economy: Escaping the Middle Income Trap, in Lim Edwin and Michael Spence (eds.), *The Medium and Long Term Development and Transformation of the Chinese Economy: An International Perspective*, Beijing: CITIC, pp. 470–501 (in Chinese).

Krugman, P. (1994). The Myth of Asia's Miracle, *Foreign Affairs*, 73(6), pp. 62–78.

Kuijs, L. (2009). China through 2020—A Macroeconomic Scenario, World Bank China Office Research Working Paper *No. 9*.

Kuijs, L., and Wang, L. (2006). China's Pattern of Growth: Moving to Sustainability and Reducing Inequality, *China & World Economy*, 14(1), pp. 1–14.

Wang, J., and Guo, C. (2004). An Improved Image Template Thinning Algorithm [J], *Journal of Image and Graphics*, 3(9), pp. 297–301.

Wang, G., and Niu, J. (2010). Composition and Development of the Chinese Education System, in F. Cai (ed.), *The China Population and Labor Yearbook Volume 2: The Sustainability of Economic Growth from the Perspective of Human Resources*, Leiden and Boston: Brill, pp. 43–62.

Williamson, J. G. (1998). Growth, Distribution, and Demography: Some Lessons from History, *Explorations in Economic History*, 35(3), pp. 241–271.

World Bank (2012). *China 2030: Building a Modern, Harmonious, and Creative High-income Society*, Washington, DC: World Bank. Available from: www.worldbank.org/content/dam/Worldbank/document/China-2030-complete.pdf.

Yang, L. (2012). China's Natural Growth Rate of Output and Its Forecast, in Cai Fang (ed.), *The China Population and Labor Yearbook No.13: Demographic Transition and Economic Rebalance in China*, Beijing: Social Sciences Academic Press, pp. 98–111.

3 Approaching a neoclassical scenario

The labor market in China after the Lewis turning point

3.1 Introduction

The three chief characteristics of a neoclassical labor market scenario, which I contrast with a dualistic labor market scenario such as described by Lewis (1954), are (1) wages are determined by marginal productivity of labor, (2) the labor market can correct its own disequilibrium in labor supply and demand over the long run, and (3) there are only three basic types of unemployment—cyclical, frictional, and structural—all of which need to be addressed with macroeconomic and labor market policies.

For a long time, the Chinese economy exemplified a dual economy characterized by unlimited labor supply, subsistence wages, and the existence of institutional barriers to labor mobility, and the resultant difficulty in labor-market clearing. Consequently, employment issues in China were understood exclusively in Lewisian, and never in neoclassical terms. Since the implementation of reform and opening-up, and in particular China's entry into the WTO in the new millennium, an enormous number of surplus laborers from the rural areas have migrated to coastal cities to take up non-agricultural jobs. It was not until very recently that the Lewis turning point arrived, signaled by widespread labor shortage and constant wage increases, particularly for unskilled workers, and facilitated by both demand and supply factors, such as demographic trends and strong growth of employment in urban areas.

While China is moving away from unlimited supply of labor and toward a neoclassical labor market scenario, today's employment problems show both neoclassical and dual economy characteristics. Some of the more prominent of these problems are (1) underemployment in the agricultural sectors has yet to be alleviated, (2) the worsening of cyclical unemployment, especially among migrant workers, (3) higher degree of vulnerability among young people and older workers in urban areas than other groups to forms of natural unemployment, including structural and frictional unemployment, and (4) inadequate protection for workers' rights, including those relating to wage negotiation and labor disputes.

This paper illustrates how China's recent demographic trends, together with fast economic growth and employment expansion, have reshaped the country's employment landscape, which is characterized no longer by unlimited supply but by a near-equilibrium. In response to this shift, we must also fundamentally change the way we understand China's employment problems and the challenges policy-makers face. In addition to promoting employment, increasingly policies must try to address problems of cyclical and natural unemployment, particularly among those that have been hardest hit by the transition and as such are especially vulnerable.

In this paper we highlight key employment issues in China by looking closely at three distinct groups: migrant workers, college graduates, and the urban working vulnerable. Each of these groups faces its own set of employment-related difficulties. Migrant workers are prone to be affected by cyclical unemployment, because when urban labor markets tighten due to economic slowdowns, many of them end up returning to agricultural work, which is a form of underemployment. College graduates are most vulnerable to structural and frictional unemployment, which partly explains why unemployment rates are often higher among this group than among some other groups. Thirdly, the vulnerability of the vulnerable workers in urban areas is due largely to inadequate education and skill, a situation for which there are deep historical reasons.

This last problem points toward major challenges in institution-building, and we will discuss it in some detail in this paper. As a result of the widespread awakening to their rights and entitlements among ordinary workers, brought by the arrival of the Lewis turning point and the continuing stress the labor market is under, labor disputes have been on the rise. The government has been quick to respond to this trend, by passing legislation and implementing policies. This is in fact yet another sign that China's labor market is on track to turning neoclassical after being Lewisian for a long time.

3.2 The demographic trend and its impacts on labor supply

Thanks to its strict implementation of the one-child policy, China has been able to complete in a very short time a demographic transition that took most developed countries much longer to complete. Since reform began, change in China's demographic profile has gone through the following stages: sharp decline in fertility rate, then in the number of young people as a percentage of total population, decreasing growth rate for people of working age, and then the rapid aging of the Chinese population. When the percentage of young people contracted at a higher rate than the growth rate of the percentage of elderly people, China began to see a sufficient labor supply, a result of productive population structure. As these demographic trends continue, working-age population will grow more slowly, while the aging process will pick up speed. These trends will surely raise many challenges.

Despite the dramatic decline in total fertility rate (TFR)—from 5.8 to 2.3 in China through the 1970s—by the early 1980s, China's TFR was still above replacement level. The drastic reduction in fertility rate that China has been

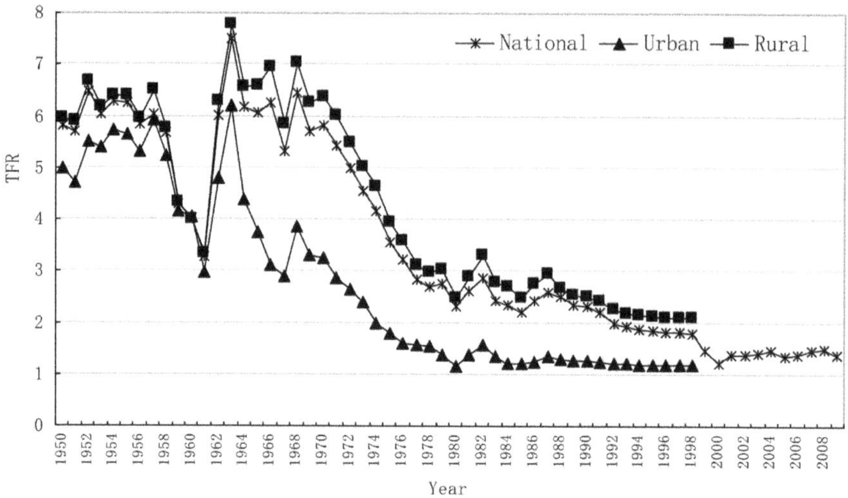

Figure 3.1 Reduction in total fertility rates: aggregate, rural and urban.

Source: Regional TFR for the period before 1998 was calculated using data from the China Center for Population Information database; national TFR post 1998 is calculated on the basis of various population survey and/or census data.

able to achieve owes very much to socioeconomic development on one hand and wide adoption of family planning on the other during the reform period. These were highly effective in arresting high fertility rates. By the dawn of the twenty-first century, not only had China successfully carried out the transition toward a modern population growth pattern, but it was able to so in less than 30 years. By comparison, it took many industrialized countries of comparable income level almost a century to do the same.

There have long been disagreements among scholars and official authorities about China's TFR. Figure 3.1 shows China's TFR from 1950 to 2009. All of the pre-1998 figures had government sources and were as such "official", but scholars treat only those for the years after 1998 as genuinely trustworthy. In Figure 3.1, one can see that the TFR in China has been below 1.5 for many years, which is quite low in international comparison (Gu and Li, 2010).

As the Chinese government began to distance itself gradually from this position, that is, that TFR in China has been below 1.5 for many years according to census data from the National Bureau of Statistics, the United Nations put China's TFR for 2006 at 1.4 in its newly published *World Fertility Pattern, 2009*, thereby placing the country among those with low fertility rates (United Nations, 2010). We may yet be hit by the consequent decline in labor supply, which will happen quite unannounced.

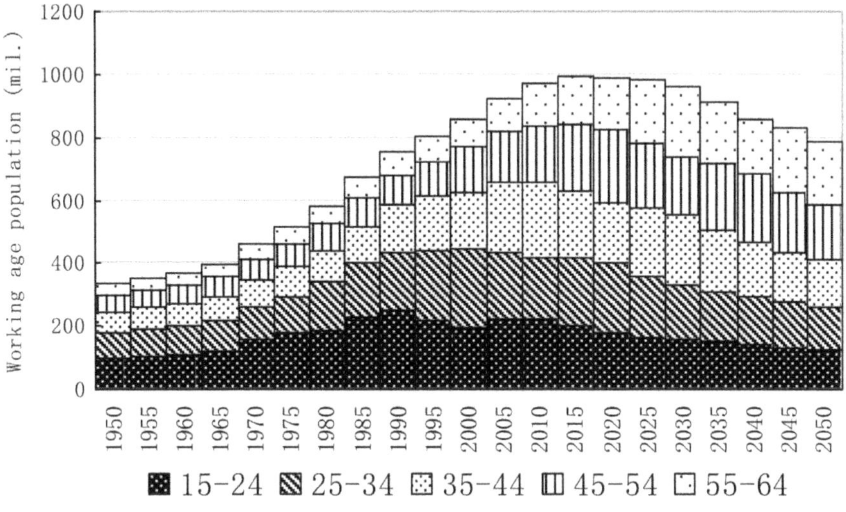

Figure 3.2 Changing age composition of working-age population.
Source: United Nations, 2011.

One repercussion of persistently low fertility rates is change in the age composition of a population. Since about 1980, the growth of the elderly population has accelerated, while that of the population of people of working age has decelerated, and the population of young people has shrunk altogether. We can conclude that under the condition of persistently low fertility rates, the growth of the working-age population will slow down before stopping altogether. These trends will lead eventually to labor shortages. According to one forecast based on the latest available statistics (United Nations, 2011), the number of Chinese between the ages of 15 and 64 will peak in 2015, after which it will begin to decrease (Figure 3.2).

Trends such as just described will lead to concomitant changes to the age structure of China's population. Our argument is based on two assumptions. First, we assume continual rise in enrolment in higher education, and have left those aged 15 to 19 outside the purview of these analyses. Secondly, we assume there will be little or no increase in the rate of labor force participation for people 65 or older, and have included in our analysis only people between the ages of 20 and 64. In the next decade, we expect to see a rise in the average age of people of working age, a slight decrease in the population size of the very young, a more significant decrease in the population size of people of ages between those of the previous two groups, and the elderly to account for 32 percent of the nation's total population by 2020.

As many previous studies have shown, among rural laborers, those with a more favorable demographic profile, for example, those who are better educated and younger, are more likely to migrate, to settle in places farther from home and for longer periods (Du and Wang, 2010). Since non-agricultural labor supply is closely linked to rural–urban labor migration, and except in cases where sufficiently strong incentives intrinsic to the labor market or the prospects for professional growth exist, people of working age tend to become less mobile as they get older. Moreover, since older urban workers tend to face greater risks of structural and frictional unemployment, and enrolment rate in higher education has continued to rise, an older labor force also means reduction in labor force participation rates.

3.3 Consequences for the labor market

An aging population presents two huge challenges to any society. On one hand, it poses a threat to the sustainability of the pension system and the elderly care infrastructure, and on the other hand, it reduces labor supply. In the period of reform, when there existed underemployment in both rural and urban sectors, the Chinese government actively helped promote employment by developing the labor market and reallocating people among different sectors and between rural and urban areas. Therefore, China's economic growth is on one hand partly attributable to the massive supply of labor, and on the other to the reallocative efficiency gained by labor mobility from agricultural to non-agricultural sectors, which constitutes the demographic dividend of total factor productivity growth (World Bank, 1997; Cai and Wang, 1999; Cai and Wang, 2005). As China enters a new era demographically, the impact on the labor market is enormous. These changes will shape the course of China's future development

3.3.1 Labor supply and demand: basic characteristics

Even though past forecasts for the annual increase in the number of new entrants to the nation's workforce never put it above 20 million, official figures for the number of new jobs needed each year to absorb the addition workers have been consistently larger. According to calculation done by the Ministry of Human Resources and Social Security, there are a total of more than 24 million people in the labor reserve. This number is arrived at by adding up the numbers for three groups of people: more than 10 million new entrants to the labor market each year, more than 8 million people currently unemployed who are looking for jobs, and over 6 million laid-off workers who need work (Zhang, 2008).

This calculation method is problematic, however. First of all, it is missing a temporal dimension and creates a false impression of timelessness. As the landscape of China's labor demand and supply has changed significantly in recent years, some of the basic categories assumed in this calculation no longer exist. For example, what used to be called "laid-off workers" were renamed in 2005 and are now referred to as the "registered unemployed". This means that, at least officially, there were no longer any laid-off workers in China but a total of 80 million "registered unemployed" in 2008. The second problem with this calculation is that it is based on the questionable assumption that all of the unemployed must be absorbed. But this assumption is neither necessary nor feasible. According to mainstream theories of employment, insofar as there is such a thing as a natural unemployment rate, it tends to stay fairly stable over the long run.

The demographic and economic trends described above have led to a changed relationship between labor supply and demand. Take the annual increase in the number of people between the ages of 16 and 64, on the supply side, and annual increase in the number of urban workers, on the demand side. When the two trends are examined together, the changing dynamics of the labor market become obvious. Since the number of agricultural workers has been falling while that of non-agricultural workers in rural areas is not expected to expand, we may treat the increases in the number of urban workers, migrant workers included, as representative of the magnitude of the overall labor demand of the Chinese economy.

In what follows, we take a closer look at the general employment situation in China by comparing the demand and the supply of labor for urban sectors. There are two parts to the statistical data on urban employment in China. The first includes the total number of urban employees, which is published by the National Bureau of Statistics (NBS). This number does not, however, cover most migrant workers in urban areas. According to estimation on the basis of micro data from 2009, only 12.5 percent of the total of 310 million urban employees were migrant workers. The second part includes the total number of people classifiable as migrant workers according to the NBS official definition. According to that definition, an individual qualifies as a "migrant worker" if s/he has been away from the town or township of their household registration for six months or more. Surveys have shown that of all migrant workers, 95.6 percent work and live in cities of varying sizes. Factoring in the overlap between these two numbers, we can calculate the actual number of urban workers inclusive of both registered urban residents and migrant workers. We can then compare this number with the total number of people of working age in the country (Table 3.1).

Between 2001 and 2011, labor demand of urban sectors, which encompasses employment among both urban residents and the migrants, grew at an annual rate of 3.2 percent. During the same period, labor supply, measured by the number of people of working age, grew by an annual rate of only 1.1 percent. For the purpose of this study, we have excluded people older than 60 from working-age population because, given China's retirement age—60 for men and 55 for women—they by default stand little chance of finding a job in the present labor market. A look at people between the ages of 15 and 59 shows that this population had begun to shrink by 2010. This suggests, among other things, that the problem of high rates of underemployment in both the rural and the urban labor markets was finally easing. As such, constant surplus

Table 3.1 Increases in demand for and supply of labor force (million, %)

	Urban resident workers		*Migrant workers*		*Working-age population*	
	Numbers	*Growth rate*	*Numbers*	*Growth rate*	*Numbers*	*Growth rate*
2001	236	-	80	-	885	-
2002	241	2.1	100	24.7	901	1.7
2003	246	2.0	109	8.8	914	1.5
2004	250	1.8	113	3.8	929	1.6
2005	254	1.7	120	6.4	944	1.6
2006	259	2.0	126	5.0	952	0.9
2007	265	2.1	131	3.7	960	0.8
2008	268	1.3	134	2.5	968	0.8
2009	272	1.4	139	3.5	974	0.7
2010	277	1.6	146	5.3	981	0.7
2011	280	1.0	152	3.7	986	0.6

Source: Authors' own calculation based on *China Statistical Yearbook* (various years), *China Yearbook of Rural Household Survey* (various years), and *China Population Yearbook* (various years).

of supply relative to demand no longer accurately describes China's labor market after the arrival of the Lewis turning point.

3.3.2 Wage increases for unskilled workers

Wages have been growing continuously in China since the late 1990s, when a huge number of workers were laid off in urban areas and labor productivity increased as a consequence. Since the beginning of this century, the average wage in major urban sectors has been rising at an annual rate of over 8 percent, which is unrivaled by any group anywhere in the world. However, understanding China's official statistical data on wages can be a challenge because of the complex ways in which they are collected and calculated. For example, data on urban wages cover only workers formally employed in formal sectors and leave out information on temporary workers and those who work in the informal sectors, therefore, such data cannot be completely relied upon if one wants to understand the dynamics of the situation in China with respect to wages. However, wage increases for migrant workers warrant close examination since they not only make up one-third of urban employment but also account for a large percentage of informal workers in non-agricultural sectors.

Until 2004, wages for migrant workers had shown little growth even though wages for urban workers who are local residents had begun to rise. In 2004, the country was hit by the first migrant labor shortage, which triggered a rapid increase in wages. As can be seen in Figure 3.3, wages for all sectors,

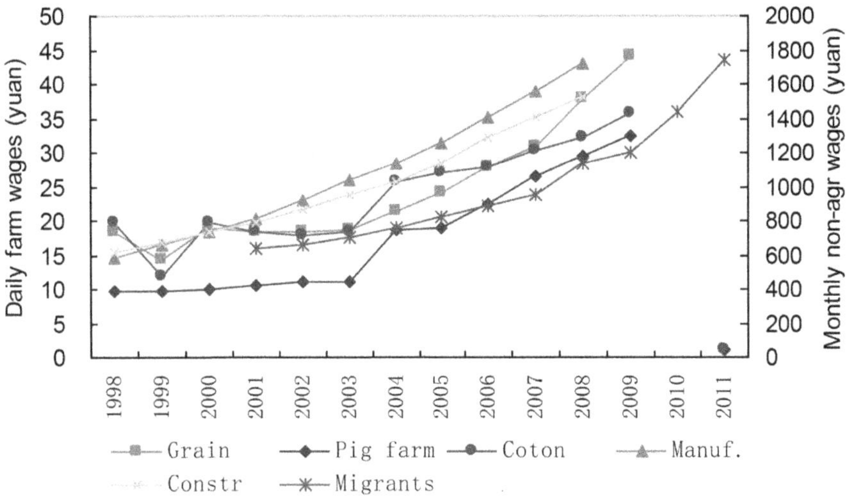

Figure 3.3 Wages increase in selected sectors.

Source: Data on the daily wages for workers in grain and cotton production and on hog farms with more than 50 hogs are from *Compilation of National Farm Product Cost-benefit Data*; monthly wages of manufacturing and construction are from *China Labor Statistics* (various years); Monthly wages of migrant workers are from *NBS Statistical Repor*t (various years).

including those dominated by migrant workers (such as manufacturing and construction), have been increasing constantly, while wage increases for migrant workers have been particularly impressive. We conclude, therefore, that observed wage increases are mainly attributable to changes in labor demand and supply. We have included here the figures for wage increases in select agricultural sectors as further evidence for the validity of this claim. Indeed, strong wage growth in agricultural sectors signals the decline of the dual economy, which, according to Lewis, is an economy characterized by surplus labor in agriculture.

Wages for migrant workers have been rising continuously since 2004, as a result of migrant labor shortage. Even the global financial crisis did not interrupt this trend. A survey done by the National Bureau of Statistics (NBS) shows that the average real monthly wage of migrant workers was 1,221 yuan in 2009, which was 90 percent higher than what it was in 2001. The real wage of migrant workers went up by 19 percent in 2010 and further increased by 21 percent in 2011. Other surveys and reports besides the one by NBS have put the figures for migrant labor wage increases even higher. For example, according to a survey conducted in early 2010 by the People's Bank of China, China's central bank, the average wage for migrant workers was 1,783.2 yuan in 2009 and was 17.8 percent higher than the year before (DSS-PBC, 2010).

In fact, because urban local workers and migrant workers tend to differ considerably with respect to their hours and pay structures, comparative analysis of the wages for the two groups must factor in both wage rates and working hours. According to a 2010 survey (China Urban Labor Survey, or CULS[1]), migrant workers worked for an average of 27 percent longer than do urban local workers per week, and their hourly wage rates were on average 88.2 percent of the average wage rate for local urban workers. This means that the reason the average monthly earning for migrant workers was higher (by 5.6 percent) than the number for urban local workers was that the former made up for lower hourly wage rates with longer hours worked.

Moreover, as the demographic profile of this population evolves, so do working habits. For example, younger workers today tend to work fewer hours than their older counterparts used to previously. Findings from CULS show that in 2010, migrant workers worked an average of almost 12.4 hours less than did migrant workers in 2005. This means that the increase in total monthly earning for migrant workers is a reflection of a substantial surge in wage rates (i.e., hourly rate).

3.3.3 Rise in labor disputes

In recent years, particularly after 2008, the year in which several labor-related laws were passed or updated, heightening workers' awareness of their rights and entitlements,[2] the incidence of labor disputes in China has sharply increased. According to official records, the total number of labor disputes in 2010 was twice what it was in 2003, and the number of severe unrests triggered by conflicts in labor relations has grown too. That is not necessarily a sign of a worsening trend in labor relations, but may be more of an indication of stronger demand for labor market institutions.

In his seminal work, Hirschman (1970) named three mechanisms—namely, exit, voice, and loyalty—by which citizens, consumers, and workers can express their dissatisfaction with conditions in the market. Here, we borrow those expressions to describe changed labor relations in China after the arrival of the Lewis turning point. As laborers in general, and migrant workers in particular (especially in China), enjoy more employment opportunities, there has also been greater room for them to exercise their rights by "voting with their feet", that is, by choosing "exit".

How individual migrant workers use their power of choice depends on what jobs they hold. For example, for workers who are dissatisfied with their jobs in small companies with poor growth prospects, they may simply quit since the odds are fairly good that they can find a better job elsewhere. But for workers who are dissatisfied with but reluctant to leave their jobs in sizable companies with some industry recognition and growth potential, efforts to seek higher pay and better working conditions may take the form of overt actions such as vocal complaints, collective bargaining, and in more extreme cases, strikes.

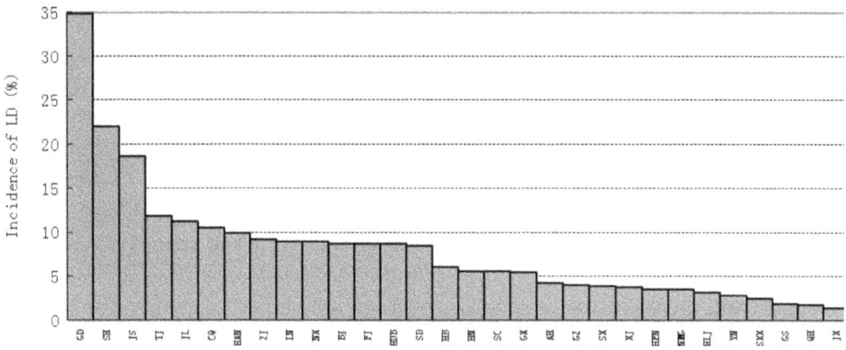

Figure 3.4 Incidence of labor dispute by province.

Note: According to China's official categorization, more developed provinces (the eastern region) include Beijing (BJ), Shanghai (SH), Tianjin (TJ), Jiangsu (JS), Zhejiang (ZJ), Guangdong (GD), Shandong (SD), Fujian (FJ), Liaoning (LN), Hainan (HAN), Hebei (HB); developmentally intermediate provinces (the central region) include Hunan (HUN), Hubei (HUB), Henan (HN), Jilin (JL), Heilongjiang (HLJ), Jiangxi (JX), Shanxi (SX), Anhui (AH); and least developed provinces (the western region) include Guangxi (GX), Shaanxi (SXX), Gansu (GS), Guizhou (GZ), Inner Mongolia (NMG), Xinjiang (XJ), Yunnan (YN), Ningxia (NX), Qinghai (QH), Sichuan (SC), Chongqing (CQ), and Tibet (XZ, omitted from Figure 3.4 due to data unavailability).

Source: National Bureau of Statistics (NBS) (2009), *China Labor Statistical Yearbook* (2009).

Figure 3.4 shows the level of labor dispute in different provinces as measured by the ratio between the number of reported cases and total employment. We can see that they happen more often in the more developed coastal regions than they do elsewhere. Of the total number of labor disputes in China in 2008, a vast majority, or 74.8 percent, took place in the eastern provinces.

There are several reasons for these regional variations in the occurrence of labor disputes. They are (1) the Lewis turning point came to the more developed regions earlier than it did elsewhere, (2) the more developed regions are also where migrant workers are most concentrated, and (3) since migrant workers are more vulnerable to abuse, they are correspondingly more likely to initiate actions in defense of their rights. The rise in labor disputes and the uneven geographical distribution of their occurrence both suggest that there has been a sharp increase both in worker awareness about rights and in the demand for the institutionalization of their protection.

3.4 Three vulnerable groups

In studying unemployment, scholars in macroeconomics and labor economics have mostly focused on two types of unemployment: cyclical unemployment and natural unemployment (which includes frictional and structural unemployment). In a typical labor market and under normal conditions, macroeconomic fluctuations are associated with temporary changes in the relationship between labor demand and supply, which generate cyclical unemployment. By contrast, natural unemployment, in either the form of frictional unemployment or the form of structural unemployment, is the effect of a mismatch between employment objectives of workers on one hand and employment opportunities employers can offer on the other. More specifically, such mismatch can reflect either the time cost of job search or changes in skill requirements.

As market mechanisms play an increasingly prominent role in labor allocation and macroeconomic business cycles in China, both cyclical and natural unemployment have existed there. According to one estimate (Cai et al., 2004), during the period between 1995 and 2002, roughly 60 to 80 percent of urban unemployment in China that had been observed was not the result of macroeconomic fluctuations and should be classified as natural unemployment.

According to Lewis (1954), as a dual economy grows, excess labor supply in agriculture is increasingly absorbed by expanding non-agricultural sectors. It is widely believed that 30 to 40 percent of China's agricultural labor force during the period between the mid-1980s and the late 1990s constituted excess supply (Taylor, 1993; Carter et al., 1996). Similarly, as a legacy of a planned economy, 30 to 40 percent of total employees of state-owned enterprises (SOEs) in urban areas were deemed dispensable (Zhang, 2008). Both of these forms of underemployment, affecting rural and urban sectors respectively, are tantamount to a kind of hidden unemployment. We can distinguish, therefore, three different forms of unemployment: cyclical, natural (frictional and structural), and hidden, and discuss changes in them separately.

When economic reform began in China, the Chinese economy was a typical dual economy characterized by a sharp rural–urban dichotomy, and high rates of hidden unemployment in both spheres. At the same time, both natural unemployment and cyclical unemployment have existed in China. The former is due to a combination of pervasive underdevelopment, inadequate public employment services, and the prevalence of mismatch between job skill and requirement; while the latter is due to macroeconomic fluctuations, which happened throughout the reform period. In order to be able to focus our analytical attention on how the transition away from a dual economy reduced hidden unemployment, the effects of urban employment policy reform, and the break-up of the "iron rice bowl" at SOEs, we shall assume that cyclical unemployment and natural unemployment stay relatively constant.

From Figure 3.5, a sketch map, one can see that since the beginning of China's reform policies, as the migration of surplus rural labor into urban areas and the reallocation of redundant urban workers continued, hidden unemployment shrank substantially in terms of both aggregate scale and percentage of total "unemployment". A number of empirical studies have shown that the massive flows of labor force from agricultural to non-agricultural

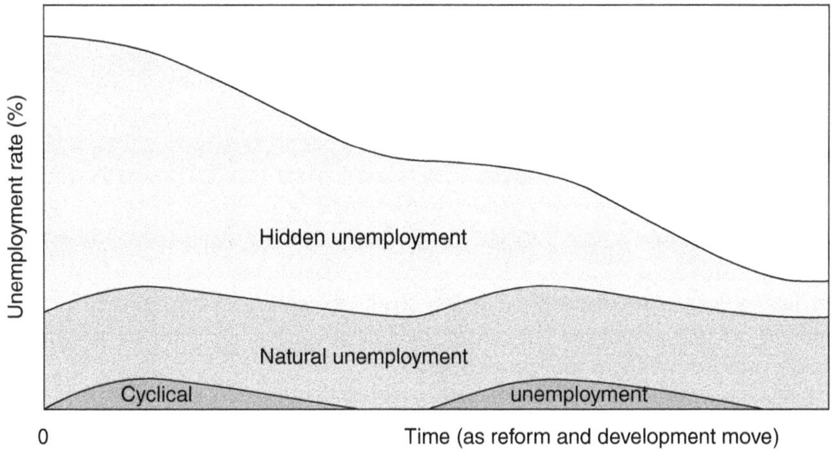

Figure 3.5 Unemployment types and their changing trends.

sectors and from rural to urban areas have contributed tremendously to the reduction in the amount of excess labor in agriculture (for example, Cai and Wang, 2008; Zhang et al., 2009). Since 2004, when the first nationwide labor shortage took place, the wage rates for ordinary workers have been rising continuously. This was by definition a Lewis turning point.

The urban labor market has been experiencing painful adjustments since the late 1990s, and a total of 40 million workers were laid off up to 2002. As the economy continues to grow and the labor market to evolve, people who had been laid off and were officially registered as unemployed have either found new jobs or retired. It seems, therefore, that while these kinds of adjustments help eliminate hidden unemployment in urban areas, older workers are more vulnerable to frictional and structural unemployment.

Three subpopulations in China are recognized by both the public and the government as being particularly vulnerable with respect to employment. These are migrant workers, college graduates, and urban workers who are relatively old and poorly educated, who suffer from unemployment or difficulty in finding jobs from time to time. By taking a closer look at each of these groups, one can begin to understand better the new challenges China is facing in this transition toward a neoclassical labor market.

A migrant worker is, literally, a "farmer-turned worker" in Chinese. Much of this population is made up of surplus labor in rural areas. One's status as a migrant worker does not necessarily mean that s/he is unwanted for agricultural production. More often, agricultural workers who choose to migrate into the cities do so because they better satisfy the personal conditions for migration than others. In other words, in comparison with those who stay behind, rural migrants have some notable advantages.

First, a higher percentage of migrants, who are mostly between the ages of 20 and 30, would have had some formal education. Many would have completed nine years of free education legally mandated in China. As such, this population is suitably prepared for most of the unskilled and/or semi-skilled jobs available in urban areas. Second, because they invariably lack access to social protection, including employment assistance, they can ill afford to stay unemployed and have no income. As a result, they tend to have a higher level of tolerance for poor pay and poor working condition and have a high rate of labor participation among them. Thirdly, since this population tends to suffer from spatial distance between where they live and where they can find a job, institutional exclusion from decision-making, and informational asymmetry between them and their employers, they tend to be cut off to a certain extent from market demand.

Today, agriculture is no longer able to reabsorb migrant returnees from the cities whenever urban labor demand crashes during an economic downturn. There are two major reasons for this. First, agricultural production has changed greatly from what it was in earlier times, in part as a result of the great labor hemorrhage; secondly, the demand for migrant workers in urban areas is now relatively inelastic. They are, therefore, no longer a reserve labor force but rather the pillar of the urban labor market. However, since they tend to receive weaker institutional protection and enjoy less of a social safety net, they are more likely to become victims of labor market volatility caused by macroeconomic fluctuations. As the macro economy goes through cycles of boom-and-bust, high rates of cyclical unemployment among migrant workers and migrant worker shortage take place alternately.

The difficulties in finding a job facing university graduates are a relatively new phenomenon. Before the massive expansion of university enrolment, university graduates were scarce human resources and tended to be highly valued in the labor market. Even though the system of job placement had largely been phased out by the end of the 1990s, as a group, college graduates had relatively little difficulty securing jobs and the unemployment rate among them remained low. This began to change, however, when the first graduates from the classes of enlarged enrolment entered the labor market. In 2001, when this group of students was yet to graduate from universities, the share of new entrants in the total unemployed who used publicly run employment services was 16.5 percent. By contrast, in 2002, when the graduates from the first class of enlarged enrolment who had spent three years or longer in colleges entered the labor market, that number increased to 20.1 percent. And in 2011, it reached 23.9 percent. Of these unemployed new entrants, 40.6 percent were that year's university graduates. A 2005 national survey shows that the unemployment rate was 8 percent among three-year college graduates and 6.1 percent for university graduates. Both these numbers were significantly higher than the urban average of 5.2 percent (Cai and Wang, 2009; Wang and Cai, 2009).

While the higher unemployment rate and the employment difficulties facing university graduates are no doubt in part caused by macroeconomic cycles of boom-and-bust, to a higher degree they are a case of frictional and structural unemployment. As human capital, university graduates in general have higher values than and are at an advantage relative to other groups, including migrant workers, (older) urban workers, and new entrants into the labor market with fewer years of formal education. They are, therefore, more likely to work in the formal sectors, to be better paid, and to enjoy more job security. However, since their training is more in specific skills than that of other groups, the job search for university graduates requires more time and more sophisticated matching mechanisms. As a result, they are more likely to face the risk of structural and frictional unemployment.

Among urban laborers, human capital deficiency is typically associated with older age, less formal education, poorer health, and outdated skills. This is another population that faces greater risks for natural unemployment. Let us consider the effect of education, for example. According to one study (Wang and Niu, 2009), for those in the 24–64 age range, each additional year of age corresponds to a 10.2 percent drop in education attainment. The correlation becomes more pronounced among older workers. For those in the 44–64 age range, each additional year of age represents a 16.1 percent reduction in the level of education attainment. Suppose there is a critical minimum to human capital—say (and not unreasonably), nine years of formal education, which is required for all Chinese citizens—the demarcation separating those who meet it and those who do not would be the age of 33.[3]

Therefore, this group of laborers is subject not only to the risks of lay-off induced by the campaign to break SOEs' "iron rice bowl" but also to the risks of frictional and structural unemployment. One silver lining for them, however, is that since most of them have urban *hukou*, or household registration, and are already living in urban communities, they tend to be counted properly in official statistics in regard to their employment status. By contrast, migrant workers are often discounted, undercounted, or uncounted altogether. This is evidenced by the fact that urban laborers have consistently accounted for a large share of the registered unemployed in official records. On the one hand, since the difficulties those laborers face are long-standing and persistent, registered unemployment in urban areas has been relatively insensitive to macroeconomic fluctuations. But on the other hand, they are also relatively well protected by the urban social security system and safety net.

3.5 Conclusions and policy implications

Thanks to rapid economic growth, fundamental changes in society, and strict implementation of family planning policies since the early 1980s, China has achieved a population transition, changing from one characterized by "high birth rate, low mortality rate, and high growth rate" to one characterized by "low birth rate, low mortality rate, and low growth rate", and has done so within a very short time. There have been a number of concomitant demographic changes, most notably with respect to age structure, which in particular has generated a demographic dividend during much of this period but this began to dissipate in the early twenty-first century. The labor market has responded to these developments, which can be clearly seen in the nationwide labor shortage and steep rises in workers' wages.

According to the literature of development economics, those phenomena signal the arrival of the Lewis turning point. Since this point marks a separation between a dual economic labor market and a neoclassical one, China faces new and fundamentally different tasks and challenges in its effort to maintain good order in its labor market and to keep unemployment rates low. In particular, instead of focusing exclusively on promoting employment, employment policies in China should also address problems of cyclical and natural unemployment, and in ways that uniquely suit the situation in China.

First, the household registration (or *hukou*) system, a unique institution that makes a sharp distinction between the rural and the urban labor markets, is a key target for reform if China's labor market is to see greater development. More specifically, one important part of this reform is to allow migrants to apply for urban resident status so they can have full access to social services. Not only can this help keep labor supply adequately large and stable, but also can it help reduce the negative effects of cyclical unemployment for migrant workers.

Second, education and training are areas in which more profound visions and more assertive government actions are urgently needed. In China, one serious problem is that wage convergence tends to generate a disincentive to complete schooling. To counter this tendency, heavier public spending toward education and better coordination between the education system and the labor market are imperative. Boosting labor force participation through, say, increasing the retirement age can only be effective if accompanied by systematic increases in continuing education and job training for older workers.

Third, the construction of labor market institutions is now of critical importance. Lessons from the experiences of both advanced countries and those of middle-income level suggest that labor market institutions, including industrial relations legislation, a minimum wage regime, laws governing collective bargaining, and unemployment protection, are instrumental for coordinating the demands of different groups and for maintaining social cohesion.

Notes

1 China Urban Labor Survey or CULS is a series of surveys conducted by the Institute of Population and Labor Economics, Chinese Academy of Social Sciences, in 2001, 2005, and 2010, respectively. It representatively sampled laborers in urban households and migrant households and surveyed both individual laborers and households in Shanghai, Wuhan, Shenyang, Fuzhou, and Xi'an.

2 In the year 2008 alone, three labor-related laws began to be implemented, of which the Employment Contract Law emphasizes enhancing employment security and providing better protection for migrant workers and the urban working vulnerable, the Employment Promotion Law clearly claims the responsibility of governments in promoting employment and in eliminating various kinds of labor market discrimination, and the Labor Disputes Mediation and Arbitration Law is intended to provide a legal framework for improving labor relations.

3 The critical age here is estimated based on data for the country as a whole. Because education attainment level in rural areas is lower than that in urban areas, it may rise a little if we examine the urban working-age population. The conclusion holds unchanged—that is, the older the less educated, and the critical point of nine years of compulsory education arrives much before the official retirement age. For a related analysis of education attainments and returns to human capital in both rural and urban areas, see Wang, 2009.

References

Cai, F. (2004). The Consistency of China's Statistics on Employment: Stylized Facts and Implications for Public Policies, *Chinese Economy*, 37(5), pp. 74–89.

Cai, F., and Wang, D. (1999). The Sustainability of China's Economic Growth and the Contributions of Labor, *Economic Research Journal*, 10, pp. 62–68.

Cai, F., and Wang, D. (2005). China's Demographic Transition: Implications for Growth, in Ross Garnaut and Song Ligang (eds.), *The China Boom and Its Discontents*, Canberra: Asia Pacific Press.

Cai, F., and Wang, M. (2008). A Counterfactual Analysis on Unlimited Surplus Labor in Rural China, *China & World Economy*, 16(1), pp. 51–65.

Cai, F., and Wang, M. (2009). The Chinese Employment Situation and Youth Employment Difficulties, in Cai Fang (ed.), *The China Population and Labor Yearbook Volume 10: The Sustainability of Economic Growth from the Perspective of Human Resources*, Beijing: Social Sciences Academic Press.

Cai, F., Yang, D., and Gao, W. (2004). Employment Elasticity, NAIRU and Macroeconomic Policies, *Economic Research Journal*, 9, pp. 18–25.

Carter, C., Zhong, F., and Cai, F. (1996). *China's Ongoing Reform of Agriculture*, San Francisco, CA: 1990 Institute.

DSS-PBC (Department of Survey and Statistics, People's Bank of China) (2010). The Fifth Monitoring Report on Migrant Workers, in Cai Fang (ed.), *The China Population and Labor Yearbook Volume 11: Labor Market Challenges in the Post-Crisis Era*, Beijing: Social Sciences Academic Press.

Du, Y., and Wang, M. (2010). New Estimate of Surplus Rural Labor Force and Its Implications, *Journal of Guangzhou University (Social Science Edition)*, 9(4), pp. 17–24.

Gu, B., and Li, J. (2010). *The Debate on China's Population Policy in the 21st Century*, Beijing: Social Sciences Academic Press.

Hirschman, A. (1970). *Exit, Voice, and Loyalty: Responses to Decline in Firms, Organizations, and States*, Cambridge, MA: Harvard University Press.

Lewis, A. (1954). Economic Development with Unlimited Supply of Labor, *Manchester School of Economic and Social Studies*, 22, 139–191.

Taylor, J. R. (1993). Rural Employment Trends and the Legacy of Surplus Labor, 1978–1989, in Y. Y. Kueh and R. F. Ash (eds.), *Economic Trends in Chinese Agriculture: The Impact of Post-Mao Reforms*, New York: Oxford University Press.

United Nations (2010). World Fertility Patterns, 2009, New York: United Nations. www.un.org/en/development/desa/population/publications/fertility/fertility-patterns.asp.

United Nations (2011). *World Population Prospects: The 2010 Revision*, CD-ROM edn, New York: United Nations.

Wang, M. (2009). Universal High School and Mass Higher Education, in Cai Fang (ed.), *The China Population and Labor Yearbook Volume 10: The Sustainability of Economic Growth from the Perspective of Human Resources*, Beijing: Social Sciences Academic Press.

Wang, D., and Cai, F. (2009). The Education and Employment of Rural and Urban Youth in China, in Cai Fang (ed.), *The China Population and Labor Yearbook Volume 10: The Sustainability of Economic Growth from the Perspective of Human Resources*, Beijing: Social Sciences Academic Press.

Wang, G., and Niu, J. (2009). Composition and Development of the Chinese Education System, in Cai Fang (ed.), *The China Population and Labor Yearbook Volume 10: The Sustainability of Economic Growth from the Perspective of Human Resources*, Beijing: Social Sciences Academic Press.

World Bank (1997). *China 2020: Development Challenges in the New Century*, Washington, DC: World Bank.

Zhang, X. (ed.) (2008). *The Reforms and Developments of Chinese Employment*, Beijing: China Labor and Social Security Press.

Zhang, X., Jin, Y., and Wang, S. (2009). Has China Reached the Lewis Turning Point? Evidence from Poor Regions, *Journal of Zhejiang University Humanities and Social Sciences*), 6, pp. 1–18.

4 China's economic slowdown from a supply-side perspective

4.1 Introduction

As a global phenomenon, economic slowdown has been widely debated in the business community and economics academia. When viewed in the context of middle-income countries, economic slowdown finds expression in another topic: the "middle-income trap". In reality, both the causes and manifestations of economic slowdown vary across countries, with each requiring a different perspective. Chinese and international scholars have put forward insightful yet different ideas on the causes of and countermeasures to global economic slowdown and its impact on world economic outlook. Their differences in views are more striking when it comes to economic slowdown in a particular country.

Regarding the reasons for China's slowdown after 2012, opinions differ and sometimes are even polar opposites of each other among opinion leaders, economists, and even decision-makers. A misunderstanding of the economic situation will lead to unjustified pessimism about China's economy as well as wrongly blaming China for the world's economic woes. Worse, the misperception will misguide China's policy options. Given the depth and persistence of the current round of economic slowdown, a correct understanding and poised reaction is not only essential for China to surmount the "middle-income trap" and build a moderately prosperous society in all respects, but is also pivotal to world economic confidence and outlook. China's three decades of uninterrupted economic surge and rags-to-riches story are inspirational to developing countries. Yet only by soundly tackling the current slowdown will the China miracle come to a perfect completion and will the Chinese experience have convincing referential value. Thus, China's economic slowdown should and deserves to be an important topic of discussion in mainstream economics.

After adoption of the reform and opening-up policy in 1978, China's economy sustained rapid growth for over three decades, with the annual growth rate averaging 9.9 percent until 2011. Despite some volatility (after the growth rate exceeded 9 percent in 1982, it fell below 8 percent in 1989–1990 and 1998–1999, respectively), the economic boom in this period was unprecedented in China's history. Considering the minimum growth target of 8 percent for this period,[1] this paper defines the first year when China's growth continually fell below 8 percent, that is, 2012, as the starting point of the slowdown. After falling to 7.7 percent in 2012 and 2013, China's growth rate further dipped to 7.3 percent and 6.9 percent respectively in 2014 and 2015.

In parallel with the overall slowdown, some positive changes have occurred in the composition of China's economic growth. First of all, the relationship among growth in the primary, secondary, and tertiary industries is better aligned, contributing to a healthier economic structure. Traditionally, China's secondary industry had been growing faster than tertiary industry since 1978. Yet in the context of slowdown, growth of the secondary industry fell by a much larger margin; in 2014, contribution by the tertiary industry to GDP growth exceeded 50 percent for the first time, and the tertiary industry thus became a major engine of growth. Secondly, regional growth and particularly growth among China's eastern, central, and western regions became more balanced. As can be seen from the decomposition of GDP growth contribution by region shown in Figure 4.1,[2] the slowdown first struck China's eastern region and persisted thereafter. On the other hand, thanks to a host of regional development strategies introduced by the Chinese government, the growth rates and contribution of China's central and western regions has continuously increased since 2000, thus narrowing the regional gaps. However, the slowdown in China's central and western regions in 2012 was a key factor behind China's slowdown to below 8 percent.

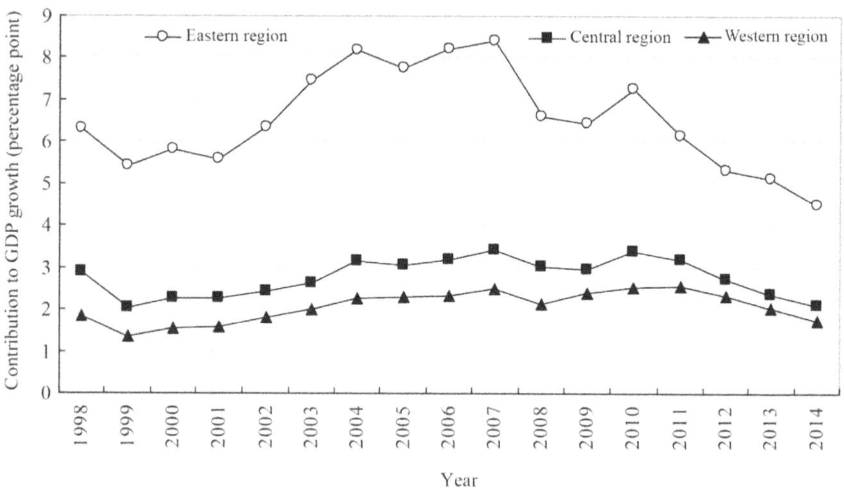

Figure 4.1 Contribution of China's eastern, central, and western regions to its GDP growth.

Source: NBS, 1998–2014.

It needs to be noted that China's economic slowdown coincided with the world economic downturn after the eruption of the global financial crisis. According to the World Bank's database, based on 2005 US dollars, global GDP growth rate plummeted in 2008 and 2009, down to 1.5 percent and –2.1 percent respectively. Despite a short-lived uptick to 4.1 percent in 2010, growth nosedived again thereafter. From 2011 to 2015, world economic growth rates registered 2.8, 2.3, 2.4, 2.5, and 2.4 percent respectively, failing to recover to the pre-crisis level.

In 2014, the low-income countries as defined by the World Bank (with gross national income or GNI per capita below US$1,035) had an average GDP growth rate of 6.3 percent; lower middle-income countries (GNI per capita between US$1,075 and US$4,086) grew by 5.7 percent; upper middle-income countries (GNI per capita between US$4,086 and US$12,616) grew by 4.6 percent; and high-income countries (GNI per capita above US$12,616) only grew by 1.7 percent. At a minimum, this group of figures suggests the following messages: first, countries in different stages of development have different sources and potentials of growth, hence their different growth rates; second, China's growth rate registered 7.3 percent in 2014, which was significantly above the average growth of 4.6 percent among countries of similar stages of development and was also much higher than the average growth rate of 6.3 percent among low-income countries; third, the shift of gears in economic growth is a milestone in China's transition from an upper middle-income status to a high-income status.

Without a doubt, China's economic slowdown is part of the world economic slowdown. However, if the above analysis still falls short of what needs to be explained, the following sections of this paper will reveal that the new normal of China's economy and the new mediocrity of the world economy are vastly different in terms of the manifestations, causes, and solutions. Over the years, the "China collapse" theory in its various versions never failed to crop up every now and then. The same authors feasted on every chance by peddling their predictions on China's economy. None of their predictions proved true. Yet this time, China's economy finally slowed down. Some observers and investors or speculators are thus once again prompted to join the camp of selling China out. Nevertheless, given the blatant defects in their arguments, this paper does not intend to discuss them unless necessary; instead it focuses only on studies that follow economics methodologies, and it will attempt to clarify some misperceptions about China's economic slowdown to shed light on the real outlook of China's economy and convince readers that the China miracle has not ended.

4.2 Cyclical perspective fails to capture the change of development stage

The most common explanation of China's slowdown is the "insufficient demand theory". For instance, Justin Yifu Lin (2011) explained the recent round of slowdown as demand-side reasons (thus also cyclical reasons) behind China's shrinking net exports after the global financial crisis. The theory believes that once demand bottlenecks are overcome by beefing up investment, a new boom will start and China's economy will return to its normal track of above 8 percent growth rates. Similar views in favor of stimulating demand hold sway among Chinese and international economists. However, unlike Justin Yifu Lin's, not many studies provide empirical evidence. By comparing the per capita GDP of an economy to the level of the United States as a measurement of the development stage, Justin Yifu Lin discovered that China's current per capita GDP is equivalent to 20 percent of that of the United States. This level of development was what Japan achieved in 1951, Singapore in 1967, Chinese Taiwan in 1975, and South Korea in 1977. Data suggest that in the two decades after reaching this level, the above-mentioned economies respectively scored annual economic growth rates of 9.2, 8.6, 8.3, and 7.6 percent. The conclusion thus arrived at is that China still enjoys great potential for rapid growth for years to come. However, such a method of comparing development stages fails to take demographics into account.

It has been proven in economic history that an increasing proportion of working-age population and falling dependency ratio will bring about demographic dividends that propel growth. Using an econometric model, Cai and Zhao (2012) decomposed China's post-1978 growth into the following factors. First, as a low dependency ratio created conditions for a high savings rate and unlimited supply of labor bolstered marginal return to capital, capital accumulation in China has been a major driver of growth. Second, an abundance of labor supply and growing levels of education (human capital) are undoubtedly conducive to economic growth. Third, the transfer of labor from agriculture to urban jobs enhances resource reallocation efficiency, which is responsible for nearly half of China's total factor productivity (TFP) improvement. All of these factors underpinning China's economic growth are a result of favorable demographics.

Hence, demographics cannot be overlooked in reckoning China's development stage and future growth outlook. Whether demographics are considered or neglected will lead to vastly different conclusions in viewing stage of development, that is, if the growth tendency of the working-age population is factored in, the conclusion will be very different from that based on per capita GDP. Specifically, if the year when China's working-age population aged between 15 and 59 years peaked is used as the benchmark of comparison, China's development stage in 2010 was actually equivalent to the level of Japan between 1990 and 1995, the level of South Korea between 2010 and 2015, and the level of Singapore between 2015 and 2020 (Figure 4.2). If the dependency ratio (population aged below 14 years plus population aged above 60 years divided by population aged between 15 and 59 years), which often serves as a proxy variable of demographic dividends in econometric modeling, is used, the time points when it bottomed for Japan, South Korea, and Singapore are much later than the time points defined by their per capita

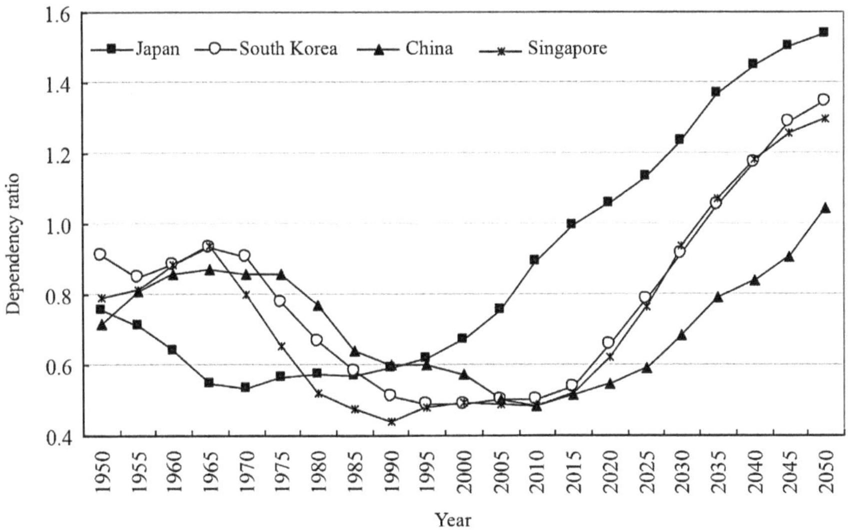

Figure 4.2 Turning points of dependency ratios for China, Japan, South Korea, and Singapore.

Source: United Nations, 2011.

income levels (Figure 2). For instance, while Japan's dependency ratio fell to the lowest point around 1970, it did not spike until the 1990s. The rising dependency ratios of South Korea and Singapore are generally synchronous with China's.

That is to say, relative to per capita GDP, China's demographic transition is much steeper and its turning point of demographic dividends arrives much earlier. Given China's three-decade reliance on demographic dividends, which are diminishing, China's potential growth rate should be estimated using another approach, which leads to different forecasts of China's economic outlook with very different policy implications. Based on the tendency of demographic change and its impact on production factors and TFP, Cai and Yang (2013) estimated China's potential GDP growth between 1979 and 2020. Judging by the average numbers of various timeframes, China's potential GDP growth was 9.66 percent between 1979 and 1994, 10.34 percent between 1995 and 2010, down to 7.55 percent between 2011 and 2015, and is projected to further dip to 6.20 percent between 2016 and 2020.

By subtracting potential growth rates from actual growth rates, we may arrive at the growth gaps for various years (Figure 4.3), which help take stock of the macroeconomic volatility since China's reform and opening-up initiated in 1978. In Figure 4.3, the cases of actual growth rates being above potential growth rates represent positive gaps, while those of real growth rates being below potential growth rates represent negative gaps. In the figure, the

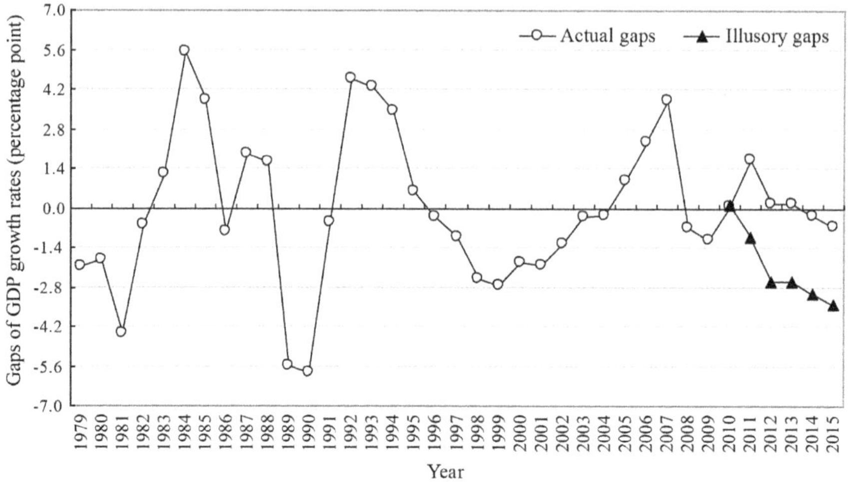

Figure 4.3 Actual and illusory gaps of GDP growth rates for China.
Source: Calculated based on the data of Cai and Yang, 2013.

years with significant negative gaps correspond to macroeconomic downturns. If potential growth rate is viewed in the context of a specific development stage, production factors supply and TFP improvement potentials that are considered endowments of a given time can support an economy to realize its potential of growth; yet negative gaps normally correspond to cyclical disturbance from the demand side, preventing actual growth from reaching its potential and production factors from being fully utilized. At these moments, such problems as insufficient utilization of production factors as reflected in cyclical unemployment will occur. By the same token, an opposite situation is positive gaps resulting from actual growth rate above potential growth rate, which corresponds to economic overheating, as reflected in inflation or economic bubbles.

Based on the potential growth rates between 1979 and 1994 and between 1995 and 2010 reckoned by Cai and Yang (2013), the gaps of growth rates for these timeframes can be calculated by subtracting the average potential growth rates from the actual growth rates in the corresponding years. In these timeframes, China's economic growth demonstrated three cycles of volatility, creating four troughs in 1981, 1990, 1999, and 2009, and the length of each cycle coincided with what was considered the "Juglar cycle". As a result of shifting stage of development, the average potential growth rates will drop to 7.55 percent and 6.2 percent for the periods between 2011 and 2015 and between 2016 and 2020, respectively. Following the same method of calculation, there is barely any gap of growth rate in the current slowdown (see the hollow circular curve tendency in Figure 4.3). However, if China's economy is habitually expected to maintain the original level of growth without recognizing declines in potential growth rate, e.g., if the 10.34 percent rate during the period between 1995 and 2010 is used as a benchmark, gaps of growth rate could be illusorily observed (see the results shown in the solid triangular curve in Figure 4.3).

Gaps of growth rate are not unique to China but represent a subject of macroeconomics and a situation that needs to be dealt with in macroeconomic policy-making. For advanced economies, long-term growth trends can be seen as potential growth rates as their economic growth is normally in the neoclassical steady state, and the gaps of growth rate stemming from faster or slower real growth are manifested as economic cycles. In this sense, frequent growth volatility is a cyclical phenomenon. When negative gaps of growth occur, attention is naturally drawn to the demand side for a way out. Despite contradictory arguments from different schools of macroeconomics, whenever the economy is in recession, governments and central banks are tempted to resort to fiscal or monetary policies or a combination of both to resist cyclical volatility.

The "real business cycle theory" attempts to eliminate the boundary between cycle and growth, recognizing that productivity shocks could change the normality of growth rate. Yet this school of theory focuses on the negation of cycles caused by demand-side shocks rather than differentiating between cyclical phenomena and growth stages. While this theory deserves our attention, as cyclical and growth issues are interchangeable and interwoven, whether in terms of theory or practice, it is necessary to classify slowdown into cyclical slowdown and change of development stage, especially when China as a fast-growing and rapid-changing case is considered.

The lesson of Japan's "lost three decades", where the economic slowdown was seen as a demand-side problem in the 1970s when the country's demographic dividend diminished, should be learned. In response to its slowdown, the Japanese government adopted an extremely loose macroeconomic policy and interventionist industrial policy. Instead of boosting the real economy and infrastructure, however, unleashed liquidity and broad money led to skyrocketing asset prices and unprecedented economic bubbles, which finally burst and dragged the economy into recession. In tackling the recession after the burst of asset bubbles, the Japanese government continued to adopt stimulus policies that protected obsolete firms and created zombie firms, which took a toll on overall innovation and TFP (Hayashi and Prescott, 2002), bringing about various supply-side hurdles to potential economic growth.

For China, the economic slowdown since 2012 has resulted from a falling potential growth rate as a result of demographic transition or change in the stage of economic development. Therefore, there were no negative gaps of growth rate. As demonstrated in another article of the author's, the slowdown did not lead to cyclical unemployment, and labor shortage continued to beleaguer China's economy (Cai, 2016). In approaching China's slowdown, macroeconomists should view a longer horizon of growth instead of being confined to the traditional cyclical perspective. On the other hand, while the problem facing us is a long-term growth phenomenon, there is no doubt that an economy could be struck by cyclical problems at any time, so we must stay vigilant and pay close attention to both changes in the development stage and cyclical volatility.

4.3 Convergence perspective has missed China's story

Economists indeed approach China's slowdown from the perspective of economic growth. For instance, Pritchett and Summers (2014) considered that any growth rate above the average level is abnormal and has to regress toward the mean, which is understood to be the average growth rate of the world economy. This methodology is based on the famous Galton's Fallacy, that is, the average height of the members of an extended family cannot stay abnormal over a long period of time and tends to regress toward the average level of the overall population. The same statistical pattern is followed in economic growth. According to their forecast, China's economic growth will fall to 5.01 percent between 2013 and 2023 and further fall to 3.28 percent between 2023 and 2033, that is, what Pritchett and Summers referred to as the "mean".

The two authors applied "regression toward the mean" to explain China's slowdown and claimed that such a statistical pattern was unavoidable. With a set of panel data, their argument overshadowed the protracted and varied growth practices of numerous countries, overlooking the catch-up attributes of developing countries. Since this argument fails to explain the spectacular growth that took place in catching-up economies like Japan, the Four Asian Tigers, and China, and since it does not provide any reasonable interpretation of China's slowdown, the "regression toward the mean" prediction is not convincing. Delineating the growth percentages of China's economy in the coming 20 years following this methodology is like making a pair of "mean-sized" shoes for everybody in the world, regardless of their gender, age, and size.

Barro (2016) arrived at a similar prediction and conclusion, that is, China's economic growth rate will swiftly fall to the level of 3 to 4 percent, thus missing the official growth targets of 6 to 7 percent set for the Thirteenth Five-Year Plan (FYP) period (2016–2020). His argument is based on his copyrighted "conditional convergence" analytical framework. In his growth regression model, the determinants of growth rate are classified into the following two types: first, the convergence effect with initial per capita GDP (in logarithm) as an independent variable; second, the group of explanatory variables that determines the steady state of growth (otherwise referred to as "X variables"). After numerous rounds of growth regression, he developed what he believed to be the "iron law of convergence", that is, it is impossible for a country to converge with a more advanced economy or its own steady state with a growth rate that deviates from 2 percent over a long period of time; now that China's growth has significantly outstripped what is predicted under this model, it is thus unlikely for China to maintain its current growth momentum in the future.

Granted, with a rising per capita income level and narrowing potentials of convergence, slowdown is undoubtedly a natural outcome. However, even if Barro's analytical framework of convergence is recognized, numerous X variables that affect growth still exist outside the law of convergence. Barro conceded that for a particular economy, there could be unique X variables or country-specific attributes that defy the so-called "iron law" or "mean". For instance, Barro and his collaborator (Barro and Sala-i-Martin, 1995) incorporated more than 100 explanatory variables into their growth regression model and discovered their significance. China's economic growth story not only has general significance but is unique as well. Overlooking China's uniqueness will cause China's growth potential to be underestimated and the timing and extent of its slowdown to be misjudged.[3]

Eichengreen et al. (2011) do not admit any iron law of economic slowdown. They made special efforts in identifying the country-specific factors of slowdown in economy and TFP. According to their findings, an economy will encounter two rounds of deceleration when its per capita GDP in 2005 purchasing power parity terms is in the range between US$10,000 and US$11,000 and between US$15,000 and US$16,000, respectively. By their definition, China has yet to reach the typical starting point of slowdown, that is, US$10,000, but partially meets the definition of slowdown, that is, its growth rate dropped from about 10 percent before 2012 to less than 8 percent afterwards, down 2 or 3 percentage points. Although comparison is conducted between the average growth rates of seven years before the slowdown and seven years after the slowdown, what we know for sure is that China's economy indeed cannot return to its 10 percent growth rate.

In another paper, Eichengreen et al. (2013) identified a few common factors related to slowdown, including, inter alia, the "regression toward the mean" effect, diminishing demographic dividend caused by population-aging, falling returns as a result of high investment rates, as well as an underestimated exchange rate that impedes the upgrade of industrial structure. They also identified some factors that can reduce the probability of slowdown, such as better human capital accumulation. However, they did not present a clear account of the causal relationship between certain factors and slowdown, nor did they distinguish cyclical factors from growth factors. On the other hand, they laid no special emphasis on the important findings in their earlier paper (Eichengreen et al., 2011), that is, TFP reduction can explain 85 percent of economic slowdown. Nevertheless, this omission was compensated for in another paper by the same authors specifically on TFP slowdown (Eichengreen et al., 2015).

The definition of economic slowdown by Eichengreen et al. is that growth rate declines by 2 or 3 percentage points before and after the turning point of slowdown. The difference between their average case in general and China's case in particular is that the decline of growth rate from 5.6 to 2.1 percent (down 3.5 percentage points) observed in the data of various countries (Eichengreen et al., 2013) has different significance from China's falling growth rate from 11.3 percent in the Eleventh FYP period to 7.8 percent in the twelfth FYP period (also down by 3.5 percentage points). That is, while the former represents a drop of 62.5 percent, the latter represents a drop of only 31.0 percent. Even at today's rate, China's economic growth still passes for rapid growth by international standards. Whereas slowdown is an inevitable result of the change in development stage, numerous opportunities exist to help prevent China's deceleration from evolving into stagnation or becoming too severe.

Demand-side disturbance to the macroeconomy is inevitable in any stage of development. What matters is to differentiate between the new normal of economy and the short-term shocks and to tackle China's slowdown from the supply side rather than the demand side. In deliberating on the long-term sustainability of China's economy, we should put aside the the national accounting identical equation $Y = C + I + G + (E - M)$, or analysis framework troika of consumption, investment, and export, and focus on the analytical methodology of production function ($Y = A * F(K, L) = K^{\alpha} * (AL)^{1-\alpha}$). Proceeding from the latter perspective, the long-term supply-side factors behind China's slowdown, which are also the areas where efforts must be made to prevent or mitigate the slowdown, are manifested in the following aspects.[4]

First, as a result of labor shortage, wage growth has outstripped productivity improvement, giving rise to spiking unit labor cost. Between 2004 and 2015, for rural migrant workers as the representative group of the unskilled and semiskilled workers, their real wage increased by 10.7 percent on an annual average basis. The shortage of labor accelerated the capital–labor substitution or the substitution of workers by machines (robots). Consequently, the capital–labor ratio spiked and return to capital dropped, while productivity growth failed to keep pace. According to the latest data of the Conference Board (2015), the annual average growth of labor productivity in China fell from 9.5 percent in the period between 2007 and 2012 to 7.3 percent in the period between 2012 and 2013, 7 percent in 2014, and foreseeably, 6.7 percent in 2015. As a result, the unit labor cost (the ratio of wage to productivity) in China increased by a much faster pace compared with major manufacturing countries in the world. According to estimates (Cai and Yang, 2015), from 2004 to 2013, the unit labor cost of China's manufacturing sector as a percentage of those of Germany, Japan (data of 2011), South Korea, and the United States climbed from 19.9 to 29.7 percent, from 24.8 to 39.5 percent, from 25.8 to 36.7 percent, and from 24.5 to 38.7 percent respectively.

Secondly, the improvement of human capital slows down due to a diminishing number of new entrants to the labor market. The distribution of the years of schooling for China's working-age population has the following characteristics: the higher the age, the less educated a workforce will be. Hence, a young workforce is a major driver of human capital accumulation. Once the number of young workers diminishes, increment in human capital will be dented. By roughly aggregating the numbers of graduates (and dropouts) at each level of education as new entrants into the workforce each year, we expect to witness a drop of the new entrants by an annual rate of 1.1 percent between 2011 and 2020. By identifying graduates after completing primary school, junior middle school, high school, college, postgraduate school, and doctoral education as having received 6 years, 9 years, 12 years, 16 years, 19 years, and 21 years of schooling, we can calculate the total increment of human capital for each year. Our forecast shows that this number will also diminish at an average speed of 1.0 percent between 2011 and 2020.

Thirdly, the economics law of diminishing return to capital began to kick in and return to investment flattened. The unlimited supply of labor under China's dual economy development underpinned the high return to capital over the past three decades. After crossing the Lewis turning point in 2004, this attribute vanished and the capital–labor ratio soared, resulting in diminishing returns to capital. According to the reckoning of Bai and Zhang (2014), return to capital in China fell from 24.3 percent in 2004 to 14.7 percent in 2013, witnessing a negative annual growth rate of 5.7 percent.

Lastly, with narrowing room for resource reallocation, TFP improvement will also slow down. In the first couple of decades after China's reform and opening up, TFP improvement played a pivotal role in China's economic growth. Research discovered that the change in the industrial structure of Asian economies is characterized by the transfer of labor from less productive sectors to more productive ones. Efficiency gains from resource reallocation serve as a major driver of TFP improvement (McMillan and Rodrik, 2011). China's economic growth and sectoral adjustment over the past three decades provide a perfect proof of this assertion. Although TFP slowdown is a global phenomenon (Eichengreen et al., 2015), China's demographic change is a unique country factor, which is depleting the potential of resource reallocation and causing TFP growth deceleration.

According to demographic analysis, whether measured by resident population or registered population, rural population aged between 16 and 19 peaked in 2014, before entering a stage of negative growth. Population of this age group comprises the vast majority of the annual increment of migrant workers. Such a demographic change inevitably slows down the transfer of rural labor. According to NBS data, the number of migrant workers increased by 4 percent on an annual average basis from 2005 to 2010. This figure dropped to 1.3 percent in 2014 and further declined to 0.3 percent in 2015. Restricted by the household registration system, migrant workers have little chance to become permanent urban residents. Therefore, labor migration between rural and urban areas demonstrates a two-way pattern. If the annual increment of migrant laborers becomes smaller than those returning from cities to their rural hometowns, the structural change will be set back, which further impedes TFP improvement.

4.4 Supply-side structural reform brings dividends

Approaching China's slowdown from a demand-side perspective will lead to policy orientation in favor of stimulus measures of macroeconomic and industrial policies. Once we come to realize that China's slowdown is mainly caused by the supply-side factors, we may deduce that the above approach will only bring the actual growth rate above the potential growth rate, which would be of no avail to improve potential growth rate. What supply-side policy strives to achieve is to raise the potential growth rate. As revealed by the above analysis, China's potential economic growth is driven by two factors. First is the maintenance of the traditional growth momentum. This does not mean that the traditional factor-driven pattern of growth must be sustained. Rather, the potentials of production factors and especially labor supply must be exploited to extend the demographic dividend. Second, new engines of growth must be kick-started by bolstering human capital accumulation and contribution of TFP growth to economic growth. These sources of growth as reflected in the following aspects must be unleashed through supply-side structural reform.

4.4.1 Increasing labor participation in high-productivity sectors

Since almost all the factors underpinning China's slowdown are related to the end of unlimited labor supply, increasing labor supply can significantly mitigate the fall of growth rate. Following the peak of the working-age population aged between 15 and 59 years, the economically active population aged between 15 and 59 years will also peak in 2017 and enter into negative growth afterwards. In this sense, China no longer has potential for labor increase and the only way to exploit labor supply potential is to increase labor participation. Given China's huge working-age population, 1 percentage point of labor participation corresponded to over 9 million economically active workers in 2015. As suggested by simulation (Cai and Yang, 2013), between 2011 and 2022, an increase of the labor participation rate in non-agricultural sectors by 1 percentage point would reap 0.88 percentage points of additional potential growth rate. The greatest potential in labor participation rate lies in reforming the household registration (*hukou*) system to increase the urbanization rate of the registered population and stabilize employment of migrant workers in the urban sectors.

4.4.2 Raising the total fertility rate to balance the future age structure

According to Chinese and international experience, a falling fertility rate is the result of economic and social development, whereas the effect of birth policy itself is minor. Still, considering China's implementation of the "one-child" policy over the past 35 years since 1980, the reform allowing couples to raise a second child will increase fertility in a certain period of time to come. It is generally believed that China's current total fertility rate is 1.5 and the adjusted birth policy should more or less move the total fertility rate toward the replacement level of 2.1. Policy simulation suggests that if the total fertility rate is increased to around 1.8, China's potential growth rate will be increased by 0.2 percentage points for the period between 2036 and 2040 as compared with the scenario of a total fertility rate of 1.6 (Cai and Yang, 2016). It needs to be noted that demographic reform must go beyond birth policy adjustments and should also encompass public service improvements to make child-raising more affordable and desirable.

4.4.3 *Maintaining the speed of human capital accumulation*

Based on experiences in East Asian economies, Masahiko Aoki (2012) discovered that a development stage featuring Kuznets structural adjustment is invariably followed by a new stage of development driven by human capital. The shift of stages is marked by the Lewis turning point that was observed in many East Asian economies, including China. According to simulation conducted by Cai and Yang (2016), based on reasonable assumptions, expected strengthening of education and training in the short and medium term will increase the potential growth rate by 0.1 percentage points. Such a reform dividend is non-trivial for China to maintain moderately high growth rates and avert medium and even lower growth rates in the short run. In addition, as revealed in a study, after the quality of education is taken into consideration, the contribution of human capital to economic growth can be substantially bigger, even outweighing the contribution of productivity (Manuelli and Seshadri, 2014).

4.4.4 *Enhancing TFP as a sustainable source of growth*

As can be expected in theory and discovered in econometric analysis (Cai and Yang, 2016), the positive effect of a higher labor participation rate on the potential growth rate will diminish over time, while the driving effect of TFP on potential growth is not only immediate but enduring as well. As a neoclassical stage of growth unfolds, China will increasingly rely upon innovation to sustain the growth momentum. On the other hand, tremendous potential exists in improving the efficiency of resource reallocation through the removal of institutional barriers. As revealed in other simulations (Cai and Yang, 2013), between 2011 and 2022, if China's TFP annual growth rate increases by 1 percentage point, the potential growth rate may increase by 0.99 percentage points.

Cai and Yang (2016) simulated different scenarios for the acquisition of reform dividends and found that whether or not the reform is carried out and with what intensity will make a big difference in potential growth

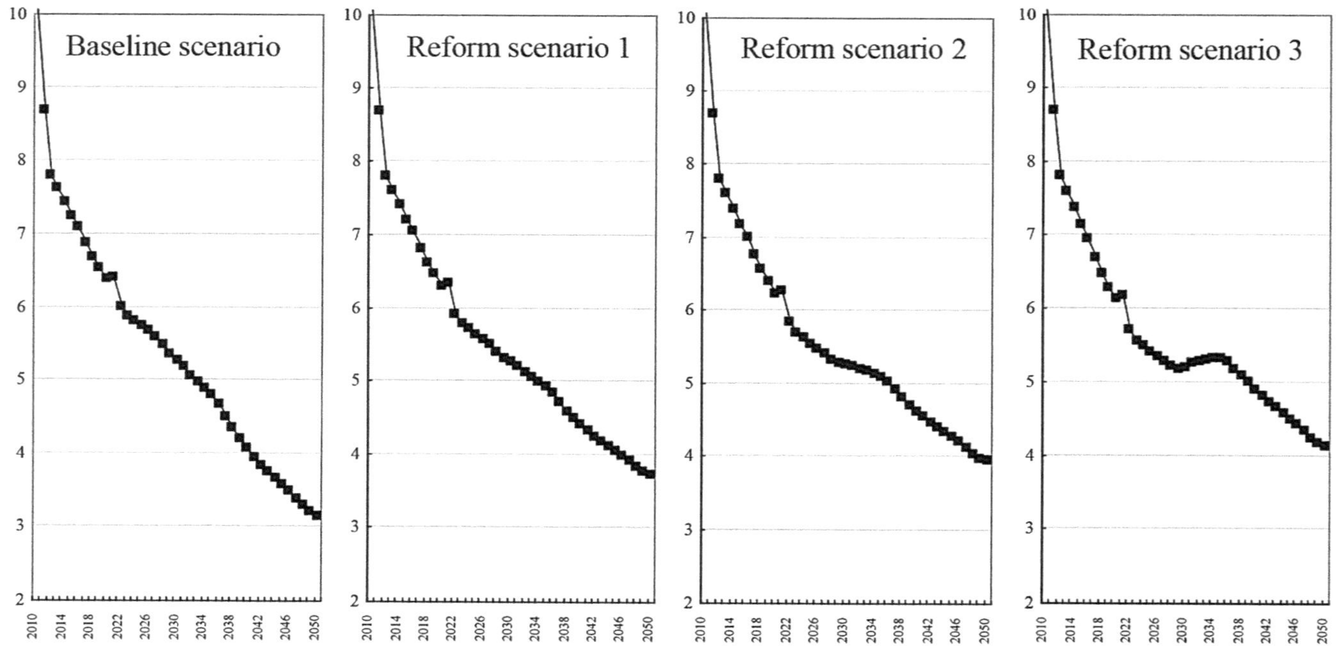

Figure 4.4 Simulation of dividends from supply-side structural reform.

Source: Cai and Yang, 2016.

rates in the short term and beyond (Figure 4.4). The simulation is based on assumptions of household registration system reform, reform of education and training systems, reform of state-owned enterprises, and other factors that may contribute to the labor participation rate, human capital, and TFP in combination with the different intensities of birth-policy adjustments (and thus different fertility scenarios). The following chart shows that based on the observation of China's long-term growth trends from supply-side factors, we cannot expect a V-shaped cyclical recovery. Under different assumptions of reform intensity and effects, dividends reaped from supply-side structural reform vary as well. If we observe Figure 4.4 from left to right, compared with the baseline scenario without reform, the deeper the reforms are, the greater will be the dividends unleashed and the closer the future potential growth rates will nudge toward the L-shaped trajectory.

4.5 Conclusions and policy recommendations

China's growth slowdown since 2012 is a new normal of economic development stemming from demographic transition and the economic development stage. In terms of both causes and manifestations, such a slowdown is drastically different from the cyclical phenomenon caused by demand-side shocks as was the case previously. Accordingly, policy targets, priorities, and instruments must be adopted differentially in order to effectively tackle it. As remarked by James Tobin, it takes a heap of "Harberger triangle" to fill an "Okun gap". Of the two economic concepts he mentioned, the former refers to welfare loss caused by institutional factors like monopoly and price distortion, while the latter refers to real growth below potential growth. Both are manifested in the decrease of GDP growth. Given their scarcity, research and policy resources should be allocated to the most needed areas according to the principle of maximal benefits. What James Tobin tried to convey is that from a utilitarian perspective, it makes more sense to pay attention to macroeconomic issues than to institutional issues; thats is, policy resources should be allocated to efforts to reduce Okun gaps caused by demand-side factors.

The problem is that instead of actual growth rate below potential growth rate, China's slowdown stemmed from the reduction of potential growth rate and is therefore free from any significant Okun gap. Therefore, the key for China to seek a sustainable path of growth in the long run lies in supply-side structural reform to unleash institutional potentials and achieve growth targets, rather than resorting to demand-side stimulus. Structural reforms include increasing production factor supply to boost quality and cut cost, transforming government functions to lower transaction costs, as well as reliance on TFP improvement to maintain the comparative advantages of industries and enterprises. The priority and intensity of these measures should be determined in light of their expected contributions to the potential growth rate.

Notes

1 In the five-year plans and annual plans, economic growth targets were generally set below 8 percent. For example, the expected growth rate was set at 7.5 percent and 7 percent during the Twelfth Five-Year Plan and Thirteenth Five-Year Plan periods. However, the 8 percent economic growth rate was identified at the central government level as a floor to be safeguarded. During the Asian financial crisis of 1997 and the global financial crisis of 2008–2009, for example, China's central government put forward the objective of ensuring an 8 percent growth rate.

2 In the accounting of China's economic growth rate, the aggregate of provincial growth rates has always been greater than the national economic growth rate. Therefore, in conducting regional decomposition, China's growth rates of various years are calculated through the aggregation of provincial GDP figures, which are obviously higher than the national growth rates released by the NBS. This paper followed this method of treatment due to data availability, rather than due to an assessment of the accuracy of the different data sources.

3 For instance, due to the wrong choice of explanatory variables and values, Barro (2016) estimated China's per capita GDP growth rate in 2015 to be 3.5 percent, which was dwarfed by the real growth rate of 6.9 percent in that year. Actually, huge differences can be found in comparing his estimates of China's per capita GDP growth for various years and the actual growth rates.

4 Richard Koo (2008) referred to the recessions in Japan since 1990 and in the United States since the 1930s as "balance sheet recessions." The fact that companies repaired their balance sheets after a plunge in asset prices was used by him as a micro-level manifestation of the economic cycle to explain why businesses were loath to borrow despite an easy monetary policy. Many Chinese scholars readily accepted this hypothesis. Whether or not such an analysis is correct, it still represents a cyclical perspective. In what follows, we will not only assert that it is the supply-side factors that affect China's economic growth, but also reveal that China's slowdown is not cyclical and provide the basis for understanding microeconomic behaviors of businesses and investors in not making anticipatory responses to monetary policy.

References

Aoki, M. (2012). Five Phases of Economic Development and Institutional Evolution in China, Japan and Korea (Part I), in M. Aoki, T. Kuran, and G. R. Roland (eds.), *Institutions and Comparative Economic Development*, Basingstoke: Palgrave Macmillan.

Bai, C., and Zhang, Q. (2014). The Return on Capital in China and Its Influencing Factors Analysis, *Journal of World Economy*, 10, pp. 3–30.

Barro, R. J. (2016). Economic Growth and Convergence, Applied Especially to China, NBER Working Paper No. 21872, Cambridge, MA: National Bureau of Economic Research.

Barro, R., and Sala-i-Martin, X. (1995). *Economic Growth*, New York: McGraw-Hill.

Cai, F. (2016). From Quantitative Issues to Structural Ones: An Interpretation of China's Labor Market. *China Economist*, 2016(1), www.chinaeconomist.com/index.php/2016/07/04/from-quantitative-issues-to-structural-ones-an-interpretation-of-chinas-labor-market-2.

Cai, F., and Yang, L. (2013). The End of China's Demographic Dividend: the Perspective of Potential GDP Growth, in Ross Garnaut, Cai Fang, and Ligang Son (eds.), *China: A New Model for Growth and Development*, Canberra: ANU Press.

Cai, F., and Yang, L. (2015). Emphasis on the Rapidly Rising Unit Labor Cost, unpublished working paper.

Cai, F., and Yang, L. (2016). Take-off, Persistence, and Sustainability: Demographic Factor of the Chinese Growth, *Asia & the Pacific Policy Studies*, 3(2), pp. 203–225.

Cai, F., and Zhao, W. (2012). When Demographic Dividend Disappears: Growth Sustainability of China, in Aoki, Masahiko and Jinglian Wu (eds.), *The Chinese Economy: A New Transition*, Basingstoke: Palgrave Macmillan.

Conference Board (2015). *The Conference Board Total Economy Database: Summary Tables*, www.conference-board.org/data/economydatabase.

Eichengreen, B., Donghyun, P., and Kwanho, S. (2011). When Fast Growing Economies Slow Down: International Evidence and Implications for China, NBER Working Paper *No. 16919*, Cambridge, MA: National Bureau of Economic Research.

Eichengreen, B., Donghyun, P., and Kwanho, S. (2013). Growth Slowdowns Redux: New Evidence on the Middle-income Trap, NBER Working Paper *No. 18673*, Cambridge, MA: National Bureau of Economic Research.

Eichengreen, B., Donghyun, P., and Kwanho, S. (2015). The Global Productivity Slump: Common and Country-specific Factors, NBER Working Paper *No. 21556*, Cambridge, MA: National Bureau of Economic Research.

Hayashi, F., and Prescott, E. (2002). The 1990s in Japan: A Lost Decade, *Review of Economic Dynamics*, 5(1), pp. 206–235.

Koo, R. C. (2008). *The Holy Grail of Macroeconomics: Lessons from Japan's Great Recession*. Hoboken, NJ: John Wiley & Sons.

Lin, Y. (2011). China and the Global Economy, *China Economic Journal*, 4(1), pp. 1–14.

Manuelli, R., and Seshadri, A. (2014). Human Capital and the Wealth of Nations, *American Economic Review*, 104(9), pp. 2736–2762.

McMillan, M. S., and Rodrik, D. (2011). Globalization, Structural Change and Productivity Growth, NBER Working Paper *No. 17143*, Cambridge, MA: National Bureau of Economic Research.

NBS (National Bureau of Statistics) (1998–2014). *China Statistics Yearbook*, Beijing: China Statistics Press.

Pritchett, L., and Summers, L. H. (2014). Asiaphoria Meets Regression to the Mean, NBER Working Paper *No. 20573*, Cambridge, MA: National Bureau of Economic Research.

United Nations (2011). *World Population Prospects: The 2010 Revision*, CD-ROM edn, New York: United Nations.

Part 2

Avoiding the middle-income trap

5 Is there a "middle-income trap"? Theories, experiences, and relevance to China

5.1 Introduction

Based on the view that East Asia is the most dynamic region in the world, the World Bank conducts a theme study of the East Asian economy every four years to summarize its unique development experiences and lessons, and to expose problems and challenges over specific time spans. In its 2007 report, *An East Asian Renaissance: Ideas for Economic Growth*, for the first time, the World Bank raises the issue of a "middle-income trap" (Gill and Kharas, 2008). The report shows that "middle-income countries have grown less rapidly than either rich or poor countries" (p. 5).

Since then, the concept of the middle-income trap has increasingly been discussed among economists. It has been used to illustrate the predicaments of certain Latin American and Asian economies, and is applied as a reference for making judgments on China's economic prospects (Wang et al., 2009; Eichengreen et al., 2011; Kharas, 2011). Its relevance to China's case, meanwhile, has drawn more attention since the Chinese Ministry of Finance, the Development Research Center of the State Council, and the World Bank jointly conducted a study on how China can overcome the middle-income trap.

Meanwhile, many researchers disagree on the use of the concept of the middle-income trap. Although systematic research is not yet available, in what follows, we touch on the nature of such disagreements. First, some researchers hold that the word "trap" is improper, because it suggests "conspiracy". How can an economy be framed? Second, some economists think that unlike the theory of the poverty trap or vicious circle of poverty, there is no economic theory available that can explain the many phenomena related to the so-called middle-income trap. Third, some suppose that the middle-income-trap theory lacks empirical evidence. It is also pointed out that over the past forty years, growth performance of middle-income countries has not been significantly lower than that of high-income and low-income countries. Last but not least, some researchers doubt the issue's relevance to China: does the concept of the middle-income trap correctly depict China's challenges and will it help China find the right solutions?

A concept or proposition is worth bringing forward so long as it can be analyzed through theoretical frameworks, and has significant empirical evidence and specific relevance, so that more thorough discussion and studies can be carried out. For that reason, this article supports the concept of the middle-income trap and holds that relevant studies should be deepened. This article starts, in Section 5.2, with a review of economic theories, of economic growth theories in particular, and demonstrates that the middle-income trap can certainly be included in existing economic growth analysis frameworks or has the potential of forming a special framework of its own. Section 5.3 introduces some empirical studies and statistical proofs of the middle-income trap and summarizes relevant characteristics of the concept. Finally, by introducing characteristics of China's economic development phase, Section 5.4 discusses the implications of the concept of middle-income trap for China's sustainable economic growth.

5.2 Theoretical basis of middle-income trap

Traditionally, the word "trap" is used to describe an economic state of superstable equilibrium that is beyond a comparative static equilibrium and cannot be changed by normal short-term outside forces. In other words, after the effect of a factor that helps improve per capita income is fully brought out, because it is somewhat unsustainable, other restraining factors will begin to work and offset that effect, bringing per capita income back to the original level. For example, the pessimistic views of Thomas Robert Malthus on the relationship between population growth and economic development are reflected in the "Malthusian trap" or the "Malthusian equilibrium". R. R. Nelson went further to combine the Malthusian model with the Harrod–Domar growth model to form a development theory which is called the low-level equilibrium trap, used as a label for the less-developed countries (Hayami and Gōdo, 2009). Moreover, not only is absolute poverty an equilibrium state; some economic historians have put forward the hypothesis of "high-level equilibrium trap" as they try to explain China's historical development and fix the Needham Puzzle. Therefore, the use of the term "equilibrium trap" has a long history in development economics.

The concept is conducive to deducing policy implications from theoretical analyses. Based on the low-level equilibrium trap hypothesis, development economics has developed the "critical minimum effort" and the "big-push" theories, among other explanatory theories, as well as their corresponding policy implications. Another example is from Theodore W. Schultz (1999), who sees traditional agriculture as a normal state of equilibrium developing countries, based on which he derives policy suggestions on reforming traditional agriculture through introducing new factors of production to break the equilibrium.

However, the aforementioned development economic theories concerning equilibrium state analysis have not been incorporated into mainstream growth theories. In reality, mainstream economists have long separated the neoclassical analysis of economic growth from the development facts observed based on the above hypotheses. Despite this, Hansen and Prescott (2002) attempt to meld the Malthusian equilibrium model and Solow's neoclassical growth model and analyze them using a unified theoretical framework. They also notice that there is a transitional phase from the Malthusian model to the Solow model. Logically, we can certainly define that transitional phase as a unique economic development phase. In reality, the dual economy defined by Arthur Lewis is just a transitional state between the Malthusian poverty trap and the Solow neoclassical growth model and it is prevalent in the developing countries. In this phase, economic growth has gone beyond the vicious poverty cycle in which income growth leads to population increase, which, in turn, drags the income level down to a basic subsistence level, and entered a phase characterized by modern sectors continually absorbing agricultural surplus labor until the economy encounters the Lewis turning point, so that there is no longer an unlimited supply of labor, and the economy becomes more and more neoclassical.

Aoki (2011) divides economic development in East Asia into the Malthusian phase of the poverty trap (M-phase), the government-led development phase (G-phase), the Kuznets process in which development is realized through structural shifts (K-phase), the human-capital-based development phase (H-phase), and the post-demographic-transition phase (PD-phase). He also acknowledges that the Kuznets phase can be called the Lewis development phase, or the Kuznets–Lewis phase. The division of development phases reveals that the shift from one development phase to another means a jump or breach, or, in other words, while shaking off the poverty trap is an important surpassing step, the shift from middle-income to high-income levels (from the K-phase to H-phase and ultimately the PD-phase) is an equally important, thrilling jump. If the latter is so challenging that some economies have long failed to break through the phase, and the phenomenon is so widespread that it has statistical significance and entails important theoretical and policy implications, then it is logical for us to use the concept of the middle-income trap.

Researchers have noticed some stylized facts that can help economists to form an initial theoretical framework to conceptualize the middle-income trap. Eeckhout and Jovanovic (2007) compare the economic growth of various economies before and after globalization, and find that in the era of globalization, the long-term growth-rate track of those economies, if they are ranked using the criterion of per capita income, is U-shaped. An explanation in the study is that laborers in rich countries possess better technologies and skills, so the number of high-skill positions has grown, particularly with the global shift in economic structures, whereas poor countries do not have the same level of skills, but the number of unskilled jobs has increased; those countries in between, meanwhile, do not have either of these labor resource advantages. Garrett (2004) goes further to explain that when rich countries become increasingly affluent because of their accelerating technological advancement, the poorest countries achieve faster growth in their manufacturing, but those countries in between fail to make headway.

This, in reality, hints at a general theoretical explanation for the middle-income trap; that is, countries at higher economic development stages obviously gain from globalization due to their comparative advantages in capital-intensive and technology-intensive industries thanks to their technological innovation capabilities. Those at lower economic development stages also gain from globalization given their comparative advantages in labor-intensive industries as a result of their rich labor resources and low labor costs. Those middle-income countries in between, however, gain less from globalization because they do not have comparative advantages in either aspect. We summarize the scenario as a "comparative advantage vacuum", which, although not completely accurate, helps to illustrate the awkward situation the middle-income countries are facing.

In addition, according to the economic growth convergence hypothesis (Barro and Sala-i-Martin, 1995), economic growth depends on multiple factors or determinants, such as investment ratio, human capital accumulation, government function, infrastructure conditions, and system and policy environments. In other words, at the initial development phase of low per capita income, improvements in these factors push economic growth convergence. However, the accumulation or improvement of those growth-favorable elements is also subject to the law of diminishing marginal effects; when all the "low-hanging fruits" have been harvested, the exogenous forces pushing economic growth will gradually lose their luster, unless the economy successfully shifts to an endogenous growth model driven mainly by total factor productivity. However, such a hypothesis generally applies to an economy that has entered the phase of a high-income country. Therefore, as the 2007 World Bank report points out, development strategies and policies that are starkly different from previous ones must be adopted during a country's transition from the middle-income to the high-income phase (Gill and Kharas, 2008).

5.3 Empirical evidence of the middle-income trap

According to the categorization of the World Bank in recent years, calculated by the "atlas method" that is similar to one for market exchange rate, those with per capita gross national income (GNI) of lower than US$975 are in the low-income group, whereas those with per capita GNI of US$976 to US$3,855 are categorized as belonging to the lower middle-income group; those with per capita GNI of US$3,856 to US$11,905 belong to the upper middle-income group and those with per capita GNI of more than US$11,906 are high-income countries. Of course, the standards of categorization are dynamic. Based on similar dynamic standards, if a country steps into the rank of middle-income countries but fails to graduate and become a high-income country after a long period of growth, then it falls into the middle-income trap.

According to such standards, in reality, if countries that have become rich through oil exports are excluded, apart from the developed economies, such as the USA and European countries, so far only Japan, Korea, Singapore, Chinese Taiwan, Hong Kong, and Macao have successfully surpassed the middle-income group. Many Latin American countries, which once had similar development levels to European countries, as well as some Asian countries that have long been middle-income countries, have failed to become members of the high-income club. Even some Latin American countries whose per capita incomes once crossed the demarcation line between middle-income and high-income groups have ultimately retrogressed to the middle-income level.

Due to technological advancement, institutional innovation, and strengthened resource mobilization capabilities, the world's production frontier has been expanding over time. Therefore, it is more appropriate to use relative, instead of absolute, per capita income to categorize income groups and, in particular, to examine the middle-income trap as a phenomenon of lingering growth. Athukorala and Wing (2011) use the purchasing power parity method of economic historian Angus Maddison to estimate the per capita GDP of particular economies and to compile the Catch-Up Index (CUI), with values presented as a percentage of the US level of per capita GDP. Using this method, to an extent, the authors prove the existence of the middle-income trap.

To be exact, they define those with a CUI higher than 55 percent as high-income countries, those with a CUI between 20 and 55 percent as middle-income countries, and those with a CUI lower than 20 percent as low-income countries. Among the 132 countries being compared, there were 32 middle-income countries in 1960 and 24 in 2008. Changes in the group show that there is a 50 percent possibility of the middle-income countries remaining in the middle-income trap. Considering cross-group movement, the possibility of moving to the lower level is higher than that of moving upward. Although there are countries from other groups moving into the middle-income group, the number of countries moving upward from the low-income group is double that of those moving downward from the high-income group.

Some studies reveal the formation of the middle-income trap from a dynamic perspective. For example, they summarize statistics of relevant economies and find that in the middle-income phase, a country's economic growth will not maintain its momentum forever. Therefore, the study of phases in which economic growth generally slows down can verify the existence of the middle-income trap. Morgan Stanley Asia/Pacific economists have conducted such a study (Wang et al., 2009). Through studying world economic history, they find that, according to history, the growth of an economy will slow down after some years of high growth. The turning point of the process comes when purchasing-power-parity-based per capita GDP reaches US$7,000. From the study of economic historian Angus Maddison, they find that over the past 100 years, 40 economies have seen their per capita GDP reach the turning point of US$7,000, 31 of which saw their growth rates decline by 2.8 percentage points on average after reaching that turning point.

Another study, conducted by Eichengreen et al., (2011), digs deeper in an analysis of relevant statistics. The question to be answered by the study is when or at what per capita income level a fast-growing economy would see its growth slow down. They find from international comparisons that based on the purchasing power parity method and the dollar value in 2005, when the per capita income reaches US$17,000, the galloping economy normally encounters an obvious slowdown, with its average annual economic growth rate generally declining by 2 percentage points.

There are also studies that attempt to prove that the middle-income trap is non-existent. Investment bank economist Jonathan Anderson (2011) chooses ten "middle-income countries" with a per capita income of US$8,000–10,000 and ten "low-income countries" with a per capita income of US$1,000–3,000, and compares their long-term economic performance. His findings can be summarized as follows. First, "middle-income countries" performed well in the first decade of this century, despite the fact that they stagnated during the previous decade. Second, "low-income countries" have failed to show better growth performance compared with their middle-income counterparts. Third, the average growth rates of the countries in the two groups are almost the same. From those findings, Anderson comes to the conclusion that the middle-income trap does not exist. In reality, however, his data and interpretation are not adequate for him to come to such a conclusion. First, his categorization of the two groups of countries differs from the typical income-based categorization. For example, his grouping of "middle-income countries" includes both the former planned-economy countries and those Latin American and Middle East countries heavily dependent on their oil resources for growth as well as the richest of the BRIC countries Brazil and Russia (the other two are India and China), and South Africa. Generally speaking, they are the richest countries among the middle-income bloc. The "low-income countries" in his categorization are almost all those that have already fallen into the middle-income trap or risk falling into it.

Second, the middle-income trap is a historical concept and might not necessarily match the economic realities of today. Those middle-income countries that had been in trouble before the start of this century were nothing but examples of falling into the middle-income trap. Although some of them have performed well over the past ten years, they have not necessarily made a shift that is a prerequisite for them to cross out of the middle-income trap. We are also not sure that those countries that have benefited from surging demand as a result of China's strong economic growth and are heavily reliant on exports of their resource products and growth of preliminary industries will have sufficient growth sustainability to become high-income countries. There are quite a few such examples in history where a country temporarily becomes a high-income economy but, ultimately, is forced back to a lower income level.[1]

Third, the middle-income-trap model does not assume absolute convergence, and, therefore, the fact that the growth performance of lower middle-income countries fails to significantly surpass that of upper middle-income countries does not necessarily mean it is illogical; rather, it is an indication of the middle-income trap. We use the concept of middle-income trap simply and exactly to indicate that countries hoping to become rich economies face the challenge of breaking through the middle-income equilibrium trap, just as those hoping to shake off poverty need to overcome the low-income equilibrium trap.

5.4 Implications for China's economic growth

In 2010, China became the world's second largest economy and its per capita GDP reached US$4,382, which means that it had just become an upper middle-income country, as categorized by the World Bank. Based on the Maddison standard, or the purchasing power parity method, China has surpassed the US$7,000 point of economic slowdown. If it maintains a 9 percent annual average growth rate, by 2015, China will reach the higher turning point for economic slowdown, at US$17,000. Due to many hidden problems and unsustainable factors in its economic growth, Eichengreen et al. (2011) warn that there is a 70 percent possibility of China being subject to the law of economic slowdown. According to some investment economists, however, a 70 percent possibility of a 2 percentage point decline in the growth rate (which is actually 1.4 percentage points) is not daunting for an economy that has maintained a growth rate of 9–10 percent for a long time.

Population-aging is an important cause of the slowing down of economic growth. The growth rate of the working-age population slows and the absolute quantity decreases, and the ratio of the working-age population to the whole population will stop rising before it declines. Accordingly, the economy will no longer benefit as a result of having an ample labor supply and a high savings rate. In 1990, the ratio of people aged 65 years and above to the whole population in Japan was 11.9 percent. Since then, the dependency ratio, or the ratio of the dependent population to the working-age population, has been rising fast. While experiencing such a population structure shift, Japan has seen its economic growth trend suddenly reversed: it first slowed down before stalling (Figure 5.1). In 2010, the ratio of people aged 65 years and above to the whole population was 8.9 percent in China, which was very close to Japan's level of aging in 1990, when the Japanese economy began to weaken. In the years of the Twelfth Five-Year Plan period (2011–2015), like Japan, China will see its dependency ratio rise rapidly.

We should draw lessons from history and work out solutions to prevent abnormal economic slowdown. Let us consider Japan again. What we should focus on is not the fact that its growth slowed down from a previous high-rate expansion, but, given the inevitability of the growth slowdown, why it has failed to maintain a growth rate similar to those of Europe and the USA.

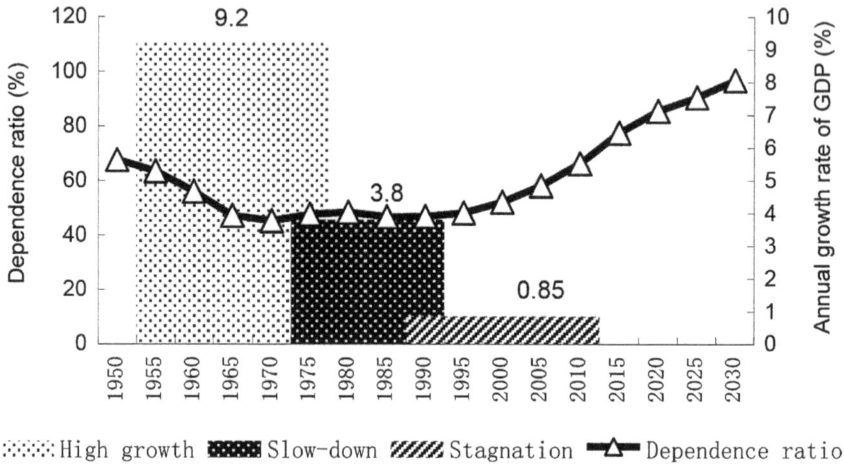

Figure 5.1 Japan's loss of population dividends and economic slowdown.

Sources: Population data from the UN database; GDP growth rates from the World Bank database and Takeo and Kashyap, 2011).

Seen from the perspective of economic growth models, China can also be situated in a special development phase. If we use the analysis framework of Hansen and Prescott (2002) and insert the Lewisian dual economy development phase in between the Malthusian growth phase and the Solow growth phase, then it is evident that as rural surplus labor decreases, labor shortage has become normal and the wage level of ordinary workers has been on the rise. As a result, China's economy has passed the Lewis turning point and has started to shift to the Solow neoclassical growth pattern.

The migrant worker shortage has been noticeable since 2004 and remains a focus of public attention. Meanwhile, wages of ordinary workers, most noticeably migrant workers, have risen continually from 2004 until today, which is in stark contrast with the previous decades, when wage growth virtually stalled. Therefore, if we must choose a year for the Lewis turning point, we would like to use 2004 as the watershed. Next, we will discuss another important point: the disappearance of population dividends (Cai, 2010). It is forecast that China's dependency ratio will stop falling in around 2013 and then start to rise rapidly. This means that China would no longer have the same high levels of saving rate and labor supply to support its dual economic development. Against that backdrop, middle-income countries face unsustainable growth.

On the one hand, rising labor costs will gradually weaken China's comparative advantage and international competitiveness in labor-intensive manufacturing sectors. A corporate survey shows that if labor costs rise by 20 percent, enterprises in the competitive industries will see their corporate profit margins decline by 20–65 percent due to the varied labor costs among different industries (Li and Meng, 2010). This will lead to labor-intensive industries moving out of the coastal regions. They might move to neighboring countries with lower labor costs, such as India and Vietnam. They might also move to China's central and western regions. According to the national manufacturing corporate statistics, the share of the labor-intensive manufacturing output of eastern regions in the national total fell from 88.9 percent in 2004 to 84.7 percent in 2008, with an average annual decline of more than 1 percentage point.

On the other hand, China still has a long way to go to gain a comparative advantage and international competitiveness in technology-intensive and capital-intensive industries. For example, according to statistics by the China Modernization Strategy Task Force and the China Center for Modernization Research at the Chinese Academy of Sciences (2010, p. 420), China's ratio of R&D to GDP is only 56 and 61 percent of the level of developed countries and the global average, respectively. The number of R&D staff for every 10,000 population is only 23 and 77 percent, respectively, of that of the developed world and the global average. The number of patents owned by every 1 million people on average is only 15 and 76 percent of the level of the developed world and the global average, respectively. In terms of educational level, the average length of education for people aged 30 years in China is only 65 and 67 percent of the level of the USA and Japan, respectively.

Although it has lost its comparative advantage in labor-intensive industries, China is yet to gain a comparative advantage in technology-intensive and capital-intensive sectors, which means the country is facing a "comparative advantage vacuum". Moreover, through its reform and opening-up, China has integrated into the world market. However, it is becoming increasingly challenging for China to further reform and open up to the outside world. These are all typical challenges facing middle-income countries. Therefore, raising the concept of the middle-income trap and thorough study of related phenomena as well as the experiences of other economies are useful for Chinese policy-makers.

5.5 Conclusion

The concept of the middle-income trap can be explained within an economic analysis framework and can be verified from economic development experiences. It is also relevant in terms of the sustainability of China's economic growth. Therefore, the concept is useful for academics and policy-makers. Figure 5.2 shows the whole process of the transition to a high-income economy, from which we can glean the tasks required to break through the poverty equilibrium trap and the middle-income trap and make a transition to becoming a high-income economy. We can also investigate the position of the middle-income-trap theory in the development economics framework and its relevant policy implications.

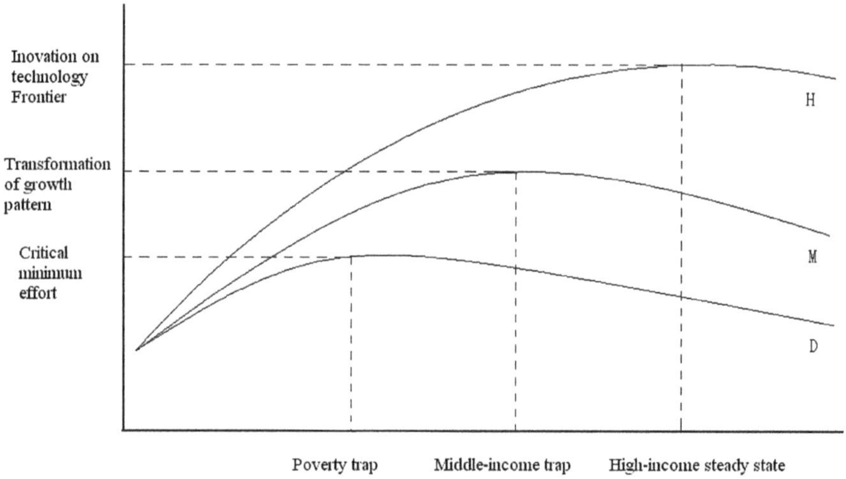

Figure 5.2 Turning point of economic growth and breaking-through strategy.

In the process of economic development, an economy initially faces the vicious cycle of the poverty trap. Its per capita output growth can be soon offset by population increases and its per capita income can be diluted by the growth of the population. The standard of living can be maintained at a subsistence level at best and savings are hard to accumulate. Even if a technological advancement in the traditional sense occurs, the "critical minimum effort" of the equilibrium trap cannot be overcome, until there is a revolutionary technological and institutional breakthrough, such as the application of technologies and market scale expansion resulting from an industrial revolution, which makes new technologies profitable (Hansen and Prescott, 2002). Only then can such an equilibrium state be broken.

Unlike the USA and European countries, most of the late-comer countries' economies grow within a dual economy framework; the unlimited labor supply itself favors accumulation of production factors while population dividends help to improve the savings rate to accelerate capital formation. Economic restructuring, featuring cross-sector labor movement and migration from rural to urban areas, also leads to reallocation of resources and improvement in total factor productivity. Therefore, in the process of globalization, the dual economy is capable of bringing about high-rate economic growth. The growth, however, ends with the advent of the Lewis turning point and the loss of the population dividends, and the economy might fall into the middle-income trap.

An indispensable prerequisite for breaking the bottleneck brought about by the Lewis turning point and loss of population dividends to avoid the middle-income trap is to upgrade the pattern of economic growth from one driven by production factor inputs and resource reallocation effects caused by transition from agriculture to non-agricultural sectors to one driven by improvement in total factor productivity and labor productivity. Once such a shift is made, long-term economic growth will be built on innovation and it will become sustainable. In this sense, many of the theoretical models and policy suggestions cited in this article are meaningful for helping China cope with the challenges of the middle-income trap.

First, it is urgent to maintain total factor productivity growth. The Solow neoclassical growth model advocated by Hansen and Prescott emphasizes that improvement in total factor productivity is the only source of maintaining sustainable economic growth. Parente and Prescott (2000) prove that the income gap between different countries is at root attributable to the differential in their total factor productivity as a result of their respective systems that either encourage or block the adoption of new technologies. Barry Eichengreen and other scholars also find that, typically, the stagnation of total factor productivity can explain 85 percent of an economy's slowdown. Hayashi and Prescott (2002) show that Japan's economic stagnation is also the result of poor total factor productivity.

Second, it is meaningful to accumulate human resource capital through education and training. Aoki (2011) holds that China has surpassed the Kuznets–Lewis phase and is shifting to the H-phase that is centered on human capital accumulation. The success of Japan and Korea in overcoming the middle-income phase is also attributable to their smooth shift from that phase. Human capital is also a source of total factor productivity improvement. Kuijs (2010) shows that in the 1978–2009 period, the annual average growth of total factor productivity was approximately 3.0–3.5 percent, 0.5 percentage points of which was attributable to improvement in human capital. Whalley and Zhao (2010) also show that human capital plays a role in offsetting the poor performance of total factor productivity.

Last but not least, it is challenging to deepen system reforms and transform government functions. Kharas (2011) provides a list of the system reforms that are unavoidable in the transition from a middle-income to a high-income phase, such as development of the capital market, acceleration of innovation, development of higher learning, improvement of urban management and city livability, formation of geographical agglomeration, effective rule of law, checks and balances, and the fight against corruption. Moreover, he points out that the real effect of such reforms will take at least years to surface. Japan's economic stagnation after 1990 shows that government function dislocation, especially the failure to establish a mechanism of creative destruction so that the most efficient enterprises can stand out in free competition, ultimately leads to stalling of the total factor productivity of the overall economy.

Note

1 Although it is not very accurate to use the current price, similar methods can still be used to examine the role of the equilibrium force. Take Argentina for example.

According to World Bank data, Argentina registered per capita GNI of US$8,140 in 1997. However, it subsequently fell below that level for many years. In 2004, its per capita income was only 44 percent of its 1997 level. Since then, its economic growth has been accelerating again and its per capita income reached an historically high level in 2010.

References

Anderson, J. (2011). Chart of the Day: Is there Really Such a Thing as a "Middle-Income Trap? *UBS Investment Research, Emerging Economic Comment*, 21 July.

Aoki, M. (2011). The Five-Phases of Economic Development and Institutional Evolution in China and Japan, Presidential Lecture at the World Congress of the International Economic Association, Beijing, http://papers.ssrn.com/sol3/papers.cfm?abstract_id=1893285.

Athukorala, P.-C., and Wing, T. W. (2011). Malaysia in the Middle-Income Trap, Paper prepared for the Asian Economic Panel Meeting at Columbia University, New York, 24–25 March.

Barro, J. R., and Sala-i-Martin, X. (1995). *Economic Growth*, New York: McGraw-Hill.

Cai, F. (2010). Demographic Transition, Demographic Dividend, and Lewis Turning Point in China, *China Economic Journal*, 3(2), pp. 107–119.

China Modernization Strategy Task Force and China Center for Modernization Research of the Chinese Academy of Social Sciences (2010). *China Modernization Report 2010—Summary of World Modernization*, Beijing: Peking University Press (in Chinese).

Eeckhout, J., and Jovanovic, B. (2007). Occupational Choice and Development, NBER Working Paper Series No. 13686, Cambridge, MA: National Bureau of Economic Research.

Eichengreen, B., Donghyun P., and Kwanho, S. (2011). When Fast Growing Economies Slow Down: International Evidence and Implications for China, NBER Working Paper Series No. 16919, Cambridge, MA: National Bureau of Economic Research.

Garrett, G. (2004). Globalization's Missing Middle, *Foreign Affairs*, 83(6), pp. 84–96.

Gill, I. S., and Kharas, H. (2008). *An East Asian Renaissance: Ideas for Economic Growth*, Beijing: CITIC (in Chinese).

Hansen, D. G., and Prescott, E. (2002). Malthus to Solow, *American Economic Review*, 92(4), pp. 1205–1217.

Hayami, Y., and Gōdo, Y. (2009). *Development Economics: From the Poverty to the Wealth of Nations*, Beijing: Social Sciences Academic Press.

Hayashi, F., and Prescott, E. (2002). The 1990s in Japan: A Lost Decade, *Review of Economic Dynamics*, 5(1), pp. 206–235.

Kharas, H. (2011). China's Shift to a High-Income Country—Method to Avoid Middle-Income Trap, in Chonggeng Lin and Andrew Michael Spence (eds.), *Long-Term Development and Transition of the Chinese Economy*, Beijing: CITIC, pp. 470–501.

Kuijs, L. (2010). China through 2020 – A Macroeconomic Scenario, World Bank China Research Working Paper *No. 9*, Washington, DC: World Bank.

Li, H., and Meng, X. (2010). Rising Labor Cost Will Change Corporate Profit Landscape—a Comparative Study of Labor Cost, Inflation and Corporate Profit, *SWS Research*, 1 July (in Chinese).

Parente, S. L., and Prescott, E. C. (2000). *Barriers to Riches*, Cambridge, MA: MIT Press.

Schultz, T. (1999). *Transforming Traditional Agriculture*, Beijing: Commercial Press (in Chinese).

Takeo, H., and Kashyap, A. (2011). Why Did Japan Stop Growing? National Institute for Research Advancement (NIRA) Working Paper, www.nira.or.jp/pdf/1002english_report.pdf.

Wang, Q., Zhang S., and Ho, E. (2009). Chinese Economy through 2020: It's Not Whether But How Growth Will Decelerate, *Morgan Stanley Research Asia/Pacific*, 20 September.

Whalley, J., and Zhao, X. (2010). The contribution of human capital to China's economic growth, NBER Working Paper *No. 16592*, Cambridge, MA: National Bureau of Economic Research.

6 How to understand income inequality in China?

Seeking common ground from the debates

> I have heard that the lord of a state or a family concerns himself not with scarcity but rather with uneven distribution, concerns himself not with poverty but with discontent.
>
> The *Analects* of Confucius

Since China reached per capita GDP of US$4,300 in 2010, which places it as an upper middle-income country, there has been a widely spread concern about whether the country can tackle the risk of falling into a middle-income trap. One of the phenomena relating to the middle-income trap is income inequality. The relationship between income inequality and middle-income trap is twofold. First, once a fast-growing economy slows down or even stagnates, so does its income growth. No evidence has ever been found that income distribution can be improved under a circumstance of economic stagnation at middle-income stage. The opposite seems from many experiences to be true: income inequality worsens when economic growth and income increase stagnate. Second, in a scenario where income inequality becomes aggravated and no policy instruments can stop it, and social stability and social cohesion are jeopardized, the inequality retards the sustainability of economic growth.

As the Chinese economy steps into its new stage, significantly improving income distribution is becoming eagerly expected by the Chinese people and an urgent challenge facing the government. Meanwhile, with the passage of the Lewis turning point signaled by labor shortage and wage increase for ordinary workers, the conditions are mature for narrowing the income gap formed during the typical dual economy period. One can therefore anticipate a Kuznets turning point—that is, a turning point at which income inequality stops increasing and begins to decline. Such a turning point, however, does not come automatically. This paper summarizes some new facts relating to the relationship between economic growth and income distribution put forward originally by Kuznets (1955), reviews competing studies on China's income distribution, elaborates the current trends of income inequality in China, and concludes with some policy suggestions on creating conditions for a Kuznets turning point to come.

6.1 New Kuznets facts

In his prominent 1955 work, *Economic Growth and Income Inequality*, Simon Kuznets devotes his analysis to answering questions of whether income inequality increases or decreases in the course of a country's economic growth and what factors determine the secular level and trends of such inequalities. Or in other words, Kuznets facts are about the observations, explanations, and empirical tests on whether or not there is a trend that income inequality first increases and then, when it reaches a certain point of time, it decreases as a country's economy grows. Because Kuznets' study was based on incomplete data of a handful of developed countries, the follow-up studies by both followers and opponents have made tremendous progress in answering those questions, though disagreements have remained wide. Based on theoretical extension and empirical testing of the Kuznets hypothesis as well as new observations of Kuznets-type facts, one can conclude that while the U-shaped curve hypothesis is a useful tool to think about the relationship between growth and distribution, factors impacting income distribution are multifaceted, and they vary in their dependence on a country's economic system, development stage, policy orientation, and the dominant forces shaping income distribution.

Literature on the nexus between economic growth and income distribution has been rich and summarized as many stylized facts (e.g., Ahluwalia, 1976). Some scholars have also tried to empirically test the Kuznets curve based on China's data, whereas there has been less discussion of the thoughtful ideas, analytical angles, and logic behind the Kuznets hypothesis. What we urgently need is to start with deep understanding of unique features of China in growth and reform, to thoroughly evaluate the reality and trends of its income distribution, and to try to find the conditions under which the Kuznets turning point can be reached.

To many Asian economies, both industrialized and developing, the application of the Kuznets analytical framework—namely, taking the reverse U-shape hypothesis as the benchmark for observing the relationship between growth and income distribution—requires starting with an understanding of the stages of dual economy development in answering the following questions: what are the factors which tend to break the Matthew effect caused by the accumulation of savings and assets, and by what mechanism can the changes of the relative shares of rural and urban populations impact the income distribution direction? In other words, observing the relationship between growth and income distribution in countries characterized by dual economy should follow a thread—namely, the basic market force related to the stages of dual economic development. This is particularly true in China's case where dual economic development has been typical and a key feature of its reform period since the late 1970s.

In what follows we summarize some new Kuznets facts—that is, the research findings relating to the explanation and testing of reverse U-shaped curves. It is worthy of note that while this paper is not able and does not intend to include all important studies, we try to choose those that are most relevant to the reality of China's income distribution.

A first fact on the Kuznets hypothesis is the coincidence or overlap between the Kuznets turning point and the Lewis turning point. Kuznets surmised that a variety of forces related to a certain phase of urbanization and industrialization may converge to bolster the economic position of the lower-income groups within the urban population, for example, migrants. Such a phase of urbanization and industrialization as he depicted is in fact the Lewis turning point manifested by significant shrinkage of surplus labor and constant increase in wages caused by labor shortage.[1] Minami and Ono (1981) find that the existence of surplus labor in agriculture can explain the long-term decline of labor's share in national income and high speed of economic growth, which results in widened income inequality. Based on the same economic logic, when the Japanese economy reached its Lewis turning point—namely, the reservoir of agricultural surplus labor significantly shrinking—overall increase in wages, and wage convergence between skilled and unskilled workers, were accompanied by the reduction of general income inequality (Minami, 2010). Another study Moriguchi and Saez, 2009) adds more evidence to indicate that while a drastic deconcentration of income took place during the World War II period, income concentration remained low after the War. The improvement of income distribution in Japan has been consistent with the changes of development stage, especially with the passage of the Lewis turning point in around 1960.

A second fact relating to the Kuznets hypothesis is that whether income distribution improves or deteriorates largely depends on how governments intend to tackle the problem of inequality and how policy and institutional change are implemented. In trying to interpret how the cumulative effect of the concentration of savings could be counteracted, Kuznets pointed to the roles of legislative interference and "political" decisions. A host of new findings show that a sound income distribution does not come naturally, but is influenced by policies and institutions. By reviewing the different policy intentions and actions on income distribution between alternate administrations, Krugman (2007) concludes that distribution policies absolutely matter, and they influence the outcomes of income distribution significantly.

Despite conflicting opinions on the impacts of labor market institutions on labor market flexibility and labor participation incentives, there is more agreement on the role of labor market institutions in reducing income inequality. Empirical studies in both developed and developing countries show that relative completion of such institutions plays a significant role in reducing income inequality.

A third fact concerning the Kuznets hypothesis is that income distribution is affected by industrial and technological structures and their changes. Although Kuznets mentioned the industrial opportunities resulting from technological progress and the development of the services sector as less obvious factors reducing income inequality, they have become more and more obvious factors influencing income distribution today as the world becomes characterized by unprecedented speed of technological progress and industrial changes in the context of globalization. There has been a rich literature that provides empirical evidence in this respect.

In explaining the widened income gap in the United States, Cowen (2011, pp. 22–22), an American economist, points out that as the rate of technological advancement slows down, the newly emerged technologies tend to feature as private goods in the country. That is, those innovations use resources from the government to grasp economic and political privilege and lobby for protections, and they do not benefit ordinary people. Similar is the scenario in which income generated by asset holdings dominates, which does not serve to improve income distribution.

Samuelson (2004) demonstrates that free trade globalization does not necessarily always benefit all trade partners. Since workers within a country are not homogenous, those with low education and skills may become permanent losers in such a globalization. This consequence is related directly to the nature of human capital accumulation—that is, due to individual or overall failures of education, the skills, as well as ability to obtain new skills, for the group of less-educated workers cannot catch up with the rapid changes in domestic sectoral structure brought about by offshoring. For example, the polarization of the US labor market—that is, the expansion of high-wage jobs and low-wage jobs at the expense of middle-wage jobs (Autor et al., 2006), gives rise to the polarization of human capital. As a result of job outflows in tradable sectors, a large fraction of US workers without the skills necessary for upgraded industries could not find a job. In other words, those American workers whose educational attainment and skills do not fit themselves to technological progress and economic globalization have become the victims of the new division of labor. That can also be a good explanation of the widened income gap in the United States in the past decade or so.

A fourth fact that helps answer the Kuznets puzzle is that economic and social policies focusing on income redistribution but overlooking a host of factors that impact economic performance produce much less obvious outcomes in narrowing income gap than economic growth per se does. In some Latin American countries, as Dornbusch and Edwards put it (1989), populist economic policies emphasizing growth and redistribution and deemphasizing the risk of inflation, external constraints, and the reactions of economic agents to aggressive non-market policies sometimes led to disastrous consequences for those who were told they would be helped by the policies. On the other hand, a handful of Latin American countries have witnessed passable economic growth performance in the first decade of the twenty-first century, accompanied by apparent improvement in income distribution, indicated by significant reduction of Gini coefficients.

Another instance is the so-called Mezzogiorno phenomenon. In trying to eliminate the insistent disparity between northern Italy and southern Italy (the Mezzogiorno region), the Italian central government implemented policies that overwhelmingly relied on redistributive tools such as income transfers and wage equalization, which strengthened the reliance of the lagging Mezzogiorno region on the central government and the richer north, directed resources toward non-productive (rent-seeking) use, and depressed private investment. Such policies further reduced the competitiveness of the regional economy and the flexibility of the labor market. As a consequence, productivity did not converge between north and south, the regional disparity even widened, and the low-income groups did not actually benefit from the policies at all. After the reunification of Germany, the initial experience in East Germany raised a worry that the country might recommit the same mistakes as Italy (Boltho et al., 1997). Later on, German regional policies became focused on encouraging private investment and building institutions to strengthen labor market flexibility and prevent rent-seeking activities, and so far have avoided Mezzogiorno-type mistakes.

6.2 Income distribution in China's rapid growth period

We now turn to focus on China. With the most impressive growth rate of 10 percent per annum since the 1980s, the Chinese economic development can be characterized as a Lewisian type—that is, a typical dual economic development. Such a process of economic development, accompanied by economic reform and opening-up unprecedented in China's history, has resulted in substantial changes in economic and social systems and deep integration of the Chinese economy into globalization. Therefore, the mass migration of labor force from the agricultural sector to non-agricultural sectors and the expansion of urban employment characterize the Chinese dual economic development in the context of globalization and institutional transformation. The increase in employment participation in rural and urban China, therefore, needs to be examined, as it is an important factor affecting income distribution.

Chinese urban employment consists of two sets of statistics. First is the total number of urban employees, published by National Bureau of Statistics (NBS). This does not, however, include most migrant workers in urban areas. Based on estimation from micro data, of the 310 million urban employees reported by such data, only 12.5 percent are migrant workers. Second is the NBS reported numbers of total migrant workers defined as those who left their home township for six months or longer. The survey indicates that 95.6 percent of those migrant workers work and live in various cities. Based on that information, after dealing with the overlap, we can sum the two datasets to actual urban employment covering both urban resident workers and migrant workers and compare them with the working-age population of the country as a whole (Table 6.1).

From the table, one can see that in the period 2001 to 2011, the growth of total urban employment—that is, the sum of urban resident employment and migrant employment—was faster than the growth of the working-age population of the country as a whole, and the ratio of urban employment (read as

Table 6.1 Changing dynamics of labor supply and labor demand (million, %)

	Urban resident employment (1)	*Migrant workers in cities (2)*	*Working-age population (3)*	*Ratio of demand to supply (1+2)/(3)*
2001	236	80	885	35.7
2002	241	100	901	37.9
2003	246	109	914	38.8
2004	250	113	929	39.1
2005	254	120	944	39.7
2006	259	126	952	40.5
2007	265	131	960	41.2
2008	268	134	968	41.6
2009	272	139	974	42.2
2010	277	146	981	43.1
2011	280	152	986	43.7

Sources: Author's calculation based on *China Statistical Yearbook* (various years); *China Rural Households Survey Yearbook* (various years); and Du and Lu, 2011.

demand for labor) to working-age population (read as supply of labor) tended to increase, which indicates that labor surplus in agriculture and workers' redundancy in urban sectors have significantly reduced, and that the dualism of the Chinese economy has been abating.[2]

In the entire period of rapid economic growth spurred by the reform and opening-up of China, there have been various forces impacting income distribution. On the one hand, government policies aiming at poverty alleviation and income redistribution, together with the expansion of labor participation, tend to reduce income inequality. On the other hand, there are some factors generated in the process of reform and growth that are more decisive in determining the trend of income distribution—namely, the increase in inequality.

First, expanded opportunity for rural laborers in non-agricultural sectors has reduced rural poverty and restrained, if not completely prevented, the rural–urban income gap from further widening. The household responsibility system, which is characterized by the even distribution of farmland among households and equal rights of residual claimants of farm production, guarantees free choice for rural laborers in search of higher pay and a better life. Therefore, even if the wage rate had remained unchanged for many years prior to the arrival of the Lewis turning point, the expansion of the scale of migration could have sufficiently increased farmers' income, which can be observed from three aspects.

A first is to examine the effect of migration on poverty alleviation. Except for those that lack a labor force, most households that fall into poverty suffer from lack of employment opportunity. Studies show that in general it is easier for those with skills and/or networks to find non-agricultural employment in rural areas, whereas poor households do not have such skills and networks. Rural-to-urban migration, therefore, is relatively a democratic opportunity for the poor to participate in the labor market and earn higher income. Du et al. (2005) find that poor households, by migrating out of rural areas, gained an 8.5 to 13.1 percent increase in per capita income. However, households short of labor force hardly benefit from migration.

A second is to look at the contribution of wage income to the increase of total household income. According to NBS categorization, net income of rural households consists of wage income, income generated by households' business operations, income from properties, and transferred income. The massive expansion of off-farm employment via labor mobility has significantly enhanced the share of wages in households' income, contributing overwhelmingly to the income growth of rural households. Official statistics show that the share of wages in rural households' income increased from 20.2 percent in 1990 to 41.1 percent in 2010, while wage income contributed 48.3 percent to the increase of households' income in 2010.

A third is to note that a significant part of migrants' earnings is missing from official statistics. When NBS conducts the household surveys in rural and urban areas separately, on the one hand, migrant households are excluded from the chosen samples of urban households because they usually do not have stable housing in destination cities and therefore they are not considered as practical survey samples; on the other hand, the sampled households in rural areas cannot fully record their income from remittance. As is explained in the notes on main statistical indicators in the *China Statistical Yearbook*, first, those households that register as rural *hukou* but all family members left their registered places for one year or more are not considered as normal rural households and thus are excluded from the sampling framework. Second, those family members who left home for six months or more are not considered as normal rural residents, unless they keep close economic relations with their family by sending the majority of their income to the household. While the exception described as "close economic relation" is practically hard to define, those who permanently live and work outside their registered place usually are not counted as normal rural residents and their income is omitted from the rural households survey.

Secondly, the characteristic of unlimited labor supply long prevented migrant workers' wage rates from increasing and the *hukou* system put migrants in a vulnerable position in the urban labor market. While labor market development allows the wage determination mechanism to function to identify human capital and work effort at places of work, institutional factors enlarge wage differentials among workers in general, and to widen the wage gap between local and migrant workers, in particular. According to a survey conducted in 2001, migrant workers' hourly wage was 39.6 percent lower than local workers', and of the wage difference, 63.9 percent can be attributed to differentials in education attainments and other demographic characteristics, while 36.1 percent can be attributed to discrimination based on *hukou* identity (Cai et al., 2011a). Such a distortion of wage determinants comes from both discrimination against migrant workers and protection of local workers. For example, Knight and Song's econometric analysis (2005, p. 108) finds that the ratio of marginal productivity of labor to wage rate is 3.86 for migrant workers and 0.81 for local workers.

Thirdly, as a consequence of the market-oriented reforms, which include promoting non-state sectors, capitalizing on natural resources, and privatizing state assets, the incomes from business operation and from properties have gained more significant shares in residents' income. While this helps increase people's income, it also tends to enlarge income inequality. Based on a survey conducted in 2002, the calculated Gini coefficient of residents' properties was 0.550, significantly higher than the Gini coefficient of residents' income (0.454) (Zhao and Ding, 2008, p. 274). Due to the lack of transparency and fairness in the marketization process, those resources and assets have been unevenly obtained by a handful of people who have power in determining the distribution procedure.

Finally, the government has achieved great success in implementing policies aiming to alleviate poverty, help the development of poor areas, and narrow the income gap. Such policies notably include the National Poverty Alleviation Strategy, the Western Development Strategy, the Strategy of Promoting Old Industrial Bases in Northeastern and Other Areas, and the Central Regions' Grow-up Strategy, the Minimum Living Standard Guarantee Program in both urban and rural areas, and policies aimed at equalizing access to public services between rural and urban areas. As a result, the number of people living below the official poverty line has been tremendously reduced and those who remain poor are better covered by the social safety net. Based on a consistent criterion, the number of rural poor decreased from 94.22 million in 2000 to 26.88 million in 2010—that is, the incidence of poverty declined from 10.2 percent to 2.8 percent. Meanwhile, the coverage rates of those programs such as the social pension, health care insurance, and the minimum living standard guarantee have substantially expanded (IOSCPRC, 2012). However, one can applaud only the achievement in alleviation of absolute poverty, because all indicators show increasingly widening income gaps—for example, the wages differentials across sectors, income disparities between rural and urban areas, and income inequality among households, which draw great attention from the public.

Manifested by the widespread labor shortage and substantial wage inflation, the Chinese economy passed through its Lewis turning point in 2004. The fundamental alteration in the relationship between labor demand and labor supply lies in population age-structure change—namely, the diminishing growth rate of the working-age population in recent years and predicted termination of that growth in 2013. According to Kuznets' speculation, at such a stage of development, a variety of forces may merge to reduce income inequality. That is, the Lewis turning point will be followed by the Kuznets turning point, as is predicted by the logic of economic development.

A first manifestation of the passage of the Lewis turning point is the concurrent increase in wages of ordinary workers, particularly of migrant workers in China's case. The wage inflation of migrant workers has several implications. First, since migrant workers have long been the overwhelmingly major component of labor supply in the urban sectors, the diminishing labor supply resulting from population age-structure change has been embodied in insufficient migration to meet the labor market demand. The increase in wages of migrant workers is a strong signal indicating the substantial reduction of surplus labor in agriculture and it therefore leads to an overall increase of wages in all sectors (Figure 6.1). Second, since compared to urban local workers, migrant workers are relatively less educated, the increase in their wages implies a shortage of unskilled workers. Thirdly, the convergence in wages between skilled and unskilled workers has become a notable phenomenon in the labor market, which tends to narrow the within-group income gap.

In conclusion, the passage of the Lewis turning point tends to contribute to narrowing the income gap between rural and urban areas. While decomposing the overall income inequality by its components, the Theil entropy index can be divided into the income inequality within urban areas, the income inequality within rural areas, and the income gap between rural and urban areas. The existing studies (e.g., Kanbur and Zhang, 2004; Wan, 2007) show that 40 to 60 percent of the overall income inequality can be attributed to the income gap between rural and urban areas. That is, holding the other conditions constant, the substantial reduction of the rural–urban

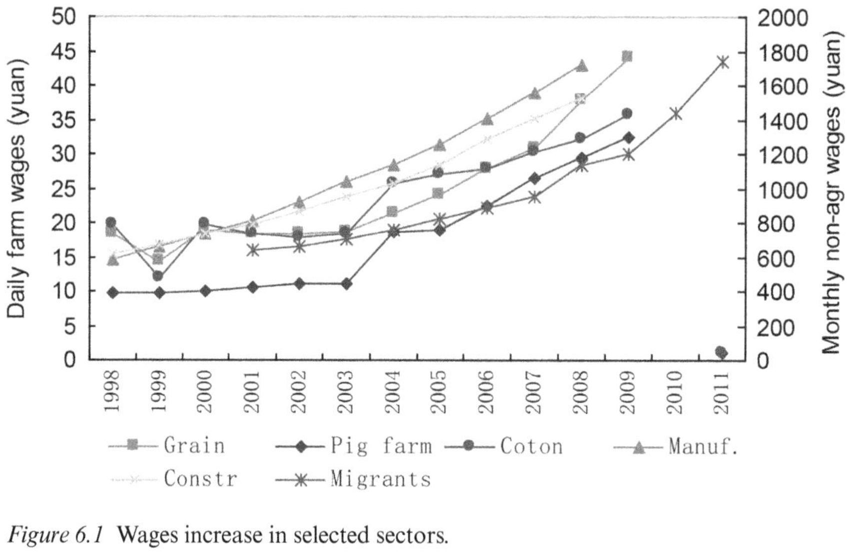

Figure 6.1 Wages increase in selected sectors.

Sources: Daily wages for grains, cotton, and pig farms with a size of over 50 pigs are from *Compilation of National Farm Product Cost-benefit Data*; monthly wages of manufacturing and construction are from *China Labor Statistics* (various years); monthly wages of migrant workers are from *NBS Statistical Report* (various years).

income gap can prevent overall income inequality from further deteriorating, if not reduce it.

Not coincidentally, the year 2004 is also a turning point at which the Chinese central and local governments strikingly strengthened the implementation of policies aimed to improve income distribution. In what follows we explain some aspects of this move. First, labor-related legislation and regulations have accelerated—most noticeably, the Employment Contract Law was put into practice in 2008, which helps to construct the labor market institutions. In parallel, local governments raised the minimum wage standard, which led to further increase of real wages. Second, the central government not only started to lessen various burdens shouldered by farmers and ended up by eliminating agricultural tax in 2006, but it has also initiated various subsidies to farmers and farming since then. Such increasingly enlarged subsidies make agriculture more profitable and therefore enhance opportunity costs of labor migration, which helps strengthen migrant workers' bargaining power in the labor market. Thirdly, the central government established the rural minimum living standard guarantee program, the new rural cooperative medical system, the new rural social pension insurance system, and other policies aimed at narrowing the gap in access to basic public services between rural and urban residents. Lastly, in some provinces and cities, the local governments began to speed up *hukou* system reform by lowering the threshold for migrant workers to become registered residents and equalizing public services provision between migrant and local residents.

6.3 The debate on current income distribution in China

Based on the Kuznets hypothesis and referring to the experiences in Japan and some other East Asian economies, the passage of the Lewis turning point should be followed by the Kuznets turning point, sooner or later. As to whether income distribution in China shows any trend corresponding to the arrival of the Lewis turning point, there are debates among researchers based on different data and methods. In what follows we summarize some relevant studies.

Some researchers found a trend of income distribution improvement by digging into and revising incomplete statistics. Trying to avoid the flaw of the present household surveys conducted separately between rural and urban areas, Gao et al. (2011) selected some households, including NBS samples and others, in Zhejiang, a developed province, and Shaanxi, a relatively underdeveloped province, to observe the degree to which migrant workers' income is being underreported. This study concludes that the existing imperfection of the statistical definition in surveying households' income alone leads to overestimation of urban residents' income by 13.6 percent and underestimation of rural households' income by 13.3 percent. That is, the income gap between rural and urban households has been overstated by 31.2 percent.

It is imaginable that the extent to which migrant workers' income is omitted became larger after the arrival of the Lewis turning point. And if such an omission can be corrected, statistically speaking, the income gap between rural and urban areas will be narrowed, which in turn improves the overall income inequality. By using micro data of from a 1 percent population sampling survey in 2005, a study by Cai et al. (2011b) shows that all indicators of income inequality actually improved after incorporating migrant workers' income into either urban income or rural income, though due to the limitation of the data, one cannot confirm the reversal of the trend of enlarged income gap between rural and urban areas.

A simulation shows that if all barriers deterring labor mobility were eliminated—representatively, the *hukou* system is completely abolished—existing income inequality would all disappear (Whalley and Zhang, 2004). Despite the *hukou* system still functioning to preventing migrants from obtaining urban residency, in taking into account the wider functions of the *hukou* system—namely, as an institutional barrier deterring labor mobility and preventing migrants from equal access to public services—the progress of *hukou* reform should be appreciated (Cai, 2011). In conclusion, if one grants that the institutional barriers of labor mobility have been eliminated to a significant extent, the trend of shrinking income inequality should be expected.

Being well aware of this feature of the Chinese data, the economists of the OECD, by employing some new methods and indicators, particularly incorporating migrant workers into observations, have confirmed the positive effects of the easing of restrictions on labor mobility between rural and urban areas and progressive introduction of the minimum subsistence allowance in rural areas, and have found that there appear to be signs that income inequality has lessened (Herd, 2010). Estimation based on household income per capita in China shows that after the Gini coefficient reached 0.492 in 2002 and climbed to its peak in 2004, it declined to 0.479 in 2007 and 0.464 in 2010. In addition, this same study shows other signs of lessened income inequality measured by wages differentials, income ratios between groups, and income disparities among provinces (Herd, 2012).

The Chinese statistical authority also confirmed the reduction of the Gini coefficient. In his press conference held on January 18 of 2013, Mr. Ma Jiantang, the Commissioner of the State Bureau of Statistics of China, provided the calculated Gini coefficients between 2003 and 2012. Combining this series of figures with the estimated figures by scholars for previous years, we see a changing trend in China's overall Gini coefficient in the past 31 years and find it consistent with the trend of the rural–urban income gap (Figure 6.2).

Researchers have tried to test whether there is any sign of the Kuznets turning point in China. For example, by using rural and urban household survey data and population sampling survey data, Li (2010) conducted an empirical test, based on perspectives of both a time series and a cross section, and denied the reversed U-shaped curve between development and income inequality. However, contrary to what the author asserts, it is not

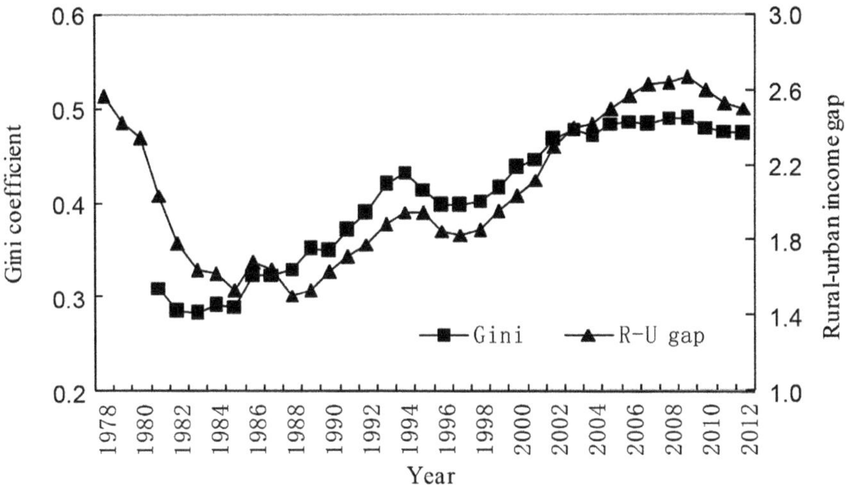

Figure 6.2 Gini coefficient and rural–urban income gap.

Sources: Rural-urban income gap is calculated based on *China Statistical Yearbook* (various years); Gini coefficients of 1981 to 2002 are cited from Li, 2010; and Gini coefficients of 2003 to 2012 are cited from the National Bureau of Statistics (NBS) official website.

the case that this test does not support the Kuznets curve hypothesis; rather, it is just the the appearance of the turning point has not yet been detected. That is not surprising, because according to the theories, we can usually expect that the Kuznets turning point is an outcome of the Lewis turning point—that is, in terms of the sequencing, the Kuznets turning point is more likely to happen after the Lewis turning point. Because the data used in Li's study are only updated to 2005, it is reasonable for him not to witness the reversal of income inequality. However, he does find that the status of income distribution of urban households is closer to the Kuznets turning point, compared to that of rural households and to the national average. This is a logical phenomenon since the major indications characterizing the Lewis turning point—notably, labor shortage and wage increase—first happened in the urban sectors.

The notable evidence that makes people believe in a strengthening trend of income inequality is that by a variety of measurements it seems to continue increasing. The World Bank estimation is that the Gini coefficient went up from 0.31 in 1981 to 0.447 in 2001 (Ravallion and Chen, 2004). According to a constant serial survey (CHIPS), the Gini coefficient increased from 0.455 in 2002 to 0.478 in 2007 (Herd, 2012). In addition, the declining trends of resident and labor income as percentage of national income have drawn wide attention. Based on the flow of funds accounts, Bai and Qian (2009) find that in both primary distribution and redistribution, resident and labor income shares have seen a declining trend since the mid-1990s, which produces a pattern of income growth unfavorable to ordinary households.

By using an unconventional method of survey and estimation, Wang (2011) finds that there is a huge amount of unreported income held by Chinese urban residents. Such hidden income amounted to 9.26 trillion yuan and was 2.19 times the reported income in 2008. It is reasonable to speculate that a significant part of this income comes from sources that cannot be testified as legal, or it often comes from sources between legal and illegal practices, thus the author refers to it as "grey income". It can also be said that this huge amount of grey income is distributed in an extremely uneven way. That is, once it is split disproportionately into different income groups, the calculated inequality indices would be substantially higher than the official data-based indices show. In fact, Wang also tried to figure out how such grey income is distributed among urban residents and concluded that 80 percent is obtained by the top 10 percent high-income group.

General observations and scholarly researches all agree that by international standards, income distribution is highly unequal in China. The intense disagreements, however, lie in whether the inequality is being aggravated or being improved, and what underlying factors determine the trends of income distribution. It is hard to find many agreements on prevailing phenomena in economic research, which is particularly true in the case of understanding income inequality in China. However, to see a bigger picture requires seeking common ground by synthesizing conflicting arguments, because all serious studies can provide useful angles to observe complicated phenomena and evidence to complement each other. In what follows we try to build a framework to thoroughly understand income distribution in China, by seeking such a common ground. That is, we use evidence provided by the competing studies to form a consistent view on the issue and to draw relevant policy suggestions.

6.4 Explaining competing observations on income inequality

Issues of income distribution can be examined from different angles at both micro and macro levels. From the perspective of the national account, one can look into distributive shares of factors of production and spatial and sectoral distributions of national income. From the perspective of individual and household income, one can examine distribution of aggregate income, distribution of income from wages and properties, and primary and secondary distribution. Overall income inequality is the comprehensive reflection of those indicators. In the present studies on income distribution, evidence and conclusion are often based on different data, and given the limitation of each dataset and different indicators chosen to measure income inequality, studies have different focuses. Since unequal distribution of households' income is a major concern and it contains sufficient information for revealing general income inequality, we mainly focus on discussing income inequality at a household level.

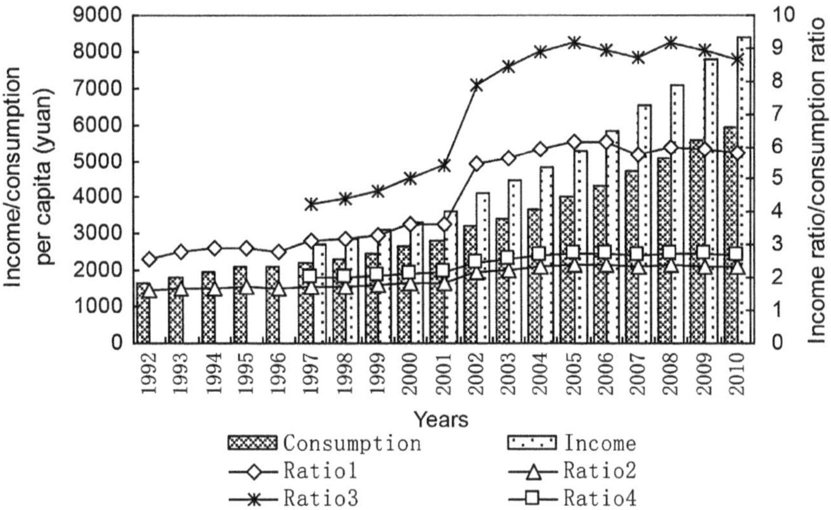

Figure 6.3 Levels and distribution of urban income/consumption per capita.
Source: *China Statistical Yearbook* (various years).

We begin with looking at the overall level and distribution of per capita income of urban households based on data published by the NBS. To make information more consistent, at the same time we also observe the level and distribution of per capita consumption expenditure (Figure 6.3). First of all, the income of urban households has grown rapidly in the past decade or so. In the period from 1997 to 2010, the annual real growth rate of per capita disposal income of urban households was 9.1 percent and that of per capita consumption expenditure was 7.3 percent. Second, the income gap began narrowing after a period of increasing. As is shown in Figure 6.3, all inequality ratios—namely, income/consumption ratios of the top 10 percent high-income group to the average income level (denoted as ratio4 and ratio2, respectively) and income/consumption ratios of the top 10 percent high-income group to the bottom 10 percent (as ratio3 and ratio1, respectively), witnessed decline after the peak in 2005.

Both public opinion and majority of researchers, however, do not agree on the conclusion to be drawn from such statistics. A serial survey shows that the issue of income inequality and polarization ranked as the third highest concern in public opinion—32.4 percent, 28.0 percent, and 31.6 percent of correspondents expressed concern on the issue in 2006, 2008, and 2011, respectively (Li et al., 2012). There is a variety of factors that impact people's views on income distribution, and people in different income groups may have different and not directly comparable feelings about it. Therefore, an immediate answer to the conflict between statistics and public opinion is that at a high level of income inequality, the initial and not obvious improvement is not enough to improve people's satisfaction about income distribution. We do not intend to stop at this answer, however.

Statistically, household income is sourced from wages, properties/assets, and transfers. The relative growth and share of those three sources of income determine the level and distribution of resident income. In the double transitions from dual economy to neoclassical growth and from planned economy to market economy, the ways by which households obtain their income are far more diversified than statistics can reveal. As with the large fraction of migrant workers' income that is missing, the income of urban residents is also greatly underreported. Since such unreported income is unevenly distributed among households, the existence of the hidden grey income can undoubtedly amplify income inequality. Apart from labor compensation and legal business income, there is a wide range of income from sources that people are unwilling to make known.

First, hidden income continues to grow in both scale and scope. Comparing two rounds of surveys on grey income conducted in 2005 and 2008, one can see a growth and, therefore, an increasing trend of income inequality (Wang, 2011). In China's transition to a market-oriented system, natural resources, minerals, and land have been capitalized in various ways in the name of enhancing efficiency of utilization. This process has brought about the transformation of income flows generated by assets and resources from public to private ownership. That is, the unequal distribution of wealth and properties has flown from the privatization of state assets, land development, and sale and lease of minerals and other natural resources.

Second, the process of capitalizing state-owned assets and resources has sometimes been characterized by untransparent, nonstandard, and even illegal practices. These include unequal opportunities and monopolized information in land-selling, restructuring of state assets, bidding for public construction projects, direct and indirect financing activities, on the one hand, and unfair operations such as tax evasion, rent-seeking activities, and corruption, on the other. The income from such activities thus tends to be concealed from official household surveys, and the higher-income groups have less willingness to report their full income. A study finds that about 70 percent of households in the top 10 percent income group expressed unwillingness to factually report their income (Wang, 2007). Furthermore, the residency of those people who have the privilege of grasping grey income often clusters in certain communities, which prevents them from appearing as samples in any survey program.

Finally, given its significant magnitude and extremely uneven distribution, grey income can dominate the degree and direction of income distribution. In addition, such a pattern tends to be fixed and hard to break, because the institutional environment of rent-seeking activities and illegal transactions still exists and those who monopolize grey income have formed vested interest groups and try to lobby for their interests. Therefore, the existence of grey income has become a key to solving the puzzle of why the Kuznets turning point has not arrived following the Lewis turning point.

According the feature of official household survey, the recorded income by sampling households are mainly generated by labor compensation, legally-run business income and transferred income, whereas the estimated grey income appears outside the statistical system. Thus, merging the two sources of income to generate an actual resident income can help us to examine the real pattern and trends of income distribution. Based on the estimated distributive share of grey income in each decile group and under some necessary and reasonable assumptions, what follows we try to build a scenario of China's income distribution, which is not necessarily real but rather symbolic in picturing the real income distribution.

We assume that grey income began to exist in 1998 and, with constant growth rate, it amplified to 9.26 trillion yuan in 2008, as estimated by Wang (2011). Based on Wang's estimate, we split grey income into each decile group of reported resident income and re-estimate time series data between 1997 and 2010, which include per capita disposable income of urban households (sum of reported and grey income) at the 1978 constant price and ratio of per capita income of the top 10 percent high-income group to that of the bottom 10 percent low-income group. Figure 6.4 shows the comparison between the estimated results and reported results.

It is worth noting that our intention is neither to question the accuracy of per capita income data published by the NBS, nor to agree with the concrete level of grey income estimated by Wang. The simulation shown in Figure 6.4 is only intended to draw two conclusions. Number one, given the significant inequity of assets and resources ownership, there is a large amount of hidden income beyond statistical coverage, which decisively determines the degree and direction of income distribution. Number two, it may well be expected that incorporating the omitted income into reported income and splitting it into different income groups will substantially increase income inequality. That is, taking into account this factor, the Kuznets turning point can hardly be observed.

As is shown in Figure 6.4, while the ratio of per capita income of the top 10 percent high-income group to that of the bottom 10 percent low-income group calculated by officially reported data has shown signs of lessening, the similar ratio calculated by estimated data—that is, the sum of grey income and reported income—continues to increase. This helps to solve the conflict between theoretical prediction and reality on income distribution. On the one hand, assuming there is no distortion by the unique economic system transformation, the distribution of urban households' reported income, in which labor income dominates, has improved, which conforms to the theoretical prediction of the Kuznets hypothesis. On the other hand, taking into account the unique factors brought about by the system transition in China—that is, the lion's share of the actual income of urban households comes from income flow from an extremely inequitable distribution of assets and properties—income inequality is increasing and the arrival of the Kuznets turning point is not within the foreseeable future. And the income inequality perceived by

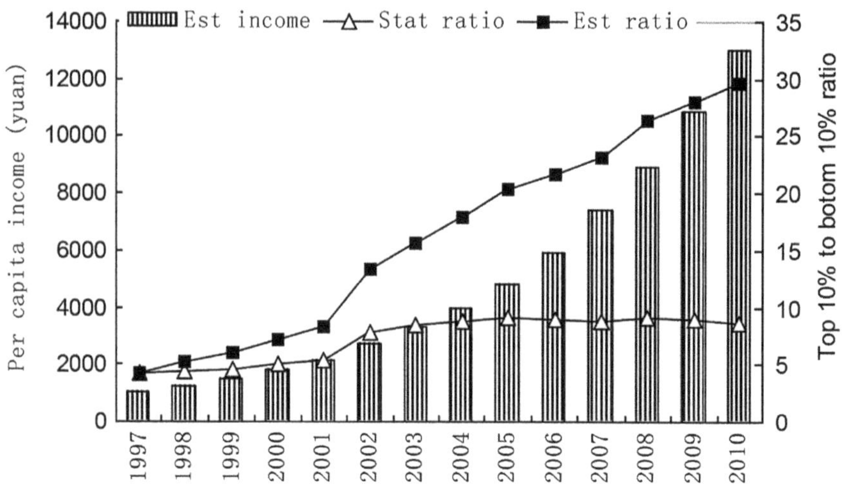

Figure 6.4 Inequality trends revealed by reported and estimated income.
Source: *China Statistical Yearbook* (2011); Wang (2011).

the public, in fact, comes mainly from the unfairness in the distribution of earning opportunities. Theoretical prediction does not fail, but it cannot be confirmed directly by the complex reality.

6.5 Conclusion and policy implications

The public debates on China's income distribution are full of dogmatism and sentimentalism, which are enemies of scientific research. That is why serious research with sound intentions and methodology is required in this area. Policy-related research, on the other hand, must not be confined by a simple-minded and one-dimensional stance—complex reality calls for sophisticated thinking. On the one hand, it is rather naïve to assert the advent of the Kuznets turning point, judged from the theoretical point of view, while ignoring the severe inequality in reality and its potential for social reaction and economic consequences. On the other hand, seeing the existing inequality without exposing its root cause behind the indices can help little with policy adjustment. It will be even worse if loud advocacy misleads the policy direction.

For example, ignoring or underestimating the inequitable distribution of resources and assets as the dominant root cause of increasing income inequality may direct policy orientation to wage equalization and over-reliance on redistribution of reported income dominated by labor compensation, which, instead of touching those groups who inequitably obtain massive resources, would hurt middle-income groups. Furthermore, such a defect of policy approach can also lead to overlooking the potential social risks caused by the severe inequity of resource distribution. In contrast, once we reveal that the major factors pushing income inequality to further increase lie in the uneven ownership of properties and assets, the policy orientation can be clearer and more focused. In conclusion, tackling income inequality should proceed with three aspects—the increment, stock, and income flows of unevenly distributed properties and assets.

To cease the increment of such inequitable distribution of assets and properties calls for stricter implementation of laws and regulations in the process of land development, mineral exploitation, and state assets selling, preventing illicit power from intruding. Accelerating the confirmation of farmers' rights on contracted farmland and homestead is an effective institutional measure to guard against infringement of farmers' property rights. To prevent state assets from leaking out into the hands of individuals and groups, property rights need to be clearly defined and the transfer of property rights should be standardized in the process of state assets restructuring. Minimizing the powers held by government officials in distributing resources via strengthening supervision and anti-corruption is the more fundamental way to cut off the increment of grey income.

To cope with the already formed stock of assets and properties of individuals and groups, the government should take taxation measures, which requires timely introduction of property tax, inheritance tax, and other taxes that aim to regulate income distribution. Taxation reform is also a way to tackle the problem with the income flow generated by inequitable holding of assets and properties. The defect of the Chinese taxation system is the high proportion of indirect taxes and low proportion of direct taxes—or in other words, the regressive nature of the taxation system prevents it from redistributing unequally distributed income among residents. In addition, encouraging employee stock ownership would also produce an outcome of equalizing holdings of assets.

After all, the factors impacting income distribution are multifaceted and the decisive factor may change over time depending on the stages of development and reform. While grasping the key to influencing income distribution today, there is still a need for institutional building to create the necessary conditions under which the Kuznets turning point matures. Now, we are in a position to come back to the Kuznets hypothesis and relevant facts for China.

First, the evolution of the labor market will continue to play an important role in improving income distribution. The constant depletion of surplus labor and, as a result, the arrival of the Lewis turning point has so far created a necessary condition for reducing income inequality. Creating jobs, equalizing opportunity of employment, and enhancing labor participation have been, and will always serve as, a reducer of income inequality through the labor market. This alone, though, will not allow the Kuznets turning point to come spontaneously; the reduction and elimination of wage differentials caused by factors irrelevant to human capital requires the establishment and perfection of labor market institutions, including a minimum-wage system, trade unions, a collective bargaining system, and the like.

Second, government policies are vital to reducing income inequity. Since 2004, a host of policies initiated by the government has been successful in improving people's livelihood, on the one hand, but the effect has been partially cancelled out by the inequitable distribution of resources that are prone to generation of grey income, on the other hand. While continuing implementing the policies aiming to enhance the equality of income distribution, the next substantive step of policy adjustment should focus on equalizing the opportunity of income earning—that is, eliminating the influence of vested interest groups on income distribution policies, and terminating the interference of administrative power and any other kinds of privileges in resource distribution and ownership. This requires reform of government to make decision-making more about equity, justice, and transparency.

Third, a more inclusive and equitable development of education is a fundamental way to narrow the income gap and to prevent poverty from becoming hereditary. Looking ahead, education, as a tool of human capital accumulation, should continue its general expansion in order to improve the general quality and skills of the entire workforce. Meanwhile, the existing unequal distribution of education resources, and as a result the unequal opportunities of education among residents, across regions, and between rural and urban areas, needs to be tackled. Given that technological advancement in the context of globalization is tends to squeeze out poorly educated laborers from job opportunities, promoting human capital through education and training is therefore a necessary safeguard to prevent such a phenomenon.

Finally, the government should focus on balancing economic growth and redistribution. Though cumulative income inequality and unequal access to basic public services among residents requires amplification of redistribution in the public services area, in which government should play a dominant role, the effects of pie distribution eventually depend on how big the pie is. That is, sustainable economic growth should be an important goal in order to enlarge the pie, whereas the redistribution policies should be implemented on the basis of law, but not in an arbitrary way, so that the policies can reach their goals—namely, to regulate high incomes, promote the middle-income class, and protect low-income groups, while avoiding the side effect of hurting the incentives to labor participation, rational consumption, capital accumulation, and investment.

Notes

1 Many scholars notice that Kuznets' analysis is based on a framework of dual economic development. See Deutsch and Silber, 2001.

2 The Sixth Census shows that in 2010, the Chinese working-age population between 15 and 59 peaked and started to shrink afterwards. See CDRF, 2012.

References

Ahluwalia, M. S. (1976). Income Distribution and Development: Some Stylized Facts, *Income Distribution in Developing Countries*, 66(2), pp. 128–135.

Autor, D. H., Katz, L. F., and Kearney, M. S. (2006). The Polarization of the US Labor Market, *NBER Working Paper No. 11986*, Cambridge, MA: National Bureau of Economic Research.

Bai, C., and Qian, Z. (2009). Analysis on China's National Income Distribution Pattern, *Social Sciences in China*, 5, pp. 99–115.

Boltho, A., Carlin, W., and Scaramozzino, P. (1997). Will East Germany Become a New Mezzogiorno? *Journal of Comparative Economics*, 24(3), pp. 241–264.

Cai, F. (2011). The *Hukou* Reform and Unification of Rural–urban Social Welfare, *China & World Economy*, 19(3), pp. 33–48.

Cai, F., Du, Y., and Wang, M. (2011a). Labor Market Institutions and Social Protection Mechanism, Background Report for the World Bank, Washington, DC: World Bank.

Cai, F., Du, Y., and Wang, M. (2011b). Rural Labor Migration and Poverty Reduction in China, *Working Paper Series No. 7*, Beijing: International Poverty Reduction Center.

CDRF (China Development Research Foundation) (2012). *China Development Report, 2012*, Beijing: China Development Publishing House.

Cowen, T. (2011). *The Great Stagnation: How America Ate All the Low-Hanging Fruit of Modern History, Got Sick, and Will (Eventually) Feel Better*, New York: Dutton.

Deutsch, J., and Silber, J. (2001). The Kuznets Curve and the Impact of Various Income Sources on the Link between Inequality and Development, Working Papers No. 2001-03, Tel Aviv: Department of Economics, Bar-Ilan University.

Dornbusch, R., and Edwards, S. (1989). Macroeconomic Populism in Latin America, NBER Working Paper No. 2986, Cambridge, MA: National Bureau of Economic Research.

Du, Y., and Lu, Y. (2011). The Natural Rate of Unemployment in China and Its Implications, *Journal of World Economy*, 34(4), pp. 3–21.

Du, Y., Park, A., and Wang, S. (2005). Migration and Rural Poverty in China, *Journal of Comparative Economics*, 33(4), pp. 688–709.

Gao, W., Zhao, W., and Cheng, J. (2011). The Impact of Rural Labor's Migration on Income Gap Statistics of Rural and Urban Residents, in F. Cai (ed.), *Reports on China's Population and Labor (No. 12): Challenges during the Twelfth Five-year Plan Period: Population, Employment, and Income Distribution*, Beijing: Social Sciences Academic Press, pp. 228–242.

Herd, R. (2010). A Pause in the Growth of Inequality in China? *Economics Department Working Papers No. 748*, Paris: OECD.

Herd, R. (2012). Recent Movements in Inequality: A Preliminary Overview, CASS Forum on Inequality, 6 January 2012, Beijing.

IOSCPRC (Information Office of the State Council of the People's Republic of China) (2012). New Progress in Development-oriented Poverty Reduction Program for Rural China (November 2011), in *White Papers of the Chinese Government* (*2009–2011*), Beijing: Foreign Languages Press.

Kanbur, R., and Zhang, X. (2004). Fifty Years of Regional Inequality in China: A Journey through Central Planning, Reform, and Openness, WIDER Working Paper Series No. 2004/50, Helsinki: World Institute for Development Economics Research.

Knight, J., and Song, L. (2005). *Towards a Labour Market in China*, Oxford: Oxford University Press.

Krugman, P. (2007). *The Conscience of a Liberal*, New York: W. W. Norton.

Kuznets, S. (1955). Economic Growth and Income Inequality, *American Economic Review*, 45(1), pp. 1–28.

Li, S. (2010). Economic Growth and Income Distribution: An Empirical Analysis on China's Experiences, in F. Cai (ed.), *Transforming the Chinese Economy, 1978–2008*, Leiden and Boston: Brill, pp. 279–315.

Li, W., Fan, L., Zhang, L., Diao, P., and Cui, Y. (2012). Report on People's Wellbeing and Urbanization in China, in X. Ru, X. Lu, and P. Li (eds.), *Society of China Analysis and Forecast, 2012*, Beijing: Social Sciences Academic Press.

Minami, R. (2010). Turning Point in the Japanese Economy, presented at the workshop Discussion on the Changes in East Asia Labor Market Based on Lewisian Turning Point Theory, Institute of Asian Cultures, Toyo University, Tokyo.

Minami, R., and Ono, A. (1981). Behavior of Income Shares in a Labor Surplus Economy: Japan's Experience, *Economic Development and Cultural Change*, 29(2), pp. 309–324.

Moriguchi, C., and Saez, E. (2009). The Evolution of Income Concentration in Japan, 1886–2005: Evidence from Income Tax Statistics, *Review of Economics and Statistics*, 90(4), pp. 713–734.

Ravallion, M., and Chen, S. (2004). China's (Uneven) Progress against Poverty, World Bank Policy Research Paper 3408, Washington, DC: World Bank.

Samuelson, P. (2004). Where Ricardo and Mill Rebut and Confirm Arguments of Mainstream Economists Supporting Globalization, *Journal of Economic Perspectives*, 18(3), pp. 135–146.

Wan, G. (2007). Understanding Regional Poverty and Inequality Trends in China: Methodological Issues and Empirical Findings, *Review of Income and Wealth*, 53(1), pp. 25–34.

Wang, X. (2007). Grey Income and Income Inequality of Chinese Residents, *Comparative Studies*, 31.

Wang, X. (2011). Grey Income and National Income Distribution, in X. Song, S. Li, X. Shi, and D. Lai (eds.) *China's Income Distribution: Researches and Debates*, China Economic Press.

Whalley, J., and Zhang, S. (2004). Inequality Change in China and (*Hukou*) Labour Mobility Restrictions, *NBER Working Paper No. 10683*, Cambridge, MA: National Bureau of Economic Research.

Zhao, R., and Ding, S. (2008). Distribution of Residents' Wealth in China, in L. Shi, T. Sicular, and B. A. Gustafsson (eds.), *Research on Income Distribution in China III*, Beijing: Beijing Normal University.

7 Labor market changes, labor disputes, and social cohesion in China*

7.1 Introduction

Thanks to the strictly implemented one-child policy, rapid economic growth, and fundamental social transformation, China has completed a demographic transition within a very short period of time compared to most developed countries (Du, 2005; Wang and Mason, 2008). During the reform period, the stage of demographic transition in China has been characterized by a sharp drop in fertility, rapid decline in the proportion of youth, slowdown of working-age population growth, and a quick increase in the proportion of elderly over time. When the pace of the decline in the proportion of youth exceeded that of the increase in the proportion of elderly, China began to enjoy a sufficient labor supply, a result of productive population structure (Cai and Wang, 2005; Cai, 2010). As the demographic transition process continues to carry forward, the growth of working-age population becomes slower and slower, whereas population-aging speeds up.

Since about 1980, the growth of the aged population has accelerated, the growth of working-age population has rapidly slowed down, and the growth of youth population has shrunk. The implication of such demographic dynamics is that long-standing low fertility leads to an inadequacy of labor supply as working-age population first slows its growth and then tapers off. According to an updated prediction (United Nations, 2009), the year 2015 is China's turning point at which the population aged 15 to 64 will stop increasing and begin shrinking.

According to a more detailed prediction (Hu, 2009), which takes into account the impacts of rural-to-urban migration, the labor demand in the urban sector has been fulfilled by rural labor migration in recent years. By 2015, the amount of incremental working-age population in urban areas will be less than that of reduced working-age population in rural areas, and the total working-age population will begin to shrink—the same conclusion as the UN prediction. This implies that, without substantial enhancement of wages and other incentives, migrant workers will not fill up the gap vacated by rapid reduction of the urban labor force.

The decline of the growth rate and of the absolute number of working-age population leads to an inevitable labor shortage, a challenge that the Chinese economy has to confront. Labor shortage first emerged in the Pearl River Delta region in 2003 and has since expanded to the Yangtze River Delta regions and to inland provinces, the general source of migrant workers. Gradually it has become a national phenomenon in China (Cai and Wang, 2005; Wang, 2005; Zhang, 2008).

With the emergence and expansion of labor shortage, wages have been growing rapidly in both agricultural and non-agricultural sectors (M. Wang, 2010). In recent years labor disputes have intensified alongside the labor shortage and wage inflation, particularly after 2008 when several Chinese labor laws were issued or updated, spurring enlightened workers to voice their various demands in the labor market.[1] Labor disputes take place in various forms, including workers' initiation of labor disputes and other collective actions such as complaints and strikes. In addition there are other events indicating employment conflicts such as chain suicides and frequent employee turnover.

According to Lewis (1972) and Ranis and Fei (1961), the Lewis turning point can be referred to as the period of time at which expansion of labor demand exceeds that of labor supply, resulting in rising wage rates of ordinary workers, while agricultural-sector wages are not yet determined by marginal productivity of labor, and a difference of marginal productivity of labor between agricultural and non-agricultural sectors remains. The commercial point occurs when the wage rates in agricultural and non-agricultural sectors are both determined by their marginal productivity of labor and the gap in productivities disappears. Only at this time does the dual economy ends.

The appearance of unskilled labor shortage and wage increases in China imply the advent of the Lewis turning point, which is empirically confirmed to be accompanied by the Kuznets turning point—that is, the point at which income inequality reaches its peak and starts to decrease (Minami and Ono, 1981). However, the existing income distribution setup cannot alter itself spontaneously.

The intensified labor disputes of recent years have drawn much attention from scholars and policy-makers. Some claim that it is a sign of labor relations' deterioration. We borrow Hirschman's framework (Hirschman, 1970) to interpret the newly emerged phenomenon. Hirschman uses three expressions—exit, voice, and loyalty—to illustrate mechanisms by which citizens, consumers, and workers express their dissatisfaction. When members of an organization perceive that the organization is demonstrating a decrease of quality or benefit to them, they can exit or they can voice.

According to Hirschman (1970), exit and voice also interact in unique and sometimes unexpected ways. Exit might be reduced if greater opportunity for feedback and criticism are provided. With the coming of the Lewis turning point, laborers face more employment opportunities and they then obtain the power to "exit" or the right to "vote with their feet". When workers are dissatisfied with their jobs, they have two choices. One choice is simply to choose to quit. The other choice is to take action to voice their claims in front of employers, such as labor disputes, complaints, collective bargaining, and (more extremely) strikes, in order to seek higher pay and better working conditions without leaving the firms.

Since more employment opportunities give workers more bargaining power with their employers, the increase of labor dispute cases need not be seen as a sign of aggravation of labor relations. Instead it is an inevitable result of labor market changes with the coming of the Lewis turning point. Intensified labor disputes are without a doubt an indication of stronger demand for labor market institutions, which are expected to be helpful for maintaining and improving social cohesion, resulting in an urgent and challenging task for the Chinese government.

The rest of this paper is organized as follows: Section 7.2 introduces the data and describes the situations of labor disputes; Section 7.3 examines the determinants of labor disputes from both macro and micro perspectives; Section 7.4 analyzes how government employment policies and labor market institutions help foster social cohesion; Section 7.5 concludes and suggests policy priorities and reform directions so as to strengthen social cohesion after the Lewis turning point via labor market institution-building.

7.2 Description of labor disputes

In this paper, we employ both macro and micro data. The macro data are from *China Labor Statistical Yearbook*, *China Compendium of Statistics 1949–2008*, and *China Statistical Yearbook*. The micro data employed include three micro survey datasets.

The first dataset is the China Urban Labor Survey (CULS). There are three waves of CULS, which are called CULS1, CULS2, and CULS3. They were conducted by the Institute of Population and Labor Economics at the Chinese Academy of Social Sciences in 2001, 2005, and 2010. In this paper we will only utilize CULS3, which was conducted in six big cities (Shanghai, Wuhan, Shenyang, Fuzhou, Xi'an, and Guangzhou). The cities were chosen to provide regional diversity and variation in the size of the state versus private sectors. Within each city, 700 urban households and 600 migrant households were interviewed.

The second micro dataset is a survey of manufacturing enterprises (MES), conducted by the People's Bank of China from September to November 2009. It surveyed 1,644 enterprises which are located in eight provinces, including Zhejiang, Jiangsu, Guangdong, Shandong, Jilin, Hubei, Shaanxi, and Sichuan.

The third micro dataset this paper employs is a survey of private enterprises (PES), jointly conducted by the All-China Federation of Industry and

Commerce, the Ministry of Human Resources and Social Security, and the All-China Federation of Trade Unions from June to September in 2009. It surveyed 1,445 enterprises which are located in all provinces throughout the country except in Chongqing.

In recent years, particularly after 2008 when several Chinese labor-related laws were issued or updated, labor disputes have intensified. In the past decade, the number of labor disputes in China has been gradually increasing. It was 169,000 in 1999 and increased steadily until 2007. In 2008, the number of labor disputes increased sharply to 931,000, which was almost twice that of 2007. The number of labor disputes in 2009 was 870,000, falling slightly compared with 2008.

Labor disputes take place in various forms, including workers' initiation of labor disputes and other collective actions such as complaints and strikes. In addition there are other events indicating employment conflicts such as chain suicides and frequent employee turnover. Since only officially mediated and accepted cases of labor disputes are statistically recorded and other forms of labor dispute can only be read as individual cases through the media, we mainly use the consistent, hopefully representative, statistics to show the changes in labor disputes (Figure 7.1).

Figure 7.1 shows a significant increase of officially recorded labor disputes. The statistics of labor dispute cases have two categories: the cases accepted and cases mediated. The majority of labor dispute cases are cases accepted and only a small portion are cases mediated. Cases accepted refer to labor

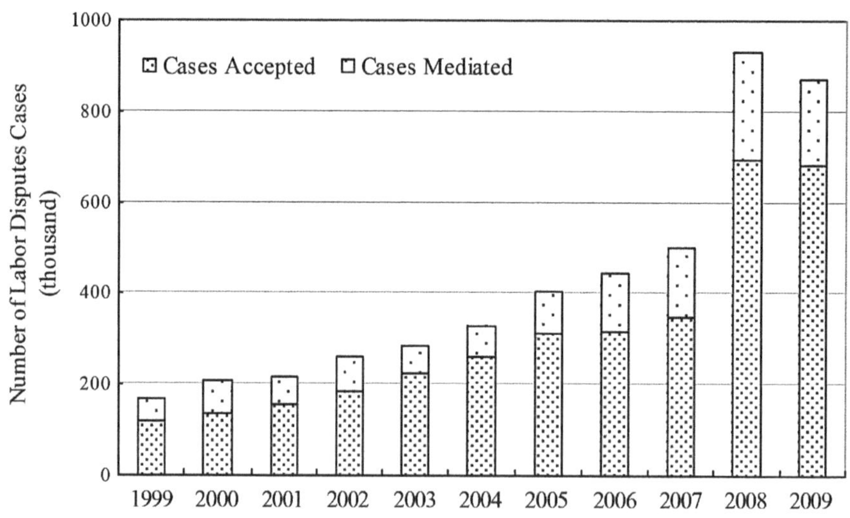

Figure 7.1 Increase in labor dispute cases.

Source: *China Labor Statistical Yearbook* (various years).

dispute cases accepted and heard by different levels of labor dispute arbitration institutions and cases mediated refer to labor dispute cases mediated before going to institutions.

While looking into the distribution and dynamics of labor dispute cases by region, we find that the number of labor disputes in the eastern region is much higher than that in the central and western regions and it grows the fastest in the eastern region (Figure 7.2). In 2008, the number of labor dispute cases in the eastern region grew by 98 percent compared to the previous year, which was much faster than in the central region (50 percent) and in the western region (61 percent). In 2009, while the number of labor disputes cases in the eastern region fell slightly, totals in the central and western regions continued to grow.

From Figure 7.2, one can also observe that the labor dispute cases in the eastern region dominate. In the period between 1999 and 2009, the share of the number of labor dispute cases in the eastern region was between 67 percent (in 1999) and 76 percent (in 2008), whereas the central region held a similar proportion as in the western region.

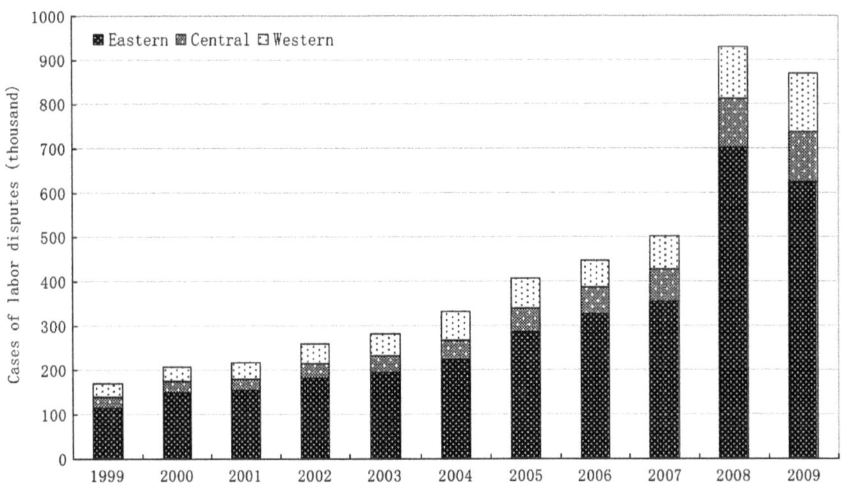

Figure 7.2 Number of labor dispute cases by region.

Note: The eastern region includes Liaoning (LN), Beijing (BJ), Tianjin (TJ), Hebei (HB), Shandong (SHD), Jiangsu (JS), Shanghai (SH), Zhejiang (ZHJ), Fujian (FJ), Guangdong (GD), and Hainan (HN); the central region includes Heilongjiang (HLJ), Jilin (JL), Shanxi (SX), Henan (HEN), Hubei (HUB), Hunan (HUN), Anhui (ANH), and Jiangxi (JX); the western region includes Inner Mongolia (NMG), Shaanxi (SHX), Gansu (GS), Qinghai (QH), Ningxia (NX), Xinjiang (XJ), Chongqing (CHQ), Sichuan (SCH), Guizhou (GZH), Yunnan (YN), Tibet (XZ), and Guangxi (GX).

Source: Calculated according to data from *China Labor Statistical Yearbook*.

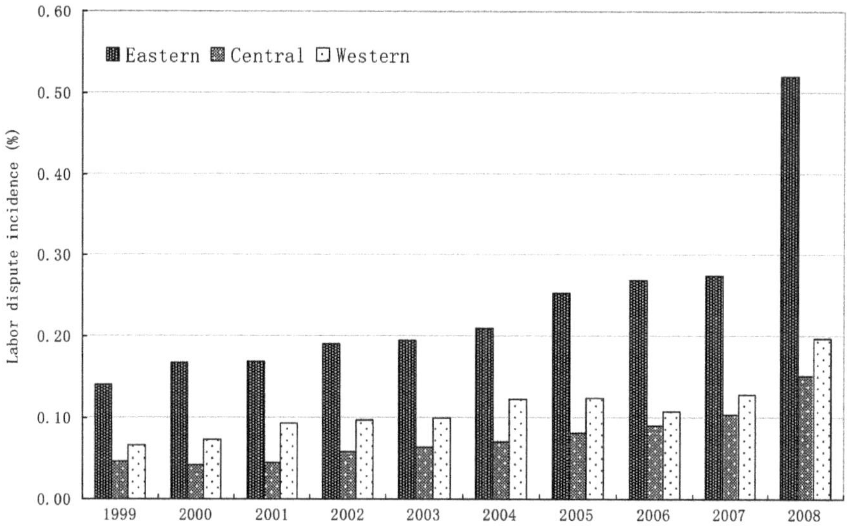

Figure 7.3 Labor dispute incidence by region.

Note: Labor dispute incidence refers to ratio of number of labor dispute cases to urban employment.

Source: Calculated according to data from *China Labor Statistical Yearbook* and *China Compendium of Statistics 1949–2008*.

The eastern domination in labor dispute cases is not only because of its larger share of employment, but also because the labor dispute incidence in the eastern region is higher (Figure 7.3). While the labor dispute incidences in the eastern, central and western regions have all showed an increasing trend and had a significant increase in 2008, the growth of labor dispute incidence in the eastern region in 2008 was much higher than that in the central and western regions, with incidences of 5.2, 1.5 and 2.0 per thousand workers respectively.

We can go further and examine the relationship between income level and labor dispute incidence. By looking at labor dispute incidence by province, one finds that the more developed provinces have the highest incidence of labor disputes (Figure 7.4). For example, Tianjin, Shanghai, Beijing, Guangdong, and Jiangsu, the five most developed provincial regions, stand out significantly with the highest incidence of labor disputes, whereas in poorer inland provinces such as Gansu, Inner Mongolia, and Qinghai, labor dispute incidence was relatively low.

We now take a step further to see how firm characteristics relate to labor dispute incidence. When we look at labor disputes by ownership, the situations in 2007, the first half of 2008, and the first half of 2009 were very similar (Table 7.1). More than 20 percent of state-owned and collective

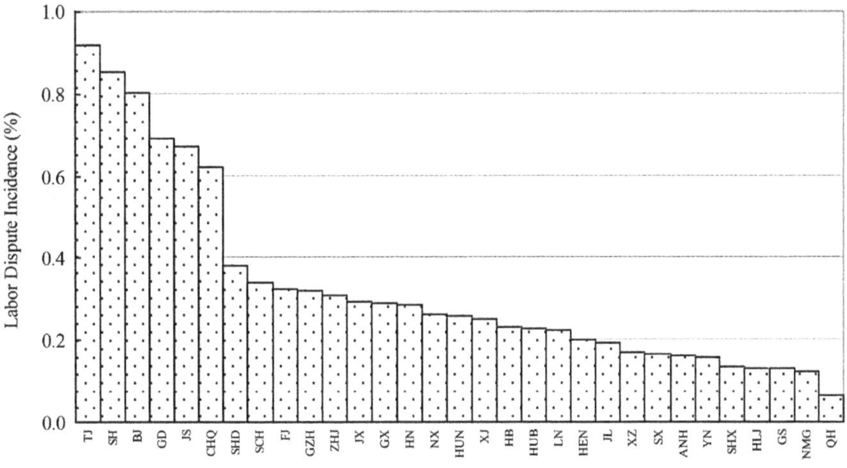

Figure 7.4 Labor dispute incidence by province in 2008.

Source: Calculated according to data from *China Labor Statistical Yearbook* and *China Compendium of Statistics 1949–2008*.

enterprises had labor disputes, which was the highest among all types of enterprises. Foreign-funded enterprise was in second place. The proportion for private enterprise was the lowest. In the second half of 2008, 15.2 percent of foreign-funded enterprises had labor disputes, which is slightly higher than state-owned and collective enterprises. For private enterprises on the one hand, and joint ownership units, joint stock companies, and limited liability corporations on the other, the proportions were 6.8 percent and 6.6 percent, respectively.

By tabulating the data of PES, we found that the proportion of private enterprises which reported labor dispute cases in the eastern region is the highest among the three regions, while that in the central region is in the middle and that in the western region is the lowest.

Looking at the proportion of enterprises which reported labor disputes by firm size, we see a U-shaped distribution (Table 7.1). In three of the periods of time observed—namely, 2007, the first half of 2008, and the first half of 2009—the situations were quite similar. In the first half of 2009, for example, more than 17 percent of enterprises with firm size above 1,000 employees had labor disputes in these three periods, which was the highest. Next were enterprises with firm size between 401 and 1,000 and enterprises with firm size at 50 and below. However, for the second half of 2008, only 2 percent of enterprises with firm size at 50 and below had labor disputes.

The PES data shows a pattern by which the larger-sized enterprises have a higher proportion of labor dispute incidence (Table 7.2). In terms of the proportions of enterprises which reported having labor disputes in 2007 and

Table 7.1 Proportion of enterprises reporting labor disputes (%)

	2007	*First half of 2008*	*Second half of 2008*	*First half of 2009*
By ownership				
State-owned and collective enterprises	23.5	20.6	14.7	25.0
Private enterprises	7.0	7.0	6.8	7.5
Foreign-funded enterprises	13.4	14.3	15.2	13.8
Other ownerships*	11.3	11.5	6.6	12.4
Total	10.9	11.0	8.2	11.8
By firm size				
50 and below	13.3	13.7	2.1	13.7
51–100	9.1	8.3	5.6	8.7
101–200	9.3	8.0	6.0	8.6
201–400	7.5	8.1	9.3	9.0
401–1,000	13.2	14.4	12.8	14.4
Above 1,000	17.0	17.6	19.2	20.3
Total	11.1	11.1	8.4	11.8

Source: Calculated from MES.

Notes

* Other ownerships includes joint ownership units, joint stock companies, and limited liability corporations.

Table 7.2 Proportion of enterprises which reported labor disputes (%)

	2007	*2008*	*The first half of 2009*
50 and below	2.9	6.2	3.3
51–100	4.0	9.7	5.1
101–200	7.6	14.1	7.6
201–400	8.9	16.5	11.0
401–1000	18.9	23.5	13.5
Above 1000	33.0	36.8	21.2
Total	12.4	17.7	10.2

Source: Calculated from PES.

in the first half of 2009, the PES data were very similar to the corresponding proportions based on MES. However, the proportion of enterprises which had labor disputes in 2008 was higher than the corresponding proportion based on MES. According to PES, enterprises with larger firm size had a higher proportion of labor disputes.

7.3 Determinants of labor dispute incidence

We use a panel dataset of 31 provinces from 1999 to 2008 to analyze the determinants of labor dispute incidence. The dataset is constructed using data from *China Labor Statistical Yearbook*, *China Statistical Yearbook*, and *China Compendium of Statistics 1949–2008*. Labor dispute incidence is measured by the ratio of number of labor dispute cases to urban employment. In order to examine the determinants of labor dispute incidence, the model is constructed as below:

$$pdispute_{i,t} = \beta_0 + \beta_1 \ln gdppc_{i,t} + \beta_2 \exp ort_{i,t} + prov_i + u_{i,t}$$

Where $pdispute_{i,t}$ is the labor dispute incidence of province i in year t, $gdppc_{i,t}$ is GDP per capita of province i in year t, $\exp ort_{i,t}$ is the proportion of export value in GDP of province i in year t, $prov_i$ is a group of province dummy variables, and $dispute = \beta_0 + \beta_1\, female + \beta_2\, age\ \beta_3\, edu + \beta_4\, contract + \beta_5\, ownership + \beta_6\, sector + \beta_7\, furnsize + \beta_8\, city + \varepsilon$ is randomly disturbing factors.

Dependent and independent variables in the model are listed in Table 7.3. The reason we add GDP per capita in the model is that we expect more developed provinces to reach the Lewis turning point earlier, and more employment opportunities motivate people's concern for their interests. At the same time, people are more aware of laws and regulations on employment and labor relations and they are more likely to be in a better position to protect their legal rights and interests. Another hypothesis is that there is better-quality employment in more developed provinces. When employees are discontent with their employers, they tend to initiate a labor dispute rather than to exit.

The proportion of export value in GDP reflects the density of export-oriented enterprises. Employees in export-oriented enterprises are usually provided with better wages and other welfare. When employees are discontent with their employers, they tend to initiate a labor dispute rather than to exit. We expect that there will be higher labor dispute incidence in provinces with a higher proportion of export value in GDP.

Table 7.3 Dependent and independent variables in the model

Dependent variable	*Variable type*	*Explanation on variables*
Labor dispute incidence	Continuous	Ratio of number of labor dispute cases to urban employment
Independent variables		
ln(gdppc)	Continuous	Natural log of GDP per capita
export	Continuous	Proportion of export value by place of origin in GDP
year2008	Dummy	year2008 = 1 if year = 2008; year2008 = 0 if year = 1999–2007
Province dummy variables	Dummy	Abbreviated

As we have seen, there was a significant increase in the number of labor dispute cases in 2008. We know that the Employment Contract Law and the Employment Promotion Law were implemented on 1 January 2008 and the Labor Disputes Mediation and Arbitration Law was implemented on 1 May 2008. The significant increase in the number of labor dispute cases in 2008 should be closely related to the implementation of these laws. We add a year2008 dummy variable (year2008 = 1 if year = 2008; year2008 = 0 if year = 1999–2007) into the model to examine whether there is a significant difference in labor dispute incidence between 2008 and previous years. The model is reconstructed as below:

$$pdispute_{i,t} = \beta_0 + \beta_1 \ln gdppc_{i,t} + \beta_2 \exp ort_{i,t} + \beta_3 y2008 + prov_i + u_{i,t}$$

The estimation results are shown in Table 7.4. Adjusted R^2 are to some extent high in all three models, which indicates that the models explain labor dispute incidence well. Also the estimation results on independent variables are consistent with our expectations. In all three models, there is significantly positive relationship between GDP per capita and labor dispute incidence. When export and year2008 are added into the model, the coefficients of GDP per capita fall. This tells us that labor dispute incidence is higher in provinces with higher GDP per capita after controlling for other factors.

There is also a significantly positive relationship between export and labor dispute incidence, which indicates that regions with higher density of export-oriented enterprises have higher labor dispute incidence. The positive coefficient of year2008 tells us that labor dispute incidence in 2008 is higher than previous years.

Now we can look into the determinants of "whether a worker has ever initiated a labor dispute" by processing micro data of CULS3. Only 0.9 percent of urban local workers and 0.8 percent of migrant workers have ever

Table 7.4 Determinants of labor dispute incidence (fixed effects model)

	Model (1)	*Model (2)*	*Model (3)*
ln(gdppc)	0.1128***	0.0761***	0.0272**
export		0.0331***	0.0355***
year2008			0.1098***
Province dummy variables	Abbreviated	Abbreviated	Abbreviated
Constant term	−0.9094***	−0.6066***	−0.1089
No. of observations	310	310	310
Adjusted R^2	0.681	0.710	0.752

Notes:
(1) *** significant at 1%; ** significant at 5%; * significant at 10%.
(2) Estimation results on province dummy variables are abbreviated for simplicity.

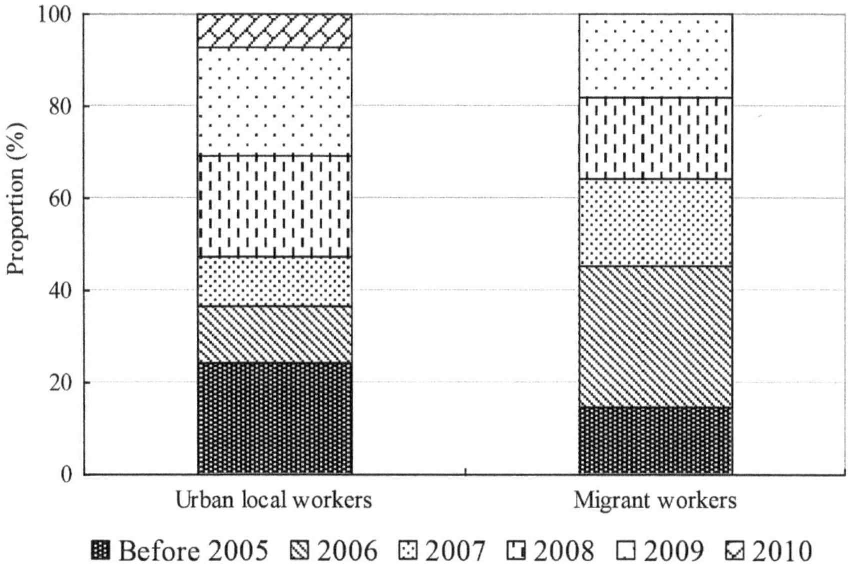

Figure 7.5 Years of the last labor dispute a worker initiated.

Note: Since CULS3 was conducted in early 2010, labor disputes initiated in 2010 were very few.

Source: Calculated from China Urban Labor Survey 3.

initiated a labor dispute. For urban local workers, 24 percent of "last labor dispute" cases happened before 2005 and three-fourths happened after 2006 (Figure 7.5). For migrant workers, only 15 percent of "last labor dispute" cases happened before 2005 and the remaining 85 percent happened after 2006. That is, most "last labor dispute" cases happened after 2006 for both urban local workers and migrant workers.

For urban local workers, 43 percent declared "wage compensation" was the main reason for initiating their last labor dispute (Table 7.5). For migrant workers, this proportion was 48.6 percent. For urban local workers, about 17.9 percent declared "ending labor contract" was the main reason and 17.1 percent declared "working time" was the main reason. For migrant workers, about 14.8 percent declared "work safety" was the main reason, and 34.4 percent declared "other" was the main reason. When we try to explore what "other" refers to, we find that all observations are of wage arrears.

In what follows we estimate by probit model to examine the factors affecting the behavior of initiating labor disputes for urban local workers and migrant workers. The dependent variable is whether a worker has ever initiated a labor dispute or not (yes = 1, no = 0). The independent variables include individual characteristics (gender, age, and educational level) and job characteristics

Table 7.5 Major reason for initiating the latest labor dispute

	Urban local workers (%)	*Migrant workers (%)*
Amending labor contract	3.8	0.0
Ending labor contract	17.9	0.6
Working time	17.1	0.0
Wage compensation	43.0	48.6
Work safety	7.0	14.8
Social welfare	2.6	1.7
Training opportunities	0.0	0.0
Other	8.5	34.4
Total	100	100

Source: Calculated from China Urban Labor Survey 3.

(contract, ownership, sector, firm size) and city dummy variables. The model is constructed as below:

$$dispute = \beta_0 + \beta_1 female + \beta_2 age + \beta_3 edu + \beta_4 contract + \beta_5 ownership + \beta_6 \sec tor \\ + \beta_7 firmsize + \beta_8 city + \varepsilon$$

Where *dispute* is whether a worker has ever initiated a labor dispute or not, *female* is female dummy variable, *edu* is a group of age group dummy variables, *edu* is a group of educational level dummy variables, *contract* is labor contract dummy variable, *ownership* is a group of ownership dummy variables, sec*tor* is a group of sector dummy variables, *firmsize* is a group of firm size dummy variables, *city* is a group of city dummy variables, and ε is the error term.

The variables in the model are listed in Table 7.6. The reason for including individual characteristics in the model is that we expect that people with higher human capital are more aware of laws and regulations on employment and labor relations and they are better at protecting their legal rights and interests. When they are discontent with their employers, they tend to initiate a labor dispute. We include job characteristics in the model to look at the impacts of job characteristics on labor dispute initiation.

For urban local workers and migrant workers, we estimate two models. In the first model, we only add individual characteristics. In the second model, job characteristics are added. In order to look at whether there is a difference in the probability of having initiated a labor dispute between urban local workers and migrant workers, we estimate models for the pooled sample. The models specification for the pooled sample is exactly the same as models for urban local workers and migrant workers, except that in the models for the pooled sample, we add a dummy variable (migrant worker = 1, urban local worker = 0). The estimation results are in Table 7.7.

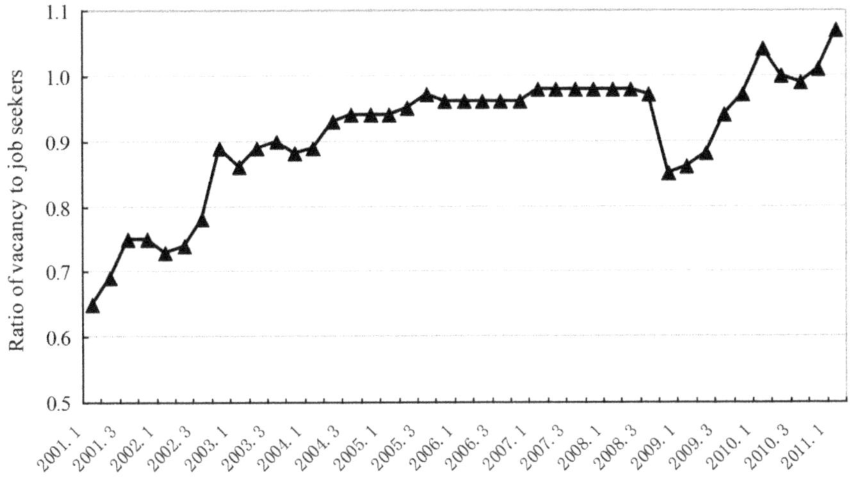

Figure 7.6 Changing labor market situation.

Source: Downloaded from the website of the Ministry of Human Resources and Social Security of the People's Republic of China.

The estimation results show that there is no significant difference in the probability of having initiated a labor dispute between urban local workers and migrant workers. For the pooled sample, there is no significant difference in the probability of having initiated a labor dispute between females and males. The probabilities of having ever initiated a labor dispute for older workers are lower and the probabilities of having ever initiated a labor dispute for more educated workers are higher. Workers having labor contracts are less likely to initiate a labor dispute. Generally, job characteristics variables do not affect whether or not a worker has ever initiated a labor dispute.

When we look at the estimation results of urban local workers and migrant workers, we find that the effects of the independent variables are very similar between urban local workers and migrant workers. For both urban local workers and migrant workers, gender and age do not much affect whether or not a worker has ever initiated a labor dispute.

For urban local workers, compared with workers with primary schooling and below, workers with junior high school, senior high or technical secondary school, and college and above have higher probability of having ever initiated a labor dispute. Among workers with junior high school, senior high or technical secondary school, and college and above, workers with junior high school have the highest probability of having ever initiated a labor dispute. Next is the probability for workers with college and above, and workers with senior high or technical secondary school have the lowest probability. For migrant workers, compared with workers with primary and below,

Table 7.6 Explanations of variables in the model

Variable	*Variable type*	*Explanation on variables*
Dependent variable		
Whether a worker has ever initiated a labor dispute or not	Dummy	Has ever initiated a labor dispute = 1 Has never initiated a labor dispute = 0
Independent variable		
Female	Dummy	Female = 1 Male = 0
31–40	Dummy	31–40 = 1 16–30 = 0
41–50	Dummy	41–50 = 1 16–30 = 0
51–60	Dummy	51–60 = 1 16–30 = 0
Junior high school	Dummy	Junior high school = 1 Primary school and below = 0
Senior high or technical secondary school	Dummy	Senior high or technical secondary school = 1 Primary school and below = 0
College and above	Dummy	College and above = 1 Primary school and below = 0
Have labor contract	Dummy	Have labor contract = 1 No labor contract = 0
State-owned enterprises	Dummy	State-owned enterprises = 1 Government agencies and institutions = 0
Private enterprises	Dummy	Private enterprises = 1 Government agencies and institutions = 0
Foreign-funded enterprises or joint ventures	Dummy	Foreign-funded enterprises or joint ventures = 1 Government agencies and institutions = 0
Other sectors in secondary industry	Dummy	Other sectors in secondary industry = 1 Manufacturing = 0
Wholesale and retail trade & hotel and catering services	Dummy	Wholesale and retail trade & hotel and catering services = 1 Manufacturing = 0
Leasing, business, personal, and other services	Dummy	Leasing, business, personal, and other services = 1 Manufacturing = 0
Other sectors in tertiary industry	Dummy	Other sectors in tertiary industry = 1 Manufacturing = 0
Firm size 2–7	Dummy	Firm size 2–7 = 1 firm size 1 = 0
Firm size 8–19	Dummy	Firm size 8–19 = 1 firm size 1 = 0
Firm size 20+	Dummy	Firm size 20+ = 1 firm size 1 = 0
Wuhan	Dummy	Wuhan = 1 Shanghai = 0
Shenyang	Dummy	Shenyang Shanghai = 0
Fuzhou	Dummy	Fuzhou Shanghai = 0
Xi'an	Dummy	Xi'an Shanghai = 0
Guangzhou	Dummy	Guangzhou Shanghai = 0

Note:
Other sectors in secondary industry refer to sectors in secondary industry except manufacturing, which include mining and quarrying, production and supply of electricity, gas and water and construction; other sectors in tertiary industry refer to sectors in tertiary industry except wholesale and retail trade & hotel and catering services, leasing, business, personal and other services, which include transport, storage, post and telecommunication services, data transmission, computer service and software, banking, real estate, scientific research, technical services and geological prospecting, water conservancy, environment and public utility management, education, public health, social securities and social welfare, culture, sports and entertainment, public administration and social organizations and international organizations.

Table 7.7 Estimation results of probit model

	Pooled sample		*Urban local workers*		*Migrant workers*	
	(1)	*(2)*	*(1)*	*(2)*	*(1)*	*(2)*
	Marginal effects	*Marginal effects*	*Marginal effects*	*Marginal effects*	*Marginal effects*	*Marginal effects*
Urban local workers						
Migrant workers	−0.0008	−0.0012				
Male						
Female	−0.0016	−0.0011	−0.0033	−0.0025	−0.0009	−0.0004
16–30						
31–40	−0.0018*	−0.0013*	−0.0042	−0.003	−0.0007	−0.0005
41–50	−0.0023*	−0.0016	−0.0065	−0.0045	−0.0007	−0.0004
51–60	−0.0023**	−0.0018**	−0.0060**	−0.0044	−0.0011	−0.0008***
Primary and below						
Junior high school	0.4958***	0.5510***	0.7537***	0.8020***	0.2681***	0.3113***
Senior high or technical secondary school	0.5476***	0.6054***	0.4998***	0.5494***	0.5489***	0.6444***
College and above	0.6565***	0.7145***	0.5041***	0.5617***	0.7567***	0.8292***
No labor contract						
Have labor contract		−0.0010*		−0.0024		−0.0002
Government agencies and institutions						
State-owned enterprises		−0.0011		−0.0045*		0.0014
Private enterprises		0.0014		0.0038		0.0006
Foreign-funded enterprises or joint ventures		0.0062***		0.0059		0.0048
Manufacturing						
Other sectors in secondary industry		0.0064		0.0012		0.0126
Wholesale and retail trade & hotel and catering services		−0.0006		−0.0049*		0.0013
Leasing, business, personal, and other services		0.0038*		0.0000		0.0061

(*continued*)

Table 7.7 Cont.

	Pooled sample		*Urban local workers*		*Migrant workers*	
	(1)	*(2)*	*(1)*	*(2)*	*(1)*	*(2)*
	Marginal effects	*Marginal effects*	*Marginal effects*	*Marginal effects*	*Marginal effects*	*Marginal effects*
Other sectors in tertiary industry		0.001		−0.0002		0.0014
Firm size 1						
Firm size 2–7		−0.0009		0.0057		−0.0010*
Firm size 8–19		0.0005		0.0058		−0.0003
Firm size 20+		0.0008		0.0037		−0.0001
City dummy variables	abbreviated	abbreviated	abbreviated	abbreviated	abbreviated	abbreviated
No. of observations	7275	7275	3104	3104	4171	4171
Pseudo R^2	0.047	0.081	0.038	0.072	0.069	0.129

Notes:
(1) *** significant at 1%; ** significant at 5%; * significant at 10%.
(2) Estimation results on city dummy variables are abbreviated for simplicity.
(3) The robust estimation and clustering within cities are used in the model to solve the problem of possibility of correlated errors within cities.

workers with higher educational levels have a higher probability of having ever initiated a labor dispute. Generally, job characteristics variables do not affect whether or not a worker has ever initiated a labor dispute.

7.4 Government initiatives

There have been three phases of employment policy in China. Before the mid-1990s, no employment policies were explicitly announced. In this period, the iron-rice-bowl dominated the urban employment pattern. That is, most urban residents at working age were guaranteed a job by the government. At the same time, labor resources reallocation accompanied by economic growth, especially by township and village enterprises development and non-agricultural industry development, promoted labor mobility from rural to urban areas. Cai and Wang (1999) break down China's economic growth between 1978 and 1998 into contributions of capital, labor, human capital, and labor transfer, finding that labor increases contributed 24 percent to China's annual growth rate of 9.5 percent and labor transfers contributed 21 percent.

Between the late 1990s and early 2000s Chinese employment was simultaneously hit by a macroeconomic downtown, the Asian financial crisis, and the system reform of breaking the iron-rice-bowl in employment. To tackle severe unemployment and lay-offs, the Chinese government began to implement proactive employment policies. Since then these policies have effectively helped urban workers to achieve reemployment, diversified employment structure, kept overall employment growth, and promoted labor migration (Cai and Wang, 2010).

Since 2003 with the coming of the Lewis Turning Point, a series of new policies aimed at promoting the establishment of labor market institutions have been implemented, though they are far from complete. The following section describes the evolution of proactive government employment policies, a collective bargaining system for wages, and a collective contract system.

6.4.1 Government proactive employment policies

To address the severe unemployment situation in the late 1990s, the government implemented a series of policies and took many measures, aimed to ease labor market pressure and involve different stakeholders, including the governments at various levels, communities, enterprises, and laborers. The focus of these policy measures can be summarized as (1) macroeconomic policy that aims to boost employment through sustained economic growth; (2) support policy that focuses on promoting the reemployment of laid-off and unemployed workers; (3) labor market policy that aims to realize rational matching between labor force and employment needs; (4) macro regulation policy that aims to reduce unemployment; and (5) social security policy that aims to effectively assure the basic standard of living for laid-off and unemployed workers and actively promote their reemployment.

Under the framework of a proactive employment policy, the central and local governments have played an important role in assisting the unemployed to become reemployed through tax exemptions, fiscal inputs, micro finance, social security subsidies, employment assistance, and even creation of community jobs. In addition, the governments have also made efforts to encourage the development of non-public-service jobs, the service sector, informal sectors, and small- and medium-sized enterprises, which were deemed and in fact served as momentous absorbers of employment. By using various effective policy measures to expand employment, the government gradually formulated and implemented the principle of giving priority to employment.

The policies aimed at promoting employment after the financial crisis in 2008 are good examples of the Chinese government's proactive employment policies. In order to reduce employment losses brought on by the financial crisis, the Chinese government has taken up a series of active labor market policies. In 2008, apart from initiating a massive fiscal stimulus package to maintain economic growth, the Chinese government specifically put forward some measures to help both employers and employees to maintain jobs.

Those measures include (1) assistance to medium-sized and small-sized enterprises by loosening market access, diversifying financing channels, and allowing enterprises with operational difficulties to delay contributions to social security programs; (2) assistance to vulnerable labor market participants—namely, migrant workers, older urban workers, and new graduates—by providing public services such as job intermediation and training; (3) encouraging enterprises to keep workers' jobs by adopting less restrictive employment, flexible working times, and on-the-job training to stabilize employment posts; (4) giving favorable tax/fee/loan policies and other policies on business registration and information consultation to migrants who return home to start their own business; and (5) guaranteeing social protection assistance such as unemployment insurance and minimum living standard programs.

Thanks to the implementation of proactive policies, the employment situation has rapidly improved. The urban registered unemployment rate reached its peak at 4.3 percent in the four quarters of 2009 and fell afterwards. Most returned migrant workers, due to factors related to the financial crisis before the 2008 Spring Festival, have returned to cities to work. With the recovery of the Chinese economy from the crisis, the labor shortage reflecting the arrival of the Lewis Turning Point has reappeared and the labor market has since tightened, as is shown in Figure 7.6 on the relationship between labor supply and demand in public service jobs.

6.4.2 Collective bargaining system and collective contract system

The collective bargaining system for wages and the collective contract system have been mapped out as important elements of labor market reform. A series of laws and regulations have provided the policy basis for developing those systems. There were regulations on collective contracts in the Labor Law of 1994. Since then, labor departments at different levels have started to pilot collective contract systems. Based on pilot programs in more than 800 enterprises in eight provinces such as Beijing, Guangdong, and Fujian in 1995, the Ministry of Labor issued Several Opinions on Collective Bargaining for Wages in Foreign-funded Enterprises in 1997, which guides foreign-funded enterprises to carry out collective bargaining for wages.

Since then more regulations on a collective bargaining system for wages and a collective contract system have been issued, such as the Guidelines on Trade Unions Participating in Collective Bargaining for Wages in 1998, Trial Procedures for Collective Bargaining System for Wages in 2000, and a revised Trade Unions Law and Notice on Further Implementing Equal Consultation and Collective Contract System in 2001. By 2002 a three-party mechanism for the coordination of labor relations was established in thirty provinces at provincial level. By 2003 more than 290,000 thousand enterprises had a collective bargaining system for wages.

In 2004 Regulations on Collective Contracts further regulated collective bargaining and collective contract signing. In 2005 the Notice on Further Promoting Collective Bargaining System for Wages was put forward so that trade unions could represent workers to negotiate with enterprises to sign collective contracts in foreign-funded enterprises, private enterprises, township and village enterprises, and in designated regions where small enterprises are relatively concentrated. By 2005 tripartite mechanisms for the coordination of labor relations were established in cities at prefecture-level and above, more than 6,600 tripartite coordination organizations were set up, and a collective bargaining system for wages was established in more than 340,000 enterprises. Tripartite coordination organizations reached 8,030 and 10,702 in 2006 and 2007.

In 2008 the Employment Contract Law gave more detailed regulations on collective contracts. A collective bargaining system for wages was mentioned by Premier Wen Jiabao in a government work report for the first session of the Eleventh National People's Congress. This was the first time that a collective bargaining system for wages was written into a government work report, highlighting the importance of this system under the new labor market situation. In 2008 and 2009 the All-China Federation of Trade Unions issued several documents on a collective bargaining system for wages.

Also in 2008 the "Rainbow Project" was put forward by the Ministry of Human Resources and Social Security. The purpose of this project is to comprehensively promote a collective bargaining system for wages and a collective contract system. In May 2010 the Deeply Promoting Collective Contract System and Implementing Rainbow Project put forward that the collective contract system should be implemented in various kinds of enterprises with established trade unions over three years (2010–2012). The coverage rate of the collective contract system should reach 60 percent and 80 percent in 2010 and 2011. The coverage rate should be improved by signing regional and industrial collective contracts in enterprises which have not yet established trade unions.

6.4.3 Statistics on trade unions and the collective contract system

The National Conference on Grassroots Trade Unions Establishment, held in 2010, motivated enterprises to establish trade unions and to implement collective bargaining for wages. The goal raised by the Conference was that more than 60 percent of legal enterprises should establish trade unions by 2010. In 2011 and 2012, this proportion is expected to reach 75 percent and 90 percent. A related goal is that 82 percent of staff and workers should become members of trade unions in 2010. In 2011 and 2012, this proportion is required to reach 87 percent and 92 percent.

The number of grassroots trade unions remained stable in the first half of the 1990s and there was a slight decrease at the end of the decade, followed by a huge jump in the early 2000s. It has been growing steadily since 2003 and reached 1.845 million in 2009. The number of members in grassroots trade unions has followed a similar pattern of growth. That is, after the stagnation in the 1990s and sudden jump in the early 2000s, it has been growing rapidly and reached 226 million in 2009 (Figure 7.7).

With the development of a collective bargaining system for wages and a collective contract system, the number of collective contracts and number of employees covered by collective contracts has been increasing (Figure 7.8).

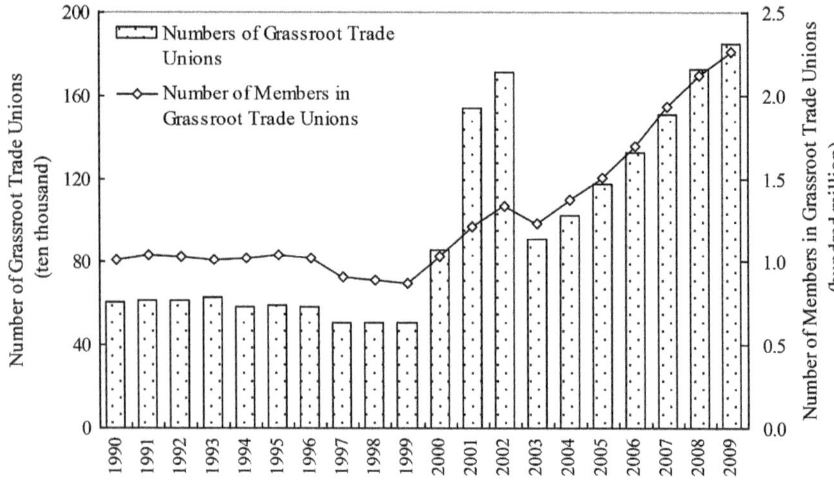

Figure 7.7 Number of grassroots trade unions and number of their members.
Note: Statistics on grassroots trade unions since 2003 have been adjusted.
Source: *China Statistical Yearbook* (2010).

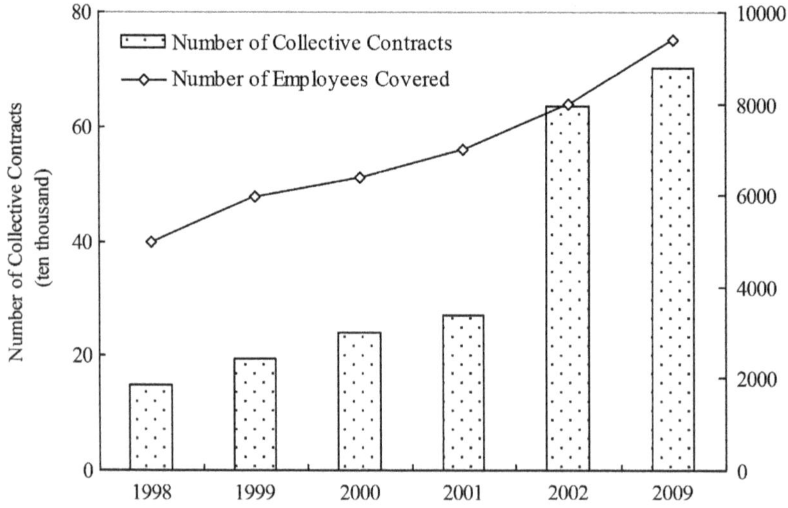

Figure 7.8 Number of collective contracts and number of employees covered.
Source: Ministry of Human Resources and Social Security, *Statistical Reports on Human Resources and Social Security Development* (various years), www.mohrss.gov.cn.

Table 7.8 Proportion of enterprises with a trade union, collective bargaining system, or staff and workers congress system (%)

	Trade union	*Collective bargaining system for wages*	*Staff and workers congress system*
Eastern region	88.5	50.8	72.0
Central region	83.0	45.3	68.7
Western region	79.4	41.2	66.0
Total	83.0	45.1	68.5

Source: Calculated from PES.

The number of collective contracts was 150,000 and the number of employees covered by collective contracts was 50 million in 1998. In 2001 the number of collective contracts increased to 270,000 and the number of employees covered by collective contracts increased to more than 70 million. There was a significant increase in the number of collective contracts in 2002 and it reached 635,000 and the number of employees covered by collective contracts reached more than 80 million. In 2009 the number of collective contracts increased to 703,000, covering more than 94 million employees.

According to PES, 83 percent of enterprises have established trade unions, 45.1 percent have established a collective bargaining system for wages, and 68.5 percent have established a staff and workers congress system (Table 7.8). the proportions of enterprises establishing trade unions, collective bargaining systems for wages, and staff and workers congress systems in the eastern region were the highest among the three regions, those in the central region were in the middle and those in the western region were the lowest.

The impacts of collective bargaining systems for wages and collective contract systems can be examined through some case studies. According to a survey conducted by Zhangjiakou Municipal Trade Union, wage growth has been achieved in most enterprises which have established a collective bargaining system for wages: 59 percent of enterprises have attained a wage growth of 5 to 10 percent and 4.6 percent of enterprises have attained a wage growth of 10 to 20 percent while 1.4 percent of enterprises have attained a wage growth of 20 to 30 percent; 33 percent of enterprises have not attained any wage growth (H. Wang, 2010).

At the Nanhai Honda Corporation located in Guangdong Province, through a collective bargaining system, an agreement between the Corporation and workers has been reached.[2] Before the agreement was reached, the monthly turnover rate was 4.9 percent. It fell to a much lower 1.2 percent after the agreement was reached. The average wages of front-line workers will increase from 1,921 yuan to 2,532 yuan. Professional and technical personnel will get a subsidy and the basic wage starting point of workers with three years' job experience will be adjusted.

7.5 Conclusions and policy suggestions

China is currently experiencing a transformation of labor market development. During most of the reform period that began in the early 1980s, the main task of labor market development was to make market forces the fundamental mechanisms for allocating the labor force and the basis of wage determination. However, the passage of the Lewis turning point has made the building of labor market institutions an urgent task.

To demonstrate its concern for social harmony, the Chinese government has embarked on building a social security system, with some success in recent years. For example, in the Twelfth Five-Year Plan approved by the National People's Congress in March 2011, the coverage rates of urban pensions and of health care were made compulsory objectives for the next five years. However, the building of labor market institutions has not been concretely scheduled in the plan.

Although labor market circumstances have been moving toward favoring ordinary workers as the Lewis turning point has been reached, the increase in wages caused by the tight labor market is insufficient to allow workers to share the benefits of enhanced labor productivity and thus to reduce income inequality among Chinese residents. That is, the wage-setting mechanism solely based on the relationship between demand for and supply of labor cannot determine a sound sharing of the outcomes between employers and employees. Therefore, there emerges a strong impetus to develop labor market institutions to maintain and improve social cohesion.

Although this paper confirms that increased labor disputes are not a result of deteriorating labor relations, the lack of mechanisms for solving disputes can cause social tension, because an arbitrary setting may neither solve the conflict nor benefit employees or employers. A lesson can be learnt from Korea. When Korea arrived at its turning point around 1970, the role of trade unions was still strictly restricted by the government and workers did not feel satisfied with their wages and working conditions. The consequence was not only a slower improvement of income distribution, comparable to Japan's similar stage of development, but also a disastrous political cost—namely, a more than decade-long collapse of social cohesion (see Freeman, 1993).

We propose three key areas of labor market institution-building. First, labor relations legislation and effective enforcement of labor-related laws are critical for building harmonious labor relations. In spite of conflicting opinions about the Employment Contract Law issued in 2008, the law has indeed enlightened workers' consciousness of interests and rights and in fact urged various levels of government to protect both urban resident workers and migrant workers.

Second, the collective bargaining system for wages is relatively weak in China while it is urgently needed. As there are no perfectly identical trade unions in any two countries, the trade union regime in China can be instrumental as a willing party in collective bargaining. The current task is to expand its coverage in various types of firms and enterprises and structure its way of working.

Lastly, as the Lewis turning point has arrived, it is an appropriate time to reorient the developmental function of the Chinese governments, both central and local, from emphasizing efforts to promote economic growth toward focusing on social protections.

Notes

* Coauthored with Wang Meiyan.

1 In the year 2008 alone, three labor-related laws began to be implemented, of which the Employment Contract Law emphasizes enhancing employment security and providing better protection for migrant workers and the urban working vulnerable, the Employment Promotion Law clearly proclaims the responsibility of governments in promoting employment and in eliminating various kinds of labor market discrimination, and the Labor Disputes Mediation and Arbitration Law is intended to provide a legal framework for improving labor relations.

2 http://business.sohu.com/20110627/n311741722.shtml.

References

Cai, F. (2010). Demographic Transition, Demographic Dividend, and Lewis Turning Point in China, *Economic Research Journal*, 45(4), pp. 4–13.

Cai, F., and Wang, D. (1999). The Sustainability of Economic Growth and the Labor Contribution, *Economic Research Journal*, 10, pp. 62–68.

Cai, F., and Wang, D. (2005). China's Demographic Transition: Implications for Growth, in Ross Garnaut and Ligang Song (eds.), *The China Boom and Its Discontents*, Canberra: Asia Pacific Press.

Cai, F., and Wang, M. (2005). An Economic Analysis on Shortage of Migrant Workers, *Guangdong Social Sciences*, 2.

Cai, F., and Wang, M. (2010). Growth and Structural Changes in Employment in Transition China, *Journal of Comparative Economics*, 38, pp. 71–81.

Du, Y. (2005). Low Fertility and Its Impacts on Long Run Economic Growth in China, *Journal of World Economy*, 12, pp.14–23.

Freeman, R. (1993). Labor Market and Institutions in Economic Development, *AEA Papers and Proceedings*, 83, pp. 403–408.

Hirschman, A. O. (1970). *Exit, Voice, and Loyalty: Responses to Decline in Firms, Organizations, and States*, Cambridge, MA: Harvard University Press.

Hu, Y. (2009). Predictions on Working Age Population of Rural and Urban China, unpublished memo.

Lewis, A. (1972). Reflections on Unlimited Labour, in L. Di Marco (ed.), *International Economics and Development*, New York, Academic Press.

Minami, R., and Ono, A. (1981). Behavior of Income Shares in a Labor Surplus Economy: Japan's Experience, *Economic Development and Cultural Change*, 29(2), pp. 309–324.

Ranis, G., and Fei, John C. H. (1961). A Theory of Economic Development, *American Economic Review*, 51(4), pp. 533–565.

United Nations (2009). The World Population Prospects: The 2008 Revision, New York: United Nations.

Wang, C. (2005). Lewis Turning Point and Chinese Transition in Dual Economy, *Population Science of China*, 6, pp. 2–10.

Wang, F., and Mason, A. (2008). The Demographic Factor in China's Transitions, in Loren Brant and Thomas Rawski (eds.), *China's Great Economic Transformations*, Cambridge: Cambridge University Press.

Wang, H. (2010). A Survey Report on the Development of a Collective Bargaining System for Wages in Zhangjiakou City, website of Zhangjiakou Municipal Trade Union.

Wang, M. (2010). The Rise of Labor Cost and the Fall of Labor Input: Has China Reached Lewis Turning Point?, *China Economic Journal*, 3(2), pp. 139–155.

Zhang, Z. (2008). Shortage of Migrant Workers: The Present and the Future, *Population and Development*, 3, p. 19.

8 Old age support system in China

Situations, challenges, and policy trends*

Expand the care of the aged in one family to that of all families.
Mencius

8.1 Introduction

Thanks to socioeconomic development and implementation of population policy, China has experienced dramatic demographic transition and thus rapid decline of fertility. Presently, both government authorities and scholars agree that the total fertility rate is 1.4.[1] Consequently, the Chinese population is aging rapidly. In 2010, working-age population aged between 15 and 59 peaked and has declined since. Even with a relaxation of population policy, the trend of population aging will not change significantly.

According to a policy simulation for the year 2030, under the unchanged birth policy, the proportion of population aged 60 and older will be 25.4 percent; under the policy that allows couples with one of the couple being the only child of her/his parents to have second child, which had already begun in 2014, the proportion of the elderly will be 24.2 percent; under the universal two-children policy, which is expected to be implemented in a few years, the proportion of the elderly will be 22.8 percent (Figure 8.1). Clearly, policy adjustment can have a moderate effect on population aging but cannot change the overall trends.

In addition, China's demographic transition has its unique characteristics. International comparison shows that as a result of rapid decline of fertility, followed by the decline of the proportion of youth population—namely, population aged 14 and younger—the speed of population aging in China began to exceed that in the rest of the less-developed countries after 1970, and it began to exceed that in more developed countries after 2010. Admitting of no doubt, China will soon catch up with its more developed counterparts in terms of population aging.

By whatever criteria, China is ranked among developing countries. For example, based on per capita GDP, the World Bank categorizes countries into a low-income group, a lower middle-income group, an upper middle-income

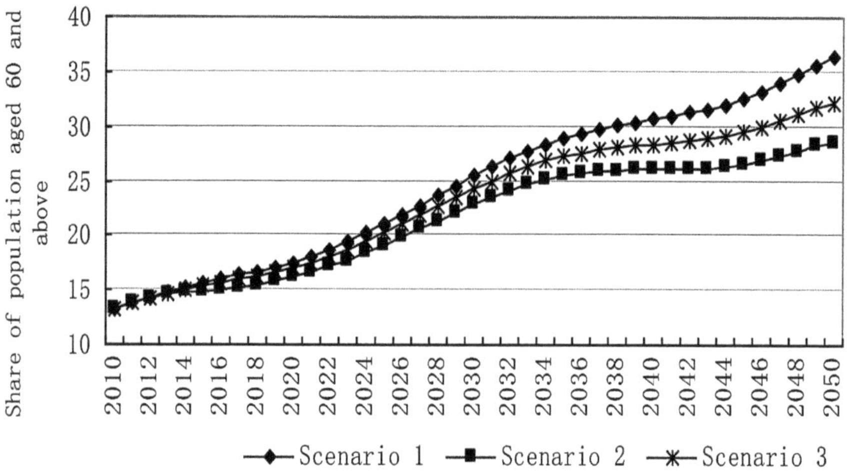

Figure 8.1 Scenarios of aging under different policies.
Source: CDRF, 2012.

group, and a high-income group. By this criterion, China now is in the upper-middle income group—that is, among developing countries. In 2010, the proportion of population aged 65 and older was 7.7 percent in the upper middle-income countries and 9.4 percent in China. That China has a higher proportion of older population implies its uniqueness in demographic transition, which we phrase as "growing old before getting rich".

The fast aging raises challenges for the old age support system in China. As a measure to tackle the challenges as well as part of reform, institution-building related to elderly support has rapidly progressed since the 1990s. Based on geographic locations, populations, and contents of security, there are six basic programs that lay the foundation of elderly support: (1) Urban Employee Basic Pension Insurance, (2) Urban Employee Basic Medical Care Insurance, (3) Urban Resident Basic Pension Insurance, (4) Urban Resident Medical Care Insurance, (5) New Rural Pension Insurance System, or NRP, and (6) New Rural Cooperative Medical Care System, or NCMS.

As a result of the establishment of those six social security programs, China has basically completed institutional transition from (urban) unit-based and (rural) family-based old age support to social security of old age support. Nowadays, those programs institutionally cover the entire population in rural and urban China. However, due to institutional and historical legacies, the unique property of China's demographic transition—namely, growing old before getting rich—and flaws of institutional design, the social security of old age support is still facing various problems and challenges. This sketch briefly depicts the formation, basic elements of programs, and operational situations, reveals fiscal and institutional challenges to the sustainability of those programs, with special focus on NRP and NCMS, summarizes related debates and policy trends, and concludes with some policy suggestions.

8.2 Current situation of pension and medical care system in urban China

China's current social security system was initiated at the end of the 1990s, with 1997 as the turning point in general. Before 1997, urban employee pension insurance and medical care insurance were mainly shouldered by enterprises and non-working urban residents had no insurance. Rural residents mainly relied on their families for support if they were old and had no medical care insurance. When state-owned enterprises met difficulties in business operation with the downturn of China's macro economy and the Asian financial crisis, a lot of urban workers were laid off or unemployed. As a part of active employment policy, urban employee pension and medical care insurance has been initiated.

In 1997, the State Council proposed to establish the Urban Employee Basic Pension Insurance system, adopting a combination of social pooling and individual accounts. The individual account is based on an 11 percent wage contribution, of which the part paid by individuals increased gradually from 4 percent to 8 percent and the rest is paid by employers. From 1990 to 2012, the number of workers participating in Urban Employee Basic Pension Insurance increased from 61.66 million to 304 million. The number of employed workers increased from 52.01 million to 230 million, which increased more than 4 times and the number of the retired increased from 9.65 million to 74.46 million, which increased more than 7 times. The number of workers participating in Urban Employee Basic Pension Insurance reached 322 million in 2013.

However, because the money in social pooling and individual accounts is managed and used collectively, individual accounts are actually empty. In 2001, the reform of the Urban Employee Basic Pension Insurance system paid attention to solving the transition cost, forming a multi-pillar system. The focus of the reform was to reduce the size of the individual account and to fully fund it. The scheme of the trial reduced the size of the individual account from 11 percent to 8 percent of wage contribution and the part paid by individuals increased from 5 percent to 8 percent. That is, the individual account was totally paid by individuals. The part paid by employers remained at 20 percent and fully funded social pooling. The trial was started in Liaoning province and expanded to Jilin and Heilongjiang province and then to some other provinces.

During almost the same period, the State Council stipulated that all urban employers, including enterprises, government departments, public institutions, social organizations, and private non-enterprise units and their employees, are required to participate in the Urban Employee Basic

Medical Care Insurance system. The basic medical care premium is borne by employers and employees. The contribution rate of employers should be controlled at about 6 percent of workers' total wages and the contribution rate of employees is usually about 2 percent of their own wages. The basic medical care premium paid by employees fully funds the individual account. The basic medical care premium paid by employers is divided into two parts: one part goes to social pooling funding and the other part goes to the individual account. Usually 30 percent of the premium paid by employers goes to the individual account.

The number of workers participating in Urban Employee Basic Medical Care Insurance has been increasing gradually since the expansion in 1999. From 1999 to 2012, it increased from 20.65 million to 265 million. The number of employed workers increased from 15.9 million to 199 million, which increased by 12 times and the number of the retired increased from 5.56 million to 66.24 million, which increased by 11 times. The number of workers participating in Urban Employee Basic Medical Care Insurance reached 299 million in 2013.

With the improvement of the urban insurance system based on employment units, a large group consisting of non-working people and people with informal employment still lack insurance. This group mainly includes the following: (1) young people who have not entered the labor market and retired people who are not covered by insurance; (2) people with informal employment, who reached 100 million in 2012 and occupied one quarter of urban employment; (3) migrant workers engaged in informal employment, who reached 166 million in 2013 and occupied 35 percent of urban employment. Under this circumstance, the emphasis of the urban social security system establishment turned to programs which secure urban residents.

The Urban Resident Basic Pension Insurance system covers people with urban *hukou* status who are not working. This system has only been established for a few years, but it is improving rapidly. The trial of the system began in 2007. The system adopted a combination of social pooling and individual accounts in 2011 and then was implemented all over the country. Urban Resident Basic Pension Insurance covered almost every resident in urban areas by 2012. The system raises funds from two channels, individual contribution and government subsidy. The urban residents participating in the system should pay a pension insurance premium according to the regulations. The contribution has ten levels, which are 100 yuan, 200 yuan, 300 yuan, 400 yuan, 500 yuan, 600 yuan, 700 yuan, 800 yuan, 900 yuan, and 1,000 yuan respectively. The local governments can add more contribution levels according to their situations. The urban residents can choose how much premium they pay and will get more if they pay more. This system is basically a transplant of the New Rural Pension Insurance System.

The Urban Resident Medical Care Insurance system covers juveniles who have not participated in Urban Employee Basic Medical Care Insurance and non-working residents with urban *hukou* status. The system was piloted in 2007 and was expanded in 2008 and expanded to the whole country in 2010, gradually covering all urban non-working residents. Students in middle school and primary school, children, and other non-working urban residents who are not covered by Urban Employee Basic Medical Care Insurance can participate in Urban Resident Medical Care Insurance on a voluntary basis.

The premium of this system is mainly paid by families, and governments provide some subsidy. On the basis of this, governments also provide some additional subsidy for the premium paid by families belonging to special disadvantaged groups. The subsidy from government increased from 40 yuan per person in 2007 to 280 yuan per person in 2013. The premium of Urban Resident Medical Care Insurance is mainly used for in-patient expense and serious illness expense of out-patient service. The financial subsidy on Urban Resident Medical Care Insurance will be improved further from 2014 and the premium paid by individuals will be adjusted accordingly. The number of persons participating in Urban Resident Medical Care Insurance increased to 221 million in 2011 and further increased to 271 million in 2012.

8.3 The current situation of China's rural pension and medical care insurance

With the reform of the enterprise employment system and the development of the labor market, an urban social insurance system has been established, which covers urban residents and even some migrants. Meanwhile, due to the long-standing dual system, the rural pension and medical care system lags far behind the urban system. With the mass migration of rural laborers, the rural population age faster than the urban population. An estimation shows that the proportion of rural population aged 65 and above was 14.7 percent in 2013, which was 4.4 percentage points higher than that of the urban population. In view of this situation, governments have begun to establish a rural pension and medical care insurance system with Chinese characteristics.

The rural insurance system established first was NCMS. NCMS is an interdependent system for the health of farmers, which is organized, guided, and supported by governments and mainly covers serious illnesses. Farmers can choose to participate in NCMS on a voluntary basis. NCMS collects funds through multiple channels, which include individual contribution, collective subsidy (rural communities, namely, villages), and government subsidy. The central and local governments arrange special funds to support the system every year. The funds of NCMS are collected and managed at county level. The focus of NCMS is to relieve farmers from poverty caused by serious illness. NCMS was launched in 2003 and government subsidies have been improving rapidly with the increase of contribution level. In 2014, the subsidy per capita from various levels of government finance reached 320 yuan and the individual contribution per capita reached 90 yuan.

The fund per capita of NCMS increased from 50 yuan in 2004 to 309 yuan in 2012 and the number of beneficiaries increased from 76 million in 2004

Table 8.1 The situation of the NCMS fund

Year	*2004*	*2005*	*2006*	*2007*	*2008*	*2009*	*2010*	*2011*	*2012*
Fund per capita (yuan)	50.4	42.1	52.1	58.9	96.3	113.4	156.6	246.2	308.5
Beneficiary-times (number of times)	0.76	1.22	2.72	4.53	5.85	7.59	10.87	13.15	17.45
Total fund (hundred million yuan)	40.3	75.4	213.6	428	784.6	944.3	1308.9	2047.6	2484.7
Fund expenditure (hundred million yuan)	26.4	61.8	155.8	346.6	662.3	922.9	1187.8	1710.2	2408
Usage rate of fund (%)	65.4	81.9	72.9	81	84.4	97.7	90.8	83.5	96.9

Source: *China Statistical Yearbook* (various years).

Note: Usage rate of fund equals to fund expenditure divided by total fund of the year.

to 170 million in 2012. The usage rate of the NCMS fund increased from 65.4 percent in 2004 to 84.4 percent in 2008. It reached 97.7 percent in 2009 and achieved a great leap. It fluctuated in 2010 and 2011 and again increased to 96.9 percent in 2012 (Table 8.1).

NCMS reimburses cost of out-patient, in-patient, and serious illness services. There is a threshold standard and a highest pay limitation. In-patient service expenses below the threshold standard should be paid by individuals.

The coverage rate of NCMS has been improving rapidly since the pilot in 2003. NCMS was implemented in 333 counties in 2004; the number of persons participating was 80 million and the participation rate was 75.2 percent. In 2007, the number of persons participating in NCMS was 730 million and the participation rate was 85.7 percent. The number of persons participating in NCMS reached 802 million and the participation rate reached 99 percent in 2013.

NRP has been established very rapidly. The aim of NRP is to secure the basic living of rural residents when they are old. NRP raises funds from multiple channels, which include individual contribution, collective subsidy, and government subsidy. The system adopts a combination of social pooling and individual accounts. It is implemented under the organization of governments and supported by other social security policies and measures such as family support, land security, and social assistance.

Rural residents aged 16 and above (excluding students at school) who have not participated in Urban Employee Basic Pension Insurance can choose to participate in NRP on a voluntary basis at their household registration place. The rural residents participating in NRP should pay a pension insurance premium according to the regulations. The contribution has five levels, which are 100 yuan, 200 yuan, 300 yuan, 400 yuan, and 500 yuan respectively. Local governments can add more contributions according to their situations. The rural residents participating in NRP can choose how much premium they pay and will get more if they pay more. The state appropriately adjusts contribution levels according to the growth of net income per capita of rural residents.

Local governments should provide a subsidy for participants to pay their premium and the subsidy is no less than 30 yuan per person per year. The local governments pay part or all the pension premium of the lowest level for persons who have difficulties in paying, such as severely disabled persons. The state establishes individual accounts for participants through their whole life. All individual contribution, collective subsidy, subsidy from other economic organizations, social organizations, and individuals, and subsidy from local government have been recorded in an individual account. The NRP fund is put in the special fiscal account of the social security fund and its revenue and expenditure are administered separately.

The pension consists of a basic pension and a pension from an individual account. The basic pension determined by the central government is 55 yuan per person per month. The governments pay the full basic pension for participants who are eligible for drawing a pension. The central government provides full subsidy for the basic pension in the central and western regions and provides 50 percent of the subsidy in eastern regions. The local government can improve the basic pension if conditions allow, and the basic pension can be improved for rural residents who pay a premium for a long time. All these are paid by local government. The monthly pension from an individual account is equal to individual account stores divided by 139.

A unified information management system for NRP all over the country has been established, which is part of the information management system of social security. It can share information with other information management systems. Every participant in NRP can get a card, which can be used for paying premiums, drawing pension, and checking their own information.

For people aged 60 and above when NRP was introduced, they can draw a monthly basic pension without paying premium if they have not participated in Urban Employee Basic Pension Insurance, but their children should participate in NRP and pay a premium. For people who are younger than pensionable age by less than 15 years, they should pay a premium annually and are allowed to pay additional premium, and total years of paying premium cannot exceed 15 years. For people who are younger than pensionable age by more than 15 years, they should pay a premium annually and total years of paying premium cannot be less than 15 years.

The pilot of NRP was started in 2009 and expanded in 2010. All residents in rural areas were fully covered by the institution by 2012. The State Council issued a document in 2014 and determined to integrate NRP and Urban Resident Basic Pension Insurance and to establish the unified urban and rural resident basic pension insurance system all over the country. The number of persons participating in NRP or Urban Resident Basic Pension Insurance reached 498 million and the number of persons drawing the two pensions reached 138 million by 2013.

8.4 Challenges to sustainability of basic old age support system in rural and urban China

Although population aging is a universal problems for all nations, social security of old age support in China faces peculiar challenges for three reasons. First, while the population aging in China is the fastest in the world, the establishment of its social security system started relatively late, giving rise to insufficiency of financial resources and incapability of institutional operation. Second, the rapid aging in China has also been accompanied by transition of economic system. As a part of transformation from planning economy to market economy, the reform of the old age support system has unique difficulties, which are especially embodied in legacy costs—namely, large amount of implicit debts of the social security funds. Third, long-lasting institutional segregation and a resulting huge income gap between rural and urban areas, along with incomplete urbanization, prevent integration of old age support programs.

In what follows we summarize fiscal and institutional challenges for the old age support system in rural and urban China.

8.4.1 Employee pension program characterized by pay-as-you-go is not sustainable

China's basic pension system is of a primarily pay-as-you-go type—that is, the pooled pension funds collected from incumbents are immediately paid to the retirees without an accumulation. Theoretically, China presently implements a two-pillar pension system for urban employees, which is supposed to allow coexistence of the social pooling program characterized by pay-as-you-go and a partially funded system with an individual account separated from the social pooling account. Because of the lack of funds, however, the two accounts have been for long mixed—participants' contributions to the individual accounts are not accumulated but used as expenditure of the social pooling account. As a result, the accumulation in the individual account was virtually zero until 2001 when a pilot reform aiming to inject money to the individual account was initiated in Liaoning, a northeast province.

As the result of the pilot reform, first in Liaoning province and then in several follow-up provinces, there has been an increase in accumulation of the

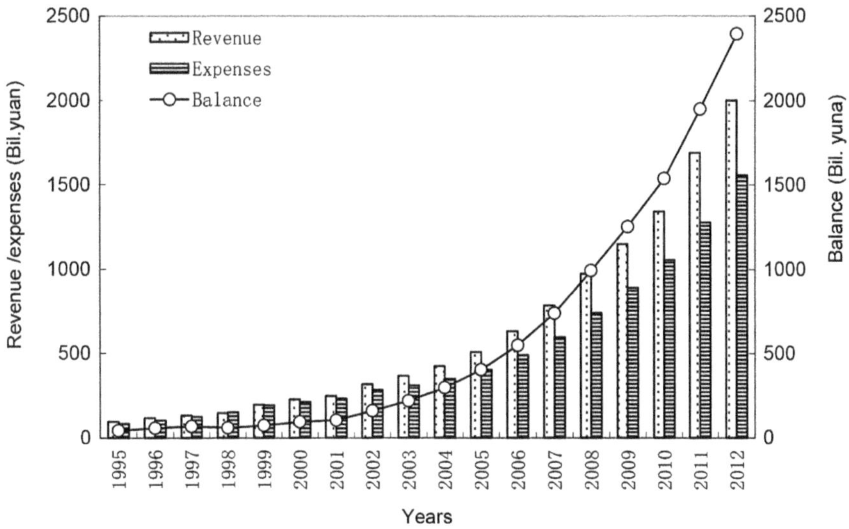

Figure 8.2 Revenue, expenses, and balance of pension funds.
Source: *China Statistical Yearbook* (2013).

overall pension fund or the difference between revenue and expenditure since 2001 (Figure 8.2). Due to the low contribution rate and limited number of provinces that implement the reform, the general accumulation in the pension funds in terms of both absolute quantity and ratio to the amount of overall expenditure is too small to declare a partially funded system.

Looking into the accumulation in individual accounts, for example, researchers find that in 2011, there were only 270.3 billion yuan accumulated in the account (Zheng, 2012). It seems that the balance shown in Figure 8.2 amounts to 1,949.7 billion yuan, a much bigger surplus than has been accumulated in the individual account; one of the reasons that the surplus could not be transferred into the empty individual accounts is because the social pension system is not yet a nationwide pooling program and the accumulated balance is highly concentrated in a few provinces.

In 2012, for example, 7 provinces hold 55.9 percent of the total balance—namely, the difference between revenue and expenses of the pension fund. In an extreme case, Guangdong, the developed coastal province and number one destination place for migrant workers, has a 16.2 percent share of the country's total pension balance, because it receives a huge volume of contributions from migrant workers without having to expend on them since they are mostly young and highly mobile among regions.

With its pay-as-you-go nature, not only is China's pension system incapable of inducing a new motive of saving and source of capital formation, but it is also bound to give rise to a crisis of old age support in the future.

8.4.2 Low coverage of urban employee social security programs

Despite old-age-support-related social security programs having virtually formed a basic safety net, the coverage rate is still low. Significant proportions of both current employees and the elderly who have quit the labor force are excluded from the coverage of those basic programs. Even the urban employee pension insurance, the relatively mature and long-implemented program, covered only 62 percent of resident workers with local *hukou* and 13 percent of migrant workers without local *hukou*, respectively, in 2012. In the same year, urban employee medical insurance covered only 54 percent of local workers and 16 percent of migrant workers. That is, of the total migrant workers who work and reside in cities, 144 million and 139 million are excluded from urban pension insurance and urban medical insurance, respectively.

The reasons causing low coverage of migrant workers are twofold. First is the informality of their employment. Although the Employment Contract Law requires employers to pay contributions to pension and medical insurance funds, highly mobile and unsecure employment characterizing migrant workers makes no incentives for either migrant workers or their employers to participate in those programs. Second is the lack of portability and continuation for those programs when workers move among cities. In most cases, when migrant workers leave a city, they have no choice but to withdraw their individual contribution. In this case, neither migrant workers nor enterprises can get back the part of the contribution made by employers to the social pooling fund. As a result, in destination places of migration such as Guangdong province, authorities have collected a large amount of revenue but spent very little, thus have accumulated a pension fund surplus, while in migrant-sending provinces, pension funds run behind their expenses. This tends to accumulate risks for old age support in the long run.

8.4.3 Problems of institutional design and implementation for NRP

First is the problem of coverage. When it was first introduced in a pilot implementation in 2009, the government scheduled a completion of the NRP by 2020. As its effect became significant, in response to various advocates, the State Council decided to bring forward the timeline of NRP's full implementation to within the Twelfth Five-year Plan period. It turned out that in 2013, when its term was about to end, the central government announced all residents in rural and urban areas were fully covered by the institution. It is worth noticing, however, that such a full coverage by the institution only means having the program introduced in all counties, but not necessarily that it covers every single resident in rural and urban China.

Given that the design for the urban resident pension program is exactly the same as for NRP and that the central government started to link up the two programs, in 2013 the official statistical authority only published the number of total participants in rural and urban programs (498 million), but not that of each of the individual programs. Adding up all participants in the urban employee pension program and rural and urban resident pension programs, we conclude they overall cover 820 million residents in rural and urban areas, accounting for 61 percent of total China's population.

Second is the problem relating to levels of contribution and benefit and of incentives. In implementing the NRP, two groups of people are typical for observing the problem. For those who are at older ages, poor, or disabled in poor rural areas, they are willing but incapable of paying the premium. Younger, active laborers, on the other hand, are capable but not willing to participate in the program, because the government subsidy doesn't provide sufficient incentives for their participation. The required minimum 30 yuan subsidy by local government is far from attractive in the more developed regions. With such a weak incentive, young people tend to withdraw from or stop their participation.

Currently, NRP has five grades of contribution, namely, 100, 200, 300, 400, and 500 yuan, respectively corresponding to five levels of benefit. As the level of governments subsidy is not significantly different among different insured grades, participants are motivated to choose the lowest grade in most cases. For example, according to the survey by the World Bank in pilot counties of Chengdu, a megacity in southwest China, in 2010, 46 percent of participants chose the lowest grade (100 yuan), and only 8 percent chose the highest grade (500 yuan). Another survey in pilot counties of Anhui, a central province, shows that more than two-thirds of participants chose the lowest grade. In some areas, all participants chose the lowest grade.

Currently, the minimum level of the basic NRP pension is 55 yuan per month or 660 yuan per year. In 2013, per capita income of Chinese rural households was 8,896 yuan. That is, the substitution rate of the basic NRP pension is only 7.4 percent. For the time being, because a large fraction of recipients are non-contributory beneficiaries whose ages were 60 or older when the program was introduced, most of them only receive the minimum basic pension of 55 yuan. For example, some surveys show that 55 percent of pension beneficiaries receive such a level, while less than 15 percent receive a pension of more than 100 yuan. As most contributors choose the lowest grade, such a low level of payment will remain unchanged in the near future.

Third is the problems related to fiscal burden and sustainability. By design, the funding of NRP consists of (1) individual contribution, (2) collective subsidy, and (3) government subsidy. However, in most rural areas, especially in the central and western regions, collective economies at village and township levels have been defunct and thus unable to provide any supplement to the fund. In addition, since there has not been concrete guidance or measures for collectives to subsidize the fund, even the able villages choose not to do so. Therefore, governments will long shoulder an overwhelming burden of NRP fundraising. For the basic pension, governments will be the sole provider. As the population ages, the balance of NRP's fund will be broken in years to come, if the institution cannot tackle this challenge in time.

Assuming a case of full coverage of NRP with the lowest benefit (55 yuan per month) and lowest subsidy (30 yuan per year), total fiscal expense was 8 billion yuan in 2009 and is predicted to exceed 100 billion yuan in 2020. Of the total fiscal expense, the amount borne by the central government will increase from 5.6 billion yuan in 2009 to 75 billion in 2020, while the amount borne by local governments will increase from 2.5 billion yuan to 27 billion yuan. In fact, the fiscal expense grows much faster than that. Based on that speed, in 2020, the accumulated fiscal expense will reach 900 billion yuan, of which the central government contributes 72 percent.

The fiscal burden of NRP is bearable in the short run and in the country as a whole. However, fiscal burdens differ from region to region given the substantial differentials in development level, fiscal situation, and population age structure. In addition, as level of payment increases in accordance with changes in per capita income and costs of living, actual fiscal expense will become heavier and heavier over time.

Currently, the NRP fund is based on a low level of pooling—namely, the funds are mostly collected and managed at county level. For that reason, its operation is characterized by difficult monitoring, high management costs and risks, and low efficiency of funds' value maintenance and appreciation.

8.4.4 Main difficulties and problems of NCMS implementation

First is the problem of fundraising. Because of the lack of a sustainable mechanism of fundraising and a low level of fund-pooling, the fund is and will be insufficient. Currently, participants contribute only small fraction of the NCMS fund—the average contribution per person was only 90 yuan in 2014, and governments at various levels take the major fiscal burden. Therefore, regional disparities in development levels result in huge difference in funds available for each person among regions. For example, in 2011, funding level per person in the central and western provinces was only one-third to one-fourth of Shanghai and Beijing (Ren and Wang, 2013). The low level of NCMS fund-pooling—namely, at county level—makes the program's implementation fragmented and weakens the ability to share risks.

Second is the problem of monopoly and moral hazard. As NCMS policies provide that only medical services at designated hospitals can be reimbursed, the designated hospitals tend to provide over-treatment and charge higher fees, which does harm to participants. Under the institutional design based on voluntary participation, there is incentive for groups of people with high risk but not for young people. The feature of serious illness reimbursement brings about a situation in which patients are willing to take over-treatment.

Third is the problem of reimbursement standards. Nationwide policies only provide general regulations but no concrete procedures. The locally formulated reimbursement policies (the floor, ceiling, and proportion of reimbursement) based on rule-of-thumb instead of actuarial standards provide very different and arbitrary standards. For example, the ratio of costs borne by participants to local levels of farmers' per capita income exceeds 0.4 in Shanxi and Shaanxi and is under 0.2 in Hunan (Ren and Wang, 2013). In addition, because there is no significant difference in reimbursement proportions among hospital levels, participants prefer to choose higher levels of hospital, leaving unused medical care resources in the countryside.

Fourth is the problem of connection between programs. In China's statistics, migrant workers are defined as those who have left their township for six months or longer. In most cases, they migrate beyond county boundaries, therefore they have to go through very complicated procedures to get reimbursed if they receive medical treatment in counties other than their own, even under the NCMS framework, which weakens incentive for more mobile groups of rural people to participate in the program. A further challenge is for migrant workers to transfer NCMS into related programs such as Urban Employee Basic Medical Care Insurance, migrant workers' medical care insurance, and the rural minimum living standard guarantee, and the other way around.

8.5 Policy debates, policy suggestions, and policy trends to improve institutions

Given the existing problems and challenges with which the social security programs related to old age support in rural and urban China are faced, policy debates on how to perfect those programs have been intense and contentious. Focusing on problems of fiscal sustainability, coverage expansion, payment level, and incentive for participation, researchers and institutions have offered various proposals on institution design and improvement. Meanwhile, the task of perfecting the social security system is blueprinted in the reform agenda of the Chinese leadership. For example, the Third Plenum points out the direction and principle for the reforms in this area.

8.5.1 Addressing the sustainability of the pay-as-you-go system

The pay-as-you-go system is usually established and operated based on the availability of a large-scale working age-population, or to put it simply, on a low dependence ratio. If such conditions no longer exist, at least one of the following adjustments must be made. That is, if a society cannot increase labor productivity at the same pace as dependence ratio change as a positive response to the situation, it has no choice but to increase contribution rate, reduce payment level, or raise retirement age as passive responses. For a country like China characterized by growing old before getting rich, however, all those are painful adjustments and hard tasks.

For one thing, China is not yet ready to postpone retirement age.[2] The overall endowments of human capital in China are remarkably heterogeneous among age groups of population. The feasibility of postponing retirement age with the aim of increasing labor force participation relies on a situation where an older worker's educational attainment is not a significant disadvantage compared to that of a younger worker, so factoring in additional work experience, the older worker has competitiveness in the labor market. While this is more or less the reality for most of the developed countries, it is not for China. For example, in the US's working-age population, the average years of schooling for the 20-year-old population is 12.6 years, that for the 60-year-old population is 13.7 years. Quite differently, at present, in China's working-age population, the older the people, the lower their educational level. For example, the average years of schooling drop from close to 10 at 24 years old to 6 at 60 years old (Wang and Niu, 2010).

At present, those Chinese workers approaching retirement are a transitional generation, shouldering the legacy from the planned period. That is, their human capital endowments allow them to be in a disadvantageous competitive position in the labor market. Once the retirement age is extended, workers in the older group will be more likely to be unemployed or to quit the labor force, as is expected from the "discouraged worker effect". In addition, being unable to receive a pension benefit before reaching the postponed legal retirement age and living a shorter life as a low-income group, they will benefit significantly less over their entire life span than they would under the current policy.

In an aging society, whether savings can be motivated and transformed as capital accumulation depends on a series of institutional settings, particularly on the properties of the old age support system (Lee and Mason, 2006). Given the reality of China, an appropriate social old age support system should be built on a multilayered and multi-pillar foundation that can simultaneously expand coverage and motivate saving. Such a system should include at least two components. First is to establish a social pension program that universally covers every senior citizen with basic financial support. Second is to transform the current pay-as-you-go system into a partially funded system in order to provide incentive for saving and develop financial sustainability of pension funds.[3]

Based on a policy option simulation, Cai and Meng (2004) suggest that if the social old age support system can be completely transformed from the currently implemented pay-as-you-go type into a fully funded type—namely, fully filled individual accounts—a much greater proportion of the retirees will not rely on social pooling pension provision in the future and the social financial burden of supporting the elderly will substantially be reduced.

A report by the World Bank and the Development Research Center of the State Council recommends a Notional Defined Contribution system (World Bank and DRC, 2013, p. 60). According to this proposal, institutional design includes the following elements. First, a non-contributory part will serve as a social pension to provide the elderly with minimum support so as to prevent them from falling into poverty. This is based on the practice of the currently implemented Urban Resident Basic Pension Insurance and New Rural

Pension Insurance System. Second, individual contribution is divided into two parts, one being compulsory Notional Defined Contribution for wage workers and another being a savings plan for those without wage income. Third, rural and urban residents voluntarily participate in annuity programs as a complementary pension.

The Third Plenum lays out the blueprint for a basic old age support system to build a fairer and more sustainable social security system. It reaffirms the combining of social pooling and individual accounts, calling for perfecting the individual account, building a closer linkage between contribution and benefit, protecting participants' rights, and accomplishing nationwide social pooling.

8.5.2 Perfecting NRP based on the principle of rural–urban integration

In establishing the social security system, various programs have been formed to target specific groups of population, and are separated from one another. Such fragmentation makes the system congenitally deficient in coordination and connection between programs. Presently, NRP has to address problems of institutional links with urban employee and resident pension programs, the migrant workers' pension program, the land-lost farmers' pension program, Old Rural Resident Pension Insurance, old age support policies for rural single-child families and for village heads, assistance policies targeting the elderly without children and direct relatives, and the minimum living standard guarantee program. For the time being, only the institutional link between NRP and urban resident pension program has been mapped out by the government.

The urgent task is to make unobstructed rural and urban old age support programs. As China urbanizes, with mass rural-to-urban migration taking place, more and more migrant workers will not only work in cities but also hold urban *hukou* status in years to come. There is increasing need for back-and-forth transfers between rural resident-based programs and urban employee-based programs.

With regard to improvement of institutional design and fiscal sustainability, China researchers propose some relevant policy suggestions. We summarize them as follows.

First, a reasonable increase in the payment level of basic pensions. Some suggest that the standard level of basic pension payment should be set as 20 percent of per capita income of local rural households, with a bias toward the vulnerable. Others suggest that apart from basic pensions, central government should also share a part of subsidies on individual accounts, depending on the development level of a region. For example, central government could cover all subsidies in poor counties as designated by the state. As institutionally full coverage is accomplished, the fund-pooling should be lifted from county level to municipality level and provincial level, so that unified institutions and standardized contribution collection and management can be realized.

Second, gradually improve the contribution mode for individual accounts. One option is proportional contribution based on per capita income of rural households. By setting a more flexible grading, contribution level can be automatically increased along with the increase of per capita income of rural households. To motivate participation, contribution level and subsidies can vary across households based on their ages and pecuniary conditions.

A differentiated contributing mechanism could be set for different age groups of residents. Meanwhile, incentive mechanisms should be designed and appropriate rewards should be provided for participants who choose higher levels of contribution and exceed the minimum years of contribution. More subsidies should be provided for disadvantaged groups such as disabled and poor people or governments must take full responsibility to pay premiums for these groups.

Third, establish long-term adjustment mechanisms for payment level. Payment level and social and economic development level should be matched. Economic development level, urban and rural resident income, wage level, prices, and financial capacity should be taken into consideration when pension level is determined. The government should follow the principle of "equality first and efficiency second" in choosing a mode of financial subsidy and should appropriately improve subsidy levels according to the economic development situation, ensuring farmers' enthusiasm for participating and equality of financial subsidy. Besides government subsidy incentives, government should explore subsidy incentive mechanisms of collective economy and enhance rural collective organizations' willingness to subsidize through quickening its shareholding system reform.

8.5.3 Improving the actual security level of NCMS

First, establish sustainable and long-term mechanism of fundraising. Government should actively explore the responsibilities of governments and individuals in NCMS financing and design scientific estimation schemes for fundraising. At present, individual contribution is limited. Whether individual contribution should be improved or what standard should be followed need to be discussed. In view of the adverse selection problem caused by the mechanism of voluntary participation, semi-mandatory mechanisms could be piloted first in some regions. That is, farmers are mandated to participate in NCMS, but they can choose their scheme according to their willingness. Pilot regions can design multi-level schemes for farmers to choose according to the local development level and characteristics. The funding level of NCMS should be further improved and a fundraising mechanism should be established which matches local economic and social development, level of income per capita, and health service development. NCMS funds should be collected and managed at higher levels, which will improve its risk-sharing ability.

Second, design a reasonable and scientific reimbursement scheme and improve reimbursement level. With the annual increase of participation rate and funds, governments should gradually improve the reimbursement level of NCMS, actively explore efficient ways of reimbursement, and set detailed and scientific standards for reimbursement mode and reimbursement scheme. The coverage scope of NCMS should gradually be expanded. NCMS should also cover chronic diseases which need long-term therapy and minor illnesses, besides mainly covering serious illnesses. This could not only improve farmers' incentive to participate in NCMS, but also reduce their burden of medical costs.

8.5.4 Integrating rural and urban old age support systems

Recognizing that both NRP and NCMS are disconnected from other programs, most discussions focus on how to integrate various programs related to old age support. For example, the Task Force of advisors for the Twelfth Five-year Plan (Lim and Spence, 2010, Chapter 6) and the World Bank and DRC (2013) both suggest introducing NRP to urban areas to establish an urban resident pension system, and formulating a social pension program that provides a basic pension to all senior citizens in rural and urban areas. Meanwhile, such a national pension program also serves as a first step toward an integrated and interconnected old age support system.

Integrating urban and rural resident basic pension insurance systems has just begun, according to a document issued by the State Council in 2014, with the aim of accomplishing full coverage with institutional sustainability and focusing on equality and portability enhancement. People aged 16 and above (excluding students at school) who are not employees of government agencies and public institutions and who are not covered by an employee basic pension insurance system can participate in an urban and rural resident pension insurance system at their household registration place. The funds of the system consist of individual contribution, collective subsidy, and government subsidy. People who participate in the system should pay a pension premium. The contribution has 12 levels, which are 100 yuan, 200 yuan, 300 yuan, 400 yuan, 500 yuan, 600 yuan, 700 yuan, 800 yuan, 900 yuan, 1,000 yuan, 1,500 yuan, and 2,000 yuan respectively.

Though it is still not a non-contributory pension system, an urban and rural resident pension insurance system achieves urban and rural integration and can be transferred among regions. People whose ages were 60 or older when the system was introduced can draw a basic pension without paying a premium. We can say that an urban and rural resident pension insurance system is a step in line with the new concept and can be the new logical starting point of future reforms.

8.6 Conclusion

Since the late 1990s, in response to rapid aging and as part of the process of economic reform, China has established six basic social security programs to provide old age support and medical care. Presently, 820 million people are covered by basic pension systems in rural and urban areas, 570 million urbanites are covered by urban medical care insurance (Urban Employee Basic Medical Care Insurance and Urban Resident Basic Medical Care Insurance), and over 800 million rural residents are covered by NCMS. With a variety of other supplementary social assistance programs, China has laid the preliminary foundations for social support of its elderly.

There exist problems of institutional design and fiscal capacity in this system that impact its long-term sustainability. These include: (1) persistent low coverage, (2) lack of fiscal guarantee and low level of payment, (3) fragmented and segregated institutions and non-transferable programs, and (4) unsustainability of the pay-as-you-go system. The Chinese government has recognized these challenges and is trying to solve them by fixing the institutions.

There are reasons that make the direction of institution-building relating to the old age support system unclear. Since there has been no clear overall design of the social security system, facing various suggestions and options, the Chinese leadership tends to take a gradual approach—that is, instead of reconstructing the overall range of institutions and making a big breakthrough, it only adds more new programs to fill the gaps in the system. However, the incremental approach to institution-building has so far not conflicted with the correct direction of future reform.

Therefore, we suggest a sequencing and roadmap of reform based on incremental adjustment under the existing framework. As a first step, the current pension programs for rural and urban residents should be taken as a basic framework to formulate a non-contributory national pension program universally covering all citizens. People might worry about the higher financial cost of this kind of program. According to a study (Lu et al., 2014), a pension which keeps most of the low-income aged out of poverty would cost between 0.7 and 1 percent of GDP over the period to 2050, with the ratio depending on assumptions about benefit indexation and the parameters of the scheme.

The second step is to expand the pilot reform of the urban employee pension system with a focus on filling up individual accounts. The same principle and practice should also be followed by other two-pillar social security programs. The third step is to centralize the social pooling from provincial level to national level through transition from contribution-based fundraising to taxation-based fundraising. In the end, a two-pillar system will be formed based on a non-contributory social pension program and fully funded individual accounts. Unit-based annuity and other supplemental programs will not be included as a major pillar of the old age support system. Government, civil society, and the private sectors should work together to ensure a decent future for the aged.

As several complementary programs help accomplish institutional coverage of rural and urban Chinese residents, the institutional building of China's old age support system has been successful, though is not finished. As a manifestation of gradualism, a term commonly adopted to characterize the approach of Chinese reform, the evolution of China's old age support system is a process of "building alongside reform", which has been overwhelmingly driven by demand for system reform and less by population aging. Such a characteristic can more or less explain both the success and shortcomings of this institutional evolution. Experiences and lessons can be summarized as follows.

As a story of success, this evolutionary approach helps institutions related to old age support develop from nothing and duly protect vulnerable groups during economic shocks. In tackling massive lay-offs and unemployment of state-owned enterprises' workers in the late 1990s, the Chinese government prioritized social security system-building. First, mainly based on two-pillar programs—namely, social pooling and individual accounts—urban employees in the formal sector have been covered by institutions. Second, in view of the fact that those formal employment-based programs cannot fully cover migrant workers, reemployed workers, those working in the informal sector or without work, and rural residents, further institutional evolution tends to cover a wider range of groups. For example, the newly issued Employment Contract Law guarantees entitlement of migrant workers to basic social insurance programs, and the establishment of resident-based social insurance programs extends coverage to those groups of people who either work in the informal sector or have no work.

In the same time, reforms have been carried out in order to accomplish the initial objective of institutions and in response to conflicts between institutions' design and changed situations or newly emerged demand for institutions. For example, reform of the Urban Employee Basic Pension Insurance system focusing on separating individual accounts from social pooling accounts and filling up accumulation in individual accounts has been piloted first in Liaoning, a northeast province, in 2001, then extended to rest two northeast provinces, Jilin and Heilongjiang, and then spread wider to several other provinces to date.

As a lesson, on the other hand, such a mode of evolution, because of lack of a master design and overall coordination, tends to result in institutional fragmentation. As the initial design of old age support institutions excluded some (vulnerable) groups of population from formal old age support programs, some patch programs remain in order to fill up the coverage gap, while there is a lack of connection mechanisms between different programs. Such fragmentation and incoordination turn out to be inefficient in resource mobilization and utilization, leading to fundraising difficulty, problems of coverage, and unsustainability of the old age support system.

Notes

* Coauthored with Wang Meiyan.

1 The total fertility rate of a population is the average number of children that would be born to a woman over her lifetime if (1) she were to experience the exact current age-specific fertility rates through her lifetime, and (2) she were to survive from birth

through the end of her reproductive life. This is obtained by summing the single-year age-specific rates at a given time.

2 In China, the legal retirement age for males is 60 years old. The legal retirement age for female workers is 50 years old and that for female cadres is 55 years old.

3 For example, a CSIS study supports the option of building a fully funded pension system. See Jackson et al., 2009.

References

Cai, F., and Meng, X. (2004). Demographic Change, System Transition, and Sustainability of Social Pension Model, *Comparative Studies*, 10, pp. .

CDRF (China Development Research Foundation) (2012). China Development Report 2011/12: Changes of Population Situation and Adjustments of Population Policies, Beijing: China Development Press.

Jackson, R., Nakashima, K., and Howe, N. (2009). *China's Long March to Retirement Reform: The Graying of the Middle Kingdom Revisited*, Washington, DC: Center for Strategic and International Studies and Prudential Foundation.

Lee, R., and Mason, A. (2006). What Is the Demographic Dividend? *Finance and Development*, 43(3), pp.16–17.

Lim, Edwin, and Michael Spence (eds.) (2010). *Thoughts and Suggestions for China's 12th Five-Year-Plan from an International Perspective*, Beijing: CITIC.

Lu, B., He, W., and Piggott, J. (2014). Should China Introduce a Social Pension? *Journal of the Economics of Ageing*, 4, pp. 76–87.

Ren, G., and Wang, Z. (2013). Empirical Research on New Rural Cooperative Medical Scheme's Regional Disparity, *Chinese Rural Health Service Administration*, 33(2), pp.121–124.

Wang, G., and Niu, J. (2010). Composition and Development of the Chinese Education System, in Cai Fang (ed.), *The China Population and Labor Yearbook Volume 2: The Sustainability of Economic Growth from the Perspective of Human Resources*, Leiden and Boston: Brill, pp. 43–61.

World Bank and DRC (Development Research Center of the State Council) (2013). *China 2030: Building a Modern, Harmonious, and Creative Society*, Beijing: China Financial and Economic Publishing House.

Zheng, B. (2012). *China Pension Report 2012*, Beijing: Economy and Management Publishing House.

Part 3

Supply-side structural reform

9 The *hukou* reform and unification of rural–urban social welfare

9.1 Introduction

The professed function of the Chinese household registration (or *hukou*) system, formed in the late 1950s, is to register population separately in rural and urban areas. Distinguishing the rural or urban birthplace determines the legitimate residence of any Chinese citizen, which is identified by the *hukou*. The alteration of *hukou* between rural and urban areas is conditional, and the criteria for such an alteration are terribly strict, constraining the rights of free migration for rural residents. *Hukou* was implemented, typically and strictly, before and during the early period of Chinese reform. While it is commonly believed that in the past thirty years, overall economic reform has been accompanied by the reform of the *hukou* system to some extent, the actual development of the *hukou* system has not been recognized fully or properly valued by academia (for example, Chan and Buckingham, 2008; Chan, 2010). In a more extreme case (Whyte, 2010), the *hukou*-related rural–urban divide has been mentioned in the same breath as the India-type caste system. Such an underrating of the progress of reform in this area originates from a narrow understanding of the *hukou* system per se. That is, if the hukou system is merely viewed as a population registration system distinguishing rural and urban residents, no significant change can be perceived.

However, when scholars advocate *hukou* reform and governments, central and local, actually conduct various reform experiments, their efforts are not confined only to eliminating the regional separation of population. To understand the essential meaning of the *hukou* system, one must explore the primary motive for its initiation, as well as its resultant characteristics (e.g., see Cai, 2010b). *Hukou* was first introduced to serve as an invisible wall to prevent the rural labor force from moving out of agriculture; thus, it is closely linked to an exclusive employment system in urban sectors. Second, it was adopted to guarantee basic living standards and minimum social welfare for urban residents, and therefore, it sought to develop an institutional arrangement in order to separate *hukou* residents' entitlements from those of migrants. In taking into account the wider functions of the *hukou* system—instead of viewing it only as population registration—it should be clear that, as the Chinese economy transitions to a market economy, *hukou* reform should not only progress simultaneously, but also should be carried out with much wider scope.

As in the other areas of Chinese economic reform, *hukou* reform has been carried out in both bottom-up and top-down ways. On the one hand, seeking higher income and improved standards of living, rural laborers have migrated beyond the resident and employment boundaries set by *hukou* during the reform period. On the other hand, as the reallocation efficiency generated by labor mobility among sectors has become apparent,[1] Chinese governments at various levels first acquiesced to rural laborers' departures from farms and villages, and have gradually altered policies over time to actually encourage farmers to leave their rural residences by actively improving the climate for workers who have moved to cities. Since *hukou* reform involves the alteration and abolition of a series of long-standing institutions, the governments' incentives and initiatives are particularly important in the process. Documenting and explaining such reforms requires exploring motives, behaviors, and the interactions of all participants—namely, rural laborers, urban residents, and central and local governments—within an analytical framework of political economy.

The Chinese economy has been undertaking double transitions: a transition from a dual economy to a more integrated economy and a transition from a planned economy to a market economy. The two transitions have imbued *hukou* reform with important characteristics and divided it into three phases. In its first phase, roughly between the early 1980s and mid-1990s, the reform was marginally carried out under the constraints of a planned economy. Spurred by the clearer market orientation of the overall reform laid out by the Chinese leadership, reform accelerated in the period between the mid-1990s and the early twenty-first century, say 2003. As the Chinese dual economy entered a new stage after 2003, a year of significance for the Chinese economy, the reform entered its more pivotal period. While in each of the phases, the reform of the *hukou* system has made some crucial progress, the latest round of reform has been much more comprehensive, aimed at completely eliminating the *hukou* system and affiliated institutions.

This chapter explains the efforts that have been made to reform the *hukou* system—as government policies respond to changing conditions—by dividing reforms into three phases. Unlike existing literature that focuses more on the unfinished aspects of reform, this paper positively evaluates progress to date and suggests further tasks by revealing the logic of reform, which is closely related to the changing economic stages. This chapter views *hukou* not only as a population residence regulation, but also as a method for examining changes in the intention and implementation of social welfare programs.

The next part of this chapter depicts *hukou* reform in the context of the transition from a planned economy to a market economy, which happened in the course of a typical dual economy development. The following section discusses the arrival of the Lewis turning point, a new stage of Chinese economic development, and its implications for migrant workers' demands for new institutional settings and the enhanced motives of governments for *hukou* reform. The final section concludes by identifying some dilemmas and proposing policy suggestions for future reform.

9.2 *Hukou* reform as institutional transition

As is commonly known, Chinese economic reform was initiated in rural areas and was characterized by the introduction of the household responsibility system, which, by solving the long-standing incentives problems, undisputedly enhanced the labor productivity of the agriculture sector, freeing up a new surplus of laborers who had accumulated during the pre-reform period. As a consequence, Chinese farmers, after fulfilling basic living needs by means of their farms, began to seek off-farm work to increase their incomes. Although economic reform at the time did not aim to relinquish the planning system, *hukou* reform actually took place without a clear blueprint of overall reform: It was represented by labor mobility, from agricultural to non-agricultural sectors in rural areas, as well as from villages to nearby towns.

It is widely believed that the labor transfer had been characterized by local relocation to township and village enterprises (TVEs) before the urbanization policy was later relaxed to allow rural-to-urban migration. It is true that, before the mid-1980s, the central government intended to create a pattern of "leaving the land without leaving the countryside". The development of TVEs, however, was confined to local villages and small towns and was extremely uneven among regions—and therefore incapable of creating adequate non-agricultural employment opportunities for the surplus laborers. In 1985, only 18.8 percent of 370 million rural laborers were engaged in TVEs. According to a scholarly estimation, at the time there were 100–150 million surplus laborers in rural areas, or 30–40 percent of the total rural workforce (Taylor, 1993). To tackle such a development challenge, farmers sought to break down institutional obstacles and migrated across regional boundaries, while the governments, both central and local, responded to the desires and actions of rural laborers by relaxing institutional constraints for labor mobility.

As reforms in urban areas were initiated in the mid-1980s, and the development of the TVEs stagnated, rural laborers began to migrate across regions, particularly from rural to urban areas in search of non-agricultural jobs. The gradual abolition of institutional obstacles has been key for increased labor mobility since the 1980s. After observing the rural sectors' narrowing capacity for absorbing surplus labor, in 1983 the government began allowing farmers to engage in long-distance transport and marketing of their products beyond local marketplaces—the first time that Chinese farmers had received legitimate rights for doing business outside their hometowns. In 1984, regulations were further relaxed and farmers were encouraged by the state to work in nearby small towns. A major policy reform took place in 1988, when the central government allowed farmers to work in enterprises or run their own businesses in cities, under the condition that they continued to be self-sufficient in terms of staples, in the light of the still-existing rationing scheme. In the 1990s, the central and local governments relaxed policies restricting migration, which also implied a certain degree of reform in the household registration system as well.

In that period, however, the planning system had not yet been abandoned and the *hukou* system was taken for granted in the institutional setting. That is, any policy adjustment or any action conducted spontaneously by laborers and acquiesced to by the governments was still circumscribed by the strict *hukou* control. In other words, all adjustments and actions outside of the institutional frame were allowed and tolerated only when they fit with certain situations, such as the need for a labor force; when they did not, they were repressed. *Hukou* reform was only marginal and reversible at the time when planning was still in effect.

The official establishment of a market economy as the goal of Chinese reform in the 1990s made the decade a turning point in terms of *hukou* reform. Symbolized by Deng Xiaoping's famous tour of South China, with his speeches during the time, as well as the Fourteenth National Congress of the Communist Party of China in the early 1990s, China's reform and opening-up entered a new era. Because of the accelerated *hukou* reform, labor market development, and population migration, we consider the mid-1990s to be the milestone that distinguishes the first and second phases of *hukou* reform.

In this period, the fast growth of labor-intensive and export-oriented sectors, mostly in the coastal provinces, and the dramatic surge of non-public sectors in urban areas, generated a huge incremental demand for labor, spurring a migratory tide of labor that moved from rural to urban sectors and from the central and western to the eastern regions. Conforming to such trends of labor market expansion and integration, a host of reform measures were carried out to eliminate the institutional barriers that deterred labor mobility. For example, the rationing system that was initiated in the mid-1950s to limit supplies of staple foods and other life necessities in cities was abolished in the early 1990s, unlocking one of the most important shackles stopping population migration from rural to urban areas.

Another manifestation of labor market development can be seen in the reform of urban employment policies. From the mid-1990s, the government granted state-owned enterprises (SOEs) autonomous powers of hiring and firing employees, which SOE managers took advantage of to break the long-standing "iron rice bowl" (jobs with guaranteed security). During the macro-economic downturn and East Asian financial crisis, which gave rise to massive layoffs and unemployment in the urban sectors in the late 1990s, the government implemented a lay-off subsidy program and built up an unemployment insurance system, a basic pension regime, and a minimum living standard program. While those measures were initiated to protect urban workers, they created an environment for labor market development and liberalized labor market regulations to encourage labor mobility across enterprises, sectors, ownerships, and regions.

In response to the matured economic conditions for labor mobility, in 1998, the Ministry of Public Security gave a green light for the entry of people into cities, such that children could carry out household registration with either parent, couples who had long been separated could get together and obtain a change of household registration, the elderly could obtain city *hukou* along with their children, and so on. Although resistance to these reforms was encountered in some major cities, the future reform of the household registration system was provided with a legitimate basis at the central government level.

China had been typified by its dual economy development before this phase ended: The rural surplus labor force endlessly migrated to urban sectors in coastal areas, seeking non-agricultural wage employment; the wage rates of migrant workers remained unchanged and low compared to their urban counterparts, partially because of the nature of the unlimited supply of labor and partially because of the *hukou* system. Despite the expanded labor mobility and a certain progress in reform, the *hukou* system still played two roles, serving its traditional function.

First, the *hukou* system guaranteed the priority of urban laborers for employment opportunities in urban sectors. Due to the coexistence of rural labor surplus and urban workforce redundancy, there existed to a certain extent job competition between migrant workers and urban unskilled workers, causing the urban governments to protect local workers and treat migrant workers discriminately via *hukou* identification. In an empirical study, Cai, Du, and Wang (2001) found that in this period, urban governments' policies toward inflows of migrants changed cyclically as employment pressures facing local governments changed over time—that is, each time the local unemployment problems became severe, in addition to regular restrictions on migrants' employment,[2] they tended to take measures to supplant migrant workers.

Second, the *hukou* system excluded migrants from obtaining equal access to urban social welfare services. In the course of tackling the employment shock in the late 1990s, the governments built a preliminary social protection system for urban workers, including programs of basic pension insurance, basic health care insurance, unemployment insurance, and a minimum living standard guarantee scheme. Whereas those programs did not provide full coverage for all urban workers, they officially included all workers with urban *hukou* and excluded rural-to-urban migrants. In addition, migrant workers were not entitled to public employment assistance programs and thus were exposed to all kinds of employment shocks without formal social protection.

In a dual economy characterized by an unlimited supply of labor, the interests of urban residents typically conflict with those of rural residents, and the urbanites have stronger bargaining power to influence policy-making and thus gain more advantageous status (Olson, 1985). That was empirically confirmed in the case of *hukou* reform in that period (Cai, 2010c)—that is, when some efforts were made by both central and local governments, they turned out to be futile in the final analysis. Initiated in 2000, *hukou* control of all Chinese small towns was relaxed by significantly lowering the thresholds for residence, while some medium and large cities, including provincial capital cities, such as Shijiazhuang of Hebei province, tried to do the same. Owing to the lack of employment opportunities and capabilities of providing equal social welfare, such as a basic pension, health care insurance, access to education, and entrance to high school for the newcomers, the reform failed to attract many to apply for local *hukou* status. In other cases, where cities abolished the distinction between agricultural and non-agricultural *hukou* identity, due to the remaining unequal social welfare among people living in rural and urban areas, the reform amounted to no more than lip service (Wang and Cai, 2010b).

9.3 The Lewis turning point and reform incentives

While the mass labor migration from rural to urban sectors has naturally reduced the degree of labor surplus in agriculture (Cai and Wang, 2008), and the demographic transition in China has reached the stage at which the growth rate of the working-age population is declining (Cai, 2010a), the fast economic growth has continued to generate huge labor demand, leading to demand for labor exceeding supply. Since 2003, the difficulty hiring migrant workers, and the labor shortage more generally, have become widespread and wages of migrant workers have significantly increased year by year. In addition, the wage rates of hired workers in agricultural sectors have also improved (Table 9.1), indicating the shrinkage of surplus labor in agriculture, the shortage of unskilled workers in urban areas, and ensuing wage increases in all sectors (Wang, 2010).

According to the definition set forth by Lewis (1954), these phenomena indicate that the Chinese economy has arrived at its Lewis turning point—a period of time in which the wages of ordinary workers increase because labor demand exceeds that of labor supply (Cai and Wang, 2010). At the

Table 9.1 Annual growth rates of selected wages, 2003–2008 (%)

	Daily wages		*Monthly wages*
Grain production	15.1	Manufacturing	10.5
Cotton production	11.7	construction	9.8
Large pig farms	21.4	Migrant workers	10.2

Sources: Wages of hired grains workers are calculated according to data from *Compilation of National Farm Product Cost-Benefit Data* (various years). Wages of manufacturing and construction workers are calculated according to data from *China Labor Statistical Yearbook* (various years). Wages of migrant workers are calculated according to data from *China's Rural Household Survey Yearbook* (various years).

same time, the *hukou* reform starts its new phase and is expected to make a more fundamental breakthrough. Because 2003 witnessed so many dramatic changes in the Chinese economy and society—for example, the first labor shortage in China's economic development, the subsequent increase in ordinary workers' wages, the rise of labor cost and fall of labor input in agriculture, and governments' efforts to improve conditions of migrants living and working in cities in response to those changes (Wang, 2010)—we take it as a symbolic year indicating the Lewis turning point and the outset of a new phase of *hukou* reform.

The essential manifestation of a Lewis turning point is the alteration of the labor market from an unlimited supply of labor to the frequent emergence of labor shortages. That is, the invariable wage rate can no longer maintain the endless supply of labor, on the one hand, and the wage rate increase alone cannot adequately satisfy the workers, who also expect policy reforms in accordance with the change of development stage. In terms of challenges facing China, this phase of reform can be characterized as follows. First, as the market orientation becomes a clear blueprint of China's overall reform, the goal set for *hukou* reform is to unify the rural and urban labor markets. Second, as the unlimited supply of labor is no longer characteristic of the Chinese economy, and structural factors rather than magnitude factors dominate the labor market, the direct conflict in employment between migrant and local workers has been eased. Third, as the social welfare provisions, mainly the social security programs, become pooled based on public finance and individual contribution, there is more compatibility than competition between newcomers and native residents in urban areas. The changes in the reform climate indicate that the governments' intentions and behaviors regarding *hukou* reform are now essentially different from those in the previous phase of reform.

Chinese governments have been conceptualized as a developmental state, in general (Walder, 1995; Oi, 1999), and local governments as competitive governments, in particular (Herrmann-Pillath and Feng, 2004). That is, governments have strong motivation to spur economic growth by various policy measures, including legislation, public policy-making, improving the climate of investment and development, helping local businesses to seek financial resources from domestic and foreign investors and subsidies from higher levels of government, intervention in enterprise management, and sometimes running businesses themselves. As they recognize that the Lewis turning point has been reached and labor becomes a constraint on economic growth, the governments begin to reorient public policy from focusing on employment opportunities to focusing on job decency, and from protecting locals to including migrants, which leads to institutional changes.

More generally, the developmental state with Chinese characteristics has been undergoing a transformation following its own logic of development stages. That is, the Chinese local governments indeed become more and more motivated by Tiebout-type incentives (Tiebout, 1956) to try to attract human resources by enriching the contents and adjusting the direction of public services. In those areas where the booming economy continues to raise demand for labor force, a silent reform has been undertaken in the building of labor market institutions and social protection mechanisms—incentives compatible with the central government's objective of building a harmonious society (Cai, 2010d).

Such a new policy climate has catalyzed the building of labor market institutions in which migrant workers are now formally included. Symbolized by the satisfactory resolution of the legislative problem behind the Sun Zhigang incident in 2003[3] and President Hu Jintao's intervention in wages arrears for migrant workers in 2004, labor-related institutions have since evolved in two directions—regulations aiming to protect all workers and deregulations aiming to liberalize labor mobility (Cai, 2010b). In tackling the problems of migrant workers' insecure employment, poor conditions of working, low coverage by social insurance, and lack of protection, governments have made various efforts related to *hukou* system reform.

First, the Employment Contract Law came into effect in 2008. This legislation, which attracted worldwide notice, requires enterprises to sign labor contracts with all employees, regardless of their *hukou* status, and to include them in basic social insurance programs. The Labor Disputes Mediation and Arbitration Law issued the same year encourages migrant workers to initiate labor disputes by cutting litigation costs to almost zero.

Second, local governments have increased the frequency and scale of minimum wage adjustments. During the early years of the implementation of this program in the 1990s, the minimum wage standard was low, rarely increased, and hardly applied to migrant workers. As the labor shortage became widespread after 2003,1 the central government required local governments to adjust the level of minimum wages every other year and to apply the program to migrant workers. Pressured by labor shortage, municipal authorities have since increased the adjustment frequency and local level of the minimum wage.

Third, one of the efforts made by the central government to enhance migrant workers' coverage in basic social insurance programs is the promulgation of Interim Measures on the Transfer of Continuation of Basic Pension for Urban Enterprises Employees in 2010, which stipulates that all workers participating in basic pension programs while migrating across provincial boundaries will be guaranteed a transfer and continuation of both individual and pooling pension accounts in their new places of work. This new regulation provides institutionally guaranteed portability for migrant workers' pension entitlements.

9.4 New wave of *hukou* reform

In a paper about *hukou* reform, Cai (2010d) identifies a dilemma—that is, the more social welfare benefits a *hukou* identity contains, the more difficult it is to push forward the reform; but without *hukou* reform, there is no way to detach social welfare benefits from *hukou* status, which has often brought the reform into stalemate. The reorientation of government functions toward public service provision, spurred by the arrival of the Lewis turning point, along with labor market institution-building, can help break such a dilemma and boost the new round of *hukou* reform. The fundamental change in the policy climate has made the new round of reform more thorough and plausible. Here, we elaborate the practice and progress of the reforms of the *hukou* system and related institutions since 2003.

The number of migrant workers leaving their home township for six months or longer increased from 114 million in 2003 to 145 million in 2009, of which 95.6 percent migrated to cities and towns. As Chinese urban residents were statistically defined as those who live in cities for six months or longer when the Fifth National Census was conducted in 2000, the migrant workers and accompanying family members make up a large part of incremental urban residents during the period. In 2009, the urbanization rate—the share of population living in cities for six months or longer—was 46.6 percent. Those migrants, however, after moving to cities, do not obtain urban *hukou* status and therefore do not have access to social welfare equal to their counterparts with urban *hukou* status. The distinction in social treatment is based on and identified by agricultural *hukou* and non-agricultural *hukou*. In 2007, the share of population with non-agricultural *hukou*, which all native urbanites hold, was 33 percent, 12 percentage points less than the statistical urbanization rate of the year (Figure 9.1).

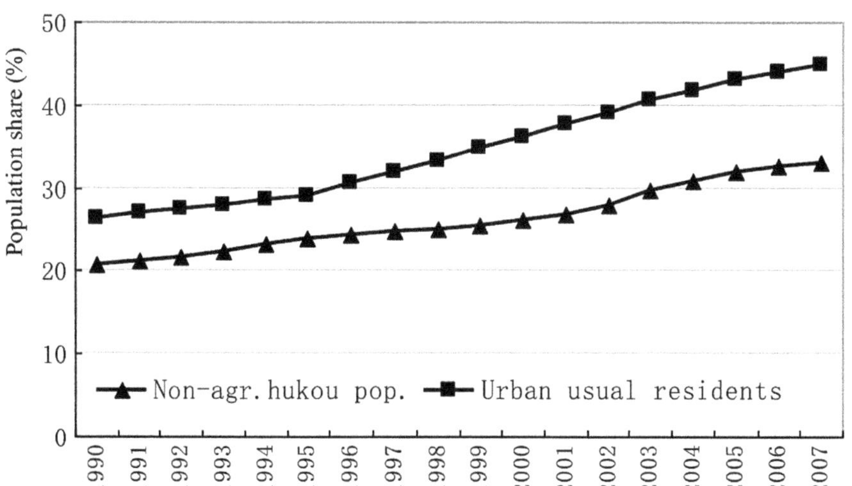

Figure 9.1 Actual urban population vs. non-agricultural *hukou* population.
Source: *China Population and Employment Statistical Yearbook* (various years).

Table 9.2 Comparison of social insurance programs between migrant and local workers (2009, %)

	Basic pension	*Basic health care*	*Unemployment insurance*	*Work injury insurance*	*Maternity insurance*
Urban workers	57.0	52.7	40.9	47.9	34.9
Migrant workers	9.8	13.1	3.7	24.1	2.0

Source: NBS (2009); Sheng (2009).

Taking account of the difference between the statistical urbanization rate and the non-agricultural rate of population, many scholars and policy researchers assert that *hukou* reform has not made noticeable progress and the urbanization level has been overestimated (for example, see Chan, 2010; Chang, 2010). Those arguments are partially correct, because whereas long-term migrant workers are counted as urban residents, they are still excluded from equitable entitlement to many public services provided by urban governments. For example, their participation rates in social insurance programs are significantly lower than those of local workers (Table 9.2); their children have difficulty enrolling in compulsory schooling, let alone entering a high school; and they are not entitled to the minimum living standard guarantee. As we noted previously, however, migrant workers and their accompanying family members now have much better access to public services than they did previously. Moreover, the *hukou* reform of formally accepting migrants as non-agricultural residents in urban areas has been accelerated.

The share of population with non-agricultural *hukou* status has increased since 2003, with faster growth than during the previous period. For example, annual growth rates of the non-agricultural population increased from 3.4 percent in 1991–2002 to 4.3 percent in 2002–2007. Given that the natural growth rate of population in both rural and urban China has declined to very low levels—that is, the natural growth of population of the country as a whole decreased from 1.3 percent in 1991 to 0.5 percent in 2007—the increase in the share of non-agricultural population is mainly attributed to mechanical growth, or the rural-to-urban migration with *hukou* change. Whereas the expansion of university enrolment may contribute to the increase, because the rural enrolled students can change their agricultural *hukou* to non-agricultural *hukou* by regulation, the share of rural origin in total enrolled students declined dramatically in recent years, meaning that the two factors cancel out each other.[4] Therefore, the majority of the new non-agricultural *hukou* population is those who have been officially accepted for migration to destination cities.

As the Chinese economy has recovered from the 2008–2009 financial crisis and then encountered unprecedented labor shortage, many provinces and cities have initiated a new round of *hukou* reform that is different from the previous ones in at least two ways. First, the motive of the new round of reform is endogenous and strong. In terms of the governments' incentives to reform *hukou*, two facts are worth attention. (1) The shortage of migrant workers, beginning in 2003 and becoming severer after the recovery from the financial crisis in 2010, has caused real difficulty for enterprises in maximizing production capacities throughout the country. In response, governments in coastal areas, where enterprises suffer the most difficulty in recruiting workers, *hukou* reform has become a policy measure to stabilize labor supply. (2) Under the strictest control over arable land use, the only way of land exploitation for the local governments who intend to boost urbanization is to reclaim plots of contracted arable land and house sites that migrated households left behind and to use the quota of those plots elsewhere in order to balance the exploitation and reclamation of land. Second, the measures of the new round of reform are more feasible. Since the century began, many areas have announced and piloted *hukou* reform. Despite its effects differing from place to place, the reforms have all been initiated locally to conform to the actual needs of the individual localities. Since the object of the reform is the institutional format of the dual societal structure, the *hukou* system, the reforms share some common features across the areas in which they have been implemented. That is, reform has been bound to equalize public service provisions and pushed by lowering the threshold-of-entry criteria for in-migrants. Neither high thresholds for migrants to obtain a local *hukou* nor segregated treatments of social welfare between newcomers and natives can make the reform successful. As local governments become more aware of the importance of *hukou* reform as an indispensable engine in pushing urbanization, they tend to substantially ease the criteria for accepting new residents.

While Guangdong, the coastal province of southern China, initiated *hukou* reform in response to labor shortage in its export-oriented sectors, the pilot reform in Chongqing, a more agrarian municipality in southwestern China, is a typical example of a city trying to obtain necessary land for urban expansion. A less-developed region, Chongqing is bottlenecked more by land than by labor in its efforts to catch up with its more developed counterparts. Since any reform needs to be boosted by incentives, and reform of *hukou* policy that relies on government initiation needs to be motivated by governments' will to it, in particular, linking *hukou* reform with land development is not only the feature but also the motive for the municipality's reform.

The *hukou* reform initiation in Chongqing is designed to properly relocate the plots of land vacated by urbanized rural families. According to the policies issued by the government, the land relocation includes three steps. First, local governments compensate for the plots of contracted arable land and house sites based on land expropriation regulations and referring to the current land voucher price.[5] Then the returned house sites are required to reclaim their original localities, their land use quota is traded within the municipality, and the quota may be used as construction land in other localities of the municipality. Next, the right to claim the land is held for the transferred households for three years in case they return for reasons of employment shock and the like. The unified utilization of the quota of land vacated by official migration from rural to urban areas is the motivation of the Chongqing municipal government in implementing the *hukou* reform.

The new round of *hukou* reform represented by the experiences in Chongqing and Guangdong in 2010 simultaneously meets the two criteria for reform—low threshold of entry and equal social welfare treatment. In Chongqing, those migrant workers who work or do business for a certain period of time, buy houses, invest, or pay taxes of a certain amount within the destination cities, are eligible to obtain local *hukou* status and to get equal access to assistance to employment, social insurance, subsidized housing, education, medical care, etc. In Guangdong, the government converts various criteria into points, such as schooling, working skills, contributions to social insurance, volunteering, and blood donation, which are accumulated to obtain urban *hukou* status. In these ways, becoming an urban citizen is no longer a random probability but the outcome of a specific procedure.

9.5 Conclusions, reflections, and policy suggestions

In the course of China's transition from planned economy to market economy, *hukou* system reform has driven labor mobility from rural to urban sectors and helped the economy reallocate resources and gain efficiency, as well as contributing to the unprecedented growth of the economy. Under the constraints of unlimited supply of labor and scarcity of resources for public services, however, discrepancies in employment opportunities and welfare provisions among urban migrant and local workers have prevented the reform from being fully accomplished, urbanization from being completed, and the floating urbanites from becoming a stable source of labor and consumption. As the Lewis turning point arrives—that is, economic growth can no longer count on cheap labor and high savings rates brought by a demographic dividend—the central and local governments, seeking a new engine for economic growth, set their sights on the potential of deepening urbanization by settling migrant workers. That creates incentives for governments to implement *hukou* reform, and the incentives are compatible between central and local governments and between migrant workers and urban native residents. As a result, *hukou* reform pushes forward in both breadth and width.

In the final analysis, different regions' governments have their own motives for carrying out *hukou* reform. They do it to attract and keep human resources in coastal areas, to tap domestic demand in central and western regions, and to break through the land bottleneck in catching-up regions. The different motives have led to dissimilar institutional designs and ways of implementing them. The diversity is not only the natural approach to such decentralized reform, it is also what the reform's advantage is based upon. Allowing diversity assures incentives, impetus, and chances of success.

Like the previous rounds of reform, the current ongoing reform has its limitations, which involve the consensus between central and local governments. That is, to initiate *hukou* reform, the local governments not only need incentives, but also legitimacy, in order to have central government's support and approval. As can be seen in the experiences of Chongqing and Guangdong, some shortcomings need to be overcome in this regard. First, the point of intersection between the central government's top concern and the local governments' legitimacy in accelerating urbanization is to retain the designated amount of arable land. Due to the extreme scarcity of arable land in China, neither industrialization nor urbanization can proceed at the expense of shifting land from agricultural to non-agricultural use. The land voucher program devised by the Chongqing government must assure that all plots of land vacated are reclaimed for cultivation in order to be approbated by the central government. The central leaders often doubt the actual reclamation of land declared by local governments, because there have been too many cases of reneging in the process of new village construction. Second, both the central government and the governments of the migrant-receiving cities are concerned about building labor market institutions and social protection mechanisms that prevent urban diseases. As the result of the advent of the Lewis turning point, migrant workers have become an indispensable source of labor for urban sectors—in other words, non-agricultural sectors' demand for migrant workers has become unvarying, or rigid, on the one hand, and agriculture has rapidly mechanized so that it no longer provides a pool of surplus labor on the other. While migrant workers as a whole cannot revert to agricultural production, individual migrant workers risk becoming urban poor. So *hukou* reform must be a comprehensive package that tackles the risks, from inclusive social protection policy in urban areas to flexible relocation policy of arable land. Third, the coordination among policy measures undertaken by local governments and a holistic vision of the entire country impact the overall effect of the reform. In the reforms of Chongqing and Guangdong, policies set for migrant workers to officially reside in cities only benefit the residents of the specific province or municipality. In 2009, of the 145 million migrant workers (and their 22 million accompanying family members), 51 percent migrated across provincial boundaries. That the inter-provincial migrants can hardly benefit from the *hukou* reform underway in many provinces implies that half of migrants, whose ancestral homes are mostly in the central and western poor areas, are still excluded from the urbanization process.

Hukou reform has so far been the initiative of local governments motivated to break through the constraints of local development. As a public policy reform, *hukou* reform requires nationwide harmonization. That is, in addition to encouraging various local reform initiatives, the central government, by generalizing the domestic and international experiences and lessons, should also put forward a general guideline regarding the contents and coverage of social security programs, ways of managing vacated plots of land, and the nexus between practical policies and the overall objectives of the reform.

Notes

1 Cai and Wang (1999) estimate that, in addition to the conventional contributions made by physical capital, labor, and education, labor mobility from low-productivity agriculture to higher-productivity non-agricultural sectors contributed 21 percent to China's GDP growth in the period 1978 to 1998. The World Bank (1997) estimated the contribution of labor mobility to GDP growth was 16 percent.

2 In the 1990s, some large cities issued policies forbidding urban enterprises from hiring migrant workers for certain jobs where they would compete with local workers (Cai, Du, and Wang, 2001).

3 A 27-year-old university graduate, Sun Zhigang, was detained by the police and beaten to death because of his lack of a local *hukou* or local temporary resident permit. This attracted widespread public criticism of the *hukou* system and led to the abolition of the State Council regulation, "Approaches to the Custody and Repatriation of Urban Vagrants and Beggars", upon which the criminal acts of the law enforcement officers were based (see Cai, 2010b).

4 Among the currently enrolled university students, the share of rural origin is 17.7 percent, a big decrease compared to that of more than 30 percent in the 1980s (Li, 2009).

5 The land voucher program, an innovative institution in Chongqing, is intended to unify land usage and development on a citywide basis. Namely, the administration issues vouchers for the increase of land area generated by reclaiming the house plots and collective construction land vacated by out-migration from villages and trades them in the government-run land exchange. Those who buy the vouchers get the quota of land use for non-agricultural development within the municipality.

References

Cai, F. (2010a). Demographic Transition, Demographic Dividend, and Lewis Turning Point in China, *Economic Research Journal*, 45(4), pp. 4–13.

Cai, F. (2010b). The Formation and Evolution of China's Migrant Labor Policy, in X. Zhang, S. Fan, and A. de Haan (eds.), *Narratives of Chinese Economic Reforms: How Does China Cross the River?* New Jersey: World Scientific Publishing.

Cai, F. (2010c). Labor Market Development and Expansion of Rural and Urban Employment, in F. Cai (ed.), *Transforming the Chinese Economy, 1978–2008*, Leiden and Boston: Brill.

Cai, F. (2010d). *Lewis Turning Point and Reorientation of Public Policy: Some Stylized Facts on Social Protection in China*, Beijing: Social Sciences Academic Press.

Cai, F., Du, Y., and Wang, M. (2001). Household Registration System and Labor Market Protection, *Economic Research Journal*, 12, pp. 41–49.

Cai, F., and Wang, D. (1999). The Sustainability of Economic Growth and the Labor Contribution, *Economic Research Journal*, 10, pp. 62–68.

Cai, F., and Wang, M. (2008). A Counterfactual Analysis on Unlimited Surplus Labor in Rural China, *China & World Economy*, 16(1), pp. 51–65.

Cai, F., and Wang, M. (2010). Growth and Structural Changes in Employment in Transition China, *Journal of Comparative Economics*, 38, pp. 71–81.

Chan, K. W. (2010). The Household Registration System and Migrant Labor in China: Notes on a Debate, *Population and Development Review*, 36(2), pp. 357–364.

Chan, K. W., and Buckingham, W. (2008). Is China Abolishing the *Hukou* System? *China Quarterly*, 195, pp. 582–606.

Chang, H. (2010). Agriculture, Countryside, and Farmers: Challenges Facing the Next Five-year Plan, *Century Weekly*, 34, pp. 40–41.

Herrmann-Pillath, C., and Feng, X. (2004). Competitive Governments, Fiscal Arrangements, and the Provision of Local Public Infrastructure in China: A Theory-Driven Study of Gujiao Municipality, *China Information*, 18(3), pp. 373–428.

Lewis, A. (1954). Economic Development with Unlimited Supplies of Labour, *Manchester School of Economic and Social Studies*, 22, 139–191.

Li, L. (2009). Why Has the Share of University Students of Rural Origins Been Halved? *Guangzhou Daily*, 24 January.

NBS (National Bureau of Statistics) (2009). *China Statistical Yearbook, 2009*, Beijing: China Statistical Publishing House.

Oi, J. C. (1999). Local State Corporatism, in J. Oi (ed.), *Rural China Takes Off: Institutional Foundations of Economic Reform*, Berkeley: University of California Press.

Olson, M. (1985). The Exploitation and Subsidization of Agriculture in the Developing and Developed Countries, Paper presented to the 19th Conference of the International Association of Agricultural Economists, Malaga, Spain.

Sheng, L. (2009), New Challenges Migrants Are Faced with on Employment during the Financial Crisis, Paper for the conference Urban–rural Social Welfare Integration, Chengdu, Sichuan Province, 16 April.

Taylor, J. R. (1993). Rural Employment Trends and the Legacy of Surplus Labor, 1978–1989, in Y.Y. Kueh and R. F. Ash (eds.), *Economic Trends in Chinese Agriculture: The Impact of Post-Mao Reforms*, New York: Oxford University Press.

Tiebout, C. (1956). A Pure Theory of Local Expenditures, *Journal of Political Economy*, 64(5), pp. 416–424.

Walder, A. (1995). Local Governments as Industrial Firms, *American Journal of Sociology*, 101(2), pp. 47–70.

Wang, M. (2010). The Rise of Labor Cost and the Fall of Labor Input: Has China Reached Lewis Turning Point? *China Economic Journal*, 3(2), pp. 139–155.

Wang, M., and Cai, F. (2010). Future Prospects of Household Registration System Reform, in F. Cai (ed.), *The China Population and Labor Yearbook, Volume 2: The Sustainability of Economic Growth from the Perspective of Human Resources*, Leiden and Boston: Brill.

Whyte, M. K. (2010). The Paradoxes of Rural–Urban Inequality in Contemporary China, in M. K. White (ed.), *One Country, Two Societies: Rural–Urban Inequality in Contemporary China*, Cambridge, MA: Harvard University Press.

World Bank (1997). *China 2020: Development Challenges in the New Century*, Washington, DC: World Bank.

10 From quantitative issues to structural issues

An interpretation of China's labor market

10.1 Introduction

Most developing countries with characteristics of a dual economy are faced with employment issues that are different from those of developed countries. In a typical dual economy where significant surplus labor exists in agriculture and other traditional sectors, employment issues are quantitative in nature and the solution is to boost economic growth to create jobs and increase the labor participation rate in the non-agricultural sectors. In developed countries where growth is neoclassical, long-term surplus labor does not exist and the problems of employment are mainly reflected in frictional and structural unemployment as well as cyclical unemployment related to macroeconomic climate. For the former, the solution lies in measures to upgrade human capital, such as education and training, and improving labor market functions. For the latter, macroeconomic policy for the adjustment of the economic cycle is the answer.

The primary contradiction of employment for developing countries is excess labor and under-employment. However, this does not mean the non-existence of natural and cyclical unemployment comprising frictional and structural unemployment. For developing countries, natural unemployment and cyclical unemployment arising from the mismatch of the labor market and macroeconomic swings are layered upon the problem of surplus labor. Yet under China's planned economy, natural and cyclical unemployment did not find full expression in overt unemployment but only intensified the degree of labor surplus and redundancy.

For most of the time after launching the reform and opening-up policy in 1978, China has been in a development stage of dual economy as defined by W. Arthur Lewis and characterized by unlimited labor supply. According to estimates by the government and academia, surplus labor in agriculture and redundant personnel in urban state-owned enterprises (SOEs) and collective enterprises accounted for one third of the total workforce in the 1990s (Carter et al., 1996; Zhang, 2008). In the meantime, economic reform was initiated to incentivize workers, enterprises, and local governments and to foster a labor market that drove the migration of labor. With the furtherance of reform and opening-up, an abundant and low-cost workforce became a comparative advantage of labor-intensive products for China in the international market.

For government officials at various levels, addressing the problem of under-employment is an arduous task, making them reluctant to break egalitarianism and the "iron rice bowl" (guaranteed lifelong employment). Employment pressures keep them up at night not only when the economy falters but during periods of growth and recovery as well. As it turned out, massive labor migration proved to be a demographic dividend for China's rapid growth during this period. Government efforts to create jobs through growth and promote labor migration through reform in turn helped boost growth and enhanced people's welfare. As a result, giving priority to job creation and GDP growth was a correct and appropriate policy for the development stage at that time.

As expected by the Lewis model, when the development of a dual economy reaches a specific juncture, growth of labor supply cannot keep up with growth of labor demand, giving rise to the shortage of average workers and the rise of wages, that is, the Lewis turning point. Based on a series of indicators such as labor market supply and demand, rising wages, and the convergence of wages, 2004 was the year of the Lewis turning point for China (Cai, 2015). Given the termination of unlimited labor supply, a fundamental feature of dual economies, the arrival of the Lewis turning point embodied the shift of China's development stage. As the new chapter of development was ushered in, the landscape of the labor market and thus the nature and characteristics of employment issues became fundamentally transformed. This new situation requires profound adjustments to China's employment policies.

Based on the latest demographic and labor data, this paper investigates the quantitative changes in China's labor supply and demonstrates that China's key employment issue is no longer a quantitative one but a structural one related to the mismatch of the labor market. Now that the real economic growth rate is consistent with the potential growth rate, cyclical unemployment is not significant, at least not in the short run. In light of domestic and international experiences, this paper offers the following policy warning: traditional policy instruments, if continued as before, will not only prove to be increasingly impotent in addressing China's employment challenges but will also harbor significant policy risks for the labor market. In conclusion, this paper proposes some policy recommendations on the key priorities of government policy-making in the context of new developments in China's labor market.

10.2 Changes in aggregate labor supply

China's rapid economic growth led to massive job creation that absorbed rural surplus labor. As a result of labor migration, the development of the urban labor market, and changing demographics, China's labor supply-and-demand equilibrium has been transformed, crossing the Lewis turning point in 2004, marked by a shortage of labor and rising wages. In 2010, China's working-age population peaked and marked a start of negative growth for the first time, which is a turning point of diminishing demographic dividends. This has further reshaped the profile of the aggregate labor supply in non-agricultural sectors. Changes in labor supply can be observed in the following aspects.

First, in the new stage of demographic transition, working-age population successively experienced a growth slowdown, zero growth rate, and negative growth. According to census data, working-age population aged between 15 and 59 peaked in 2010. Given the increase of the labor participation rate (the share of working-age population who are either employed or actively looking for work in total working-age population) over recent years, the economically active population (working-age population multiplied by the labor participation rate) has continued to grow slowly. Yet it is projected that by 2017, China's total economically active population will also peak and then decrease in absolute number. According to forecast, in 2017 China's working-age population aged between 15 and 59 will reach 980 million and the labor participation rate will be 87.2 percent. Thus, economically active population will peak at 800 million by then.

Second, the large-scale migration of rural labor to non-agricultural industries and urban sectors greatly reduced rural labor surplus. By China's official statistics, primary industry still accounts for 29.5 percent of total employment, following 29.9 percent for secondary industry and 40.6 percent for tertiary industry. Many researchers, quoting the share of agricultural labor from this source, have concluded that huge surplus labor still exists in China. Many people have thus denied the arrival of the Lewis turning point for China despite labor shortages and rising wages. Nevertheless, both the official statistics and such academic views appear to be inconsistent with at least the following realities:

(1) The argument that huge surplus labor still exists in China's agricultural sector is inconsistent with the massive labor migration that occurred after China's reform and opening-up policy was introduced in the late 1970s. According to 2015 data of the National Bureau of Statistics (NBS, 2015), the total number of rural migrant workers in China was 274 million in 2014, including 168 million migrant workers who left their townships for more than six months and 106 million migrant workers who were employed locally in the non-agricultural sectors of their townships. The result was inevitably substantial reductions in the workforce who stayed in the countryside for agriculture and in the share of agricultural labor.
(2) If official statistics are to be followed, during China's rapid growth and intense industrial restructuring, the share of China's agricultural workforce decreased at less than half the speed of Japan and South Korea in their respective development stages of a similar nature. For instance, official statistics indicate that between 1978 and 2012 the share of China's agricultural labor declined by only 2.2 percent on an annual basis while

this figure was 4.5 percent for Japan between 1953 and 1987 and 5.1 percent for South Korea between 1963 and 1997.

After adjusting the NBS definition of agricultural labor, Du and Meiyan (2010) re-estimated China's real agricultural labor in 2009 and demonstrated that official statistics overestimated the size of agricultural labor by about 13.4 percentage points. Based on this approach, we recreated China's real agricultural labor data between 1984 and 2014 and thus arrived at the conclusion that by 2014, the actual proportion of agricultural labor is at least 10 percentage points below NBS statistics (Figure 10.1). This estimate is consistent with Brandt and Zhu (2010) based on other data sources. In the figure below, the difference between official statistics and re-estimated data is treated as residual, and is distributed in secondary and tertiary industries respectively under normal labor market conditions and will often return to agriculture as a reservoir of surplus labor when non-agricultural sectors suffer shocks. Yet as a result of rising productivity due to agricultural mechanization, agriculture is losing its role as a reservoir for surplus labor.

Lastly, since urban employment reform was initiated in the late 1990s and early 2000s, corporate employment gradually became market-oriented and redundancy of personnel ceased to be a prominent phenomenon. Despite government opposition to large-scale layoffs by enterprises and especially SOEs,

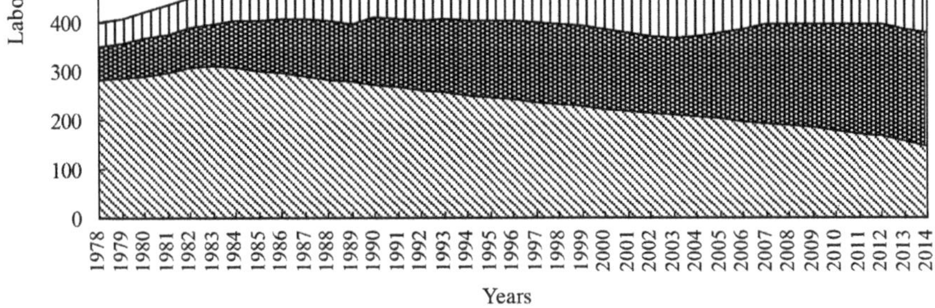

Figure 10.1 Re-estimation of workforce for the primary, secondary, and tertiary industries.

Source: Estimated by the author according to relevant data of the National Bureau of Statistics (NBS) over the years, and Du and Meiyan (2010); see Cai, 2016, for the estimation approach.

selective layoffs of certain employees still occurred when the economy faltered. As a result, workers with urban household registration became overtly jobless and rural migrant workers returned to the countryside. Prior to the reforms of the employment system for SOEs and the urban labor market in 1995, SOEs accounted for 59.1 percent of total urban employment. After radical reforms and painful adjustments, this proportion fell to a mere 16.1 percent in 2014. The difference between these percentages is an indication of redundant personnel being laid off and their reemployment in the private sector through the labor market rather than them holding onto the "iron rice bowl" provided in the planned economy. In considering the stock of urban labor supply, we should not assume that redundant personnel still exist extensively in enterprises or that they serve as reserve laborers for industries.

10.3 Employment difficulties: cyclical or structural?

Concerns of the government and researchers over the labor market arise from observations of employment difficulties facing certain population groups. Yet according to the analysis in the preceding section, we should abandon the traditional concept that these problems are still caused by an oversupply of labor. It needs to be further investigated whether such labor market performance is cyclical or structural, as employment problems of different natures need to be addressed with very different policy instruments.

In general, cyclical unemployment is caused by real growth rate below potential growth rate, that is, economic growth rate fails to reach the level of full employment of factors of production and especially labor. Based on my study, due to significant variations of growth factors such as supply of production factors and productivity (e.g., reduction of labor supply), stalling improvement of human capital, diminishing return to capital, and decelerating total factor productivity (TFP) growth, China's annual potential GDP growth rate significantly declined after 2010.

Before 2010, each and every round of economic growth deceleration suggested that real growth rate stayed below potential growth rate, causing a growth gap. For instance, in the early 1980s, the lowest point of real growth rate was recorded in 1981 at 5.2 percent while potential growth rate was 7.6 percent, with the difference being 2.3 percentage points. Between the late 1980s and early 1990s, the lowest point of real growth rate was recorded in 1990 when the growth gap was 3.0 percentage points. Under the impact of the global financial crisis between 2008 and 2009, the lowest point of real growth rate was recorded in 2009, with a growth gap of 1.4 percentage points. These years all coincided with rising employment pressures and unemployment. Thus, the three slowdowns are all typical indications of the macroeconomic cycle (Figure 10.2).

During the recent economic slowdown that started in 2012, China's real growth rate did not stay below potential growth rate, resulting in no growth gap. Correspondingly, the labor market and unemployment rate are both kept

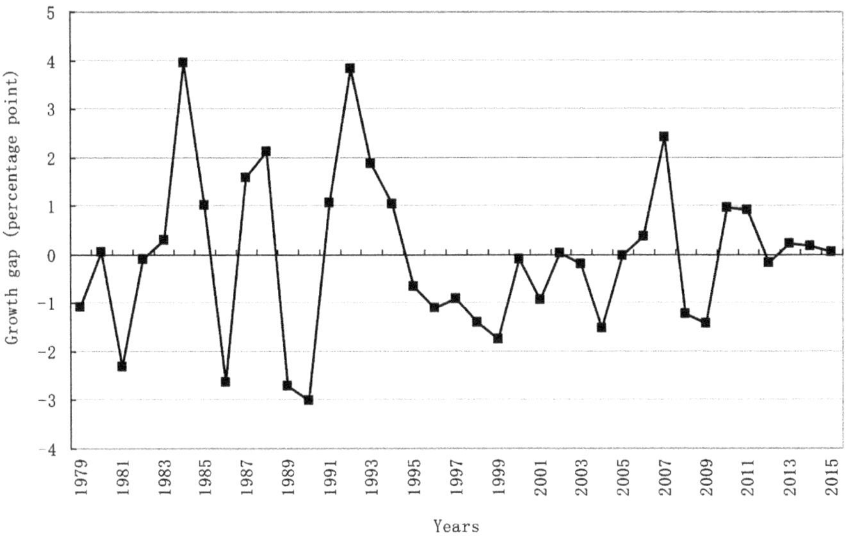

Figure 10.2 Economic growth gaps during China's reform period.
Source: Calculated by the author using data provided by Cai and Lu, 2013.

stable. Clearly, the recent growth slowdown represents a structural variation associated with the reduction of potential growth rate and is an indication that a "new normal" has been ushered in for China's economy. It is therefore not a cyclical phenomenon. According to the definition of potential growth rate and Okun's Law, growth rate in line with growth potential can achieve full utilization of factors of production and thus will not cause cyclical unemployment.

Since 2002, China's urban registered unemployment has stayed around 4.0 to 4.1 percent. It briefly reached 4.3 percent but not any higher. Coincidentally, according to the estimates of Du and Lu (2011), China's urban natural unemployment has also been between 4.0 and 4.1 percent in recent years. The aggregate unemployment rate consists of two parts: natural unemployment rate comprising frictional and structural unemployment rates, and cyclical unemployment rate caused by macroeconomic fluctuations. The question thus is whether overlapping registered and natural unemployment rates suggest the non-existence of cyclical unemployment in the urban labor market?

The problem is that registered unemployment rate statistically only includes urban households, whose unemployment is registered on a voluntary basis rather than calculated based on sample surveys. Hence, it cannot accurately reflect real unemployment in the labor market. Thus, we need to arrive at an unemployment indicator consistent with international standards—urban surveyed unemployment rate—as the basis of our analysis. Despite the lack of systematic statistics of urban surveyed unemployment released by the

NBS, Chinese officials and government reports have sporadically indicated certain data, which suggest that by the first half of 2015 the urban surveyed unemployment rate had been kept at around 5.1 percent. If this is used as an accurate measure of the aggregate urban unemployment rate, cyclical unemployment (i.e., surveyed unemployment rate minus natural unemployment rate) only stands at 1 percent.

According to experience, urban unemployment rate surveys have a limited coverage of rural-to-urban migrant workers and lack representation for this group, while their unemployment rate is greatly different from that of workers with urban household registration. For instance, according to a survey conducted by the Institute of Population and Labor Economics, Chinese Academy of Social Sciences (CASS) in six major cities in 2010, the surveyed unemployment rate stood at 4.72 percent for urban local workers and only 0.73 percent for migrant workers. Given that migrant workers already account for more than one third of urban employment (urban local employees account for less than two thirds), if this ratio is used as the weight for the adjustment of the coverage of the urban unemployment survey and conversion into overall urban surveyed unemployment rate, the result will not be much higher than the natural unemployment rate. This implies that at least for recent years, cyclical unemployment is not the major cause of employment difficulties.

Indeed, the reduction of real growth rate along with potential growth rate indicates that cyclical unemployment will not occur. Yet the reduction of potential growth rate also implies that traditional sources of growth can no longer support the previous double-digit growth rates and new sources of growth must be created. This conversion of growth drivers will be a process of upgrading and optimizing the industrial structure, featuring creative destruction. Meanwhile, the effect of creative destruction will also eliminate a considerable portion of traditional jobs when new jobs are being created. As shown in economic history, the disappearance and creation of jobs take place at the same time and are an inevitable result of upgrading and optimizing the industrial structure. For China in its "new normal" of economic development, more rapid and intense variations of industrial structure suggest that such creative destruction of jobs is inevitable.

The Ministry of Human Resources and Social Security compiled and released an indicator of labor market supply and demand—the ratio of job vacancies to job seekers—which verifies the above analysis. Based on the market supply and demand information of public employment service institutions of almost 100 cities across China, this ratio shifted from smaller than 1, that is, an undersupply of vacancies, to greater than 1, that is, an oversupply of vacancies. This transition implies that more vacancies correspond to fewer job seekers (Figure 10.3). This is consistent with the overall labor market tendency that employment contradictions are easing. On the other hand, it can be seen from the chart that after peaking at 1.15 in the fourth

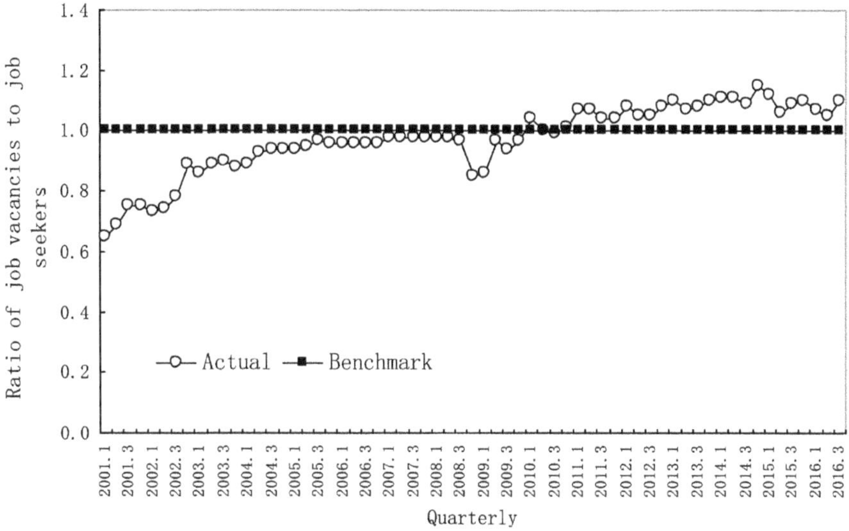

Figure 10.3 Ratio of job vacancies to job seekers in urban labor market.
Source: www.chinajob.gov.cn/DataAnalysis/node_1522.htm.

quarter of 2014, the ratio of job vacancies to job seekers started to decline, reaching 1.06 in the second quarter of 2015. Although this does not suggest a potential reversal of the tight labor market in the near future, structural unemployment contradictions tend to become more serious with the growing speed and intensity of industrial restructuring.

The "new northeast phenomenon" that made headlines recently provides a very good empirical explanation of such creative destruction of jobs. As an old industrial base, China's northeast is heavily dominated by traditional industries, particularly heavy and resource-intensive industries, making it hard to transform the regional development pattern and industrial structure. As China's economy entered into the "new normal", the growth rate of this region fell behind other parts of China. In 2014, China's national GDP growth rate registered 7.3 percent while growth rates for the three provinces of the northeast, Liaoning, Jilin, and Heilongjiang, only reached 5.8, 6.5, and 5.6 percent respectively. Despite a tight urban labor market nationwide over recent years, that is, vacancies outnumbering job seekers (ratio greater than 1), the ratio of vacancies to job seekers in such cities as Shenyang and Changchun continuously stayed below the national level (i.e., the ratio was smaller than 1). This indicates that due to sluggish traditional industries and the lack of a new industrial structure with comparative advantages, the labor market in northeast China still has more jobs destroyed than jobs newly created.

10.4 Avoid overreaction with traditional policies

There is one thing in common in the means that were employed to tackle cyclical unemployment and quantitative issues of employment: the government attempted to use macroeconomic policy, industrial policy, and regional policy to stimulate and promote economic growth in order to create more jobs. The policies aimed to either lower the unemployment rate or alleviate the degree of underemployment. These policy orientations and practices are not unfamiliar to observers of China's economy over the past three decades.

First, since the Sixteenth Congress of the CPC Central Committee was held in 2002, the CPC Central Committee and the State Council identified economic growth, job creation, stabilizing commodity prices, and maintaining the balance of international payments as the primary objectives of macroeconomic regulation. Since the then Premier Zhu Rongji announced a growth target of no less than 8 percent in response to the Asian financial crisis in 1998, 8 percent became the bottom line of economic growth for the central government, that is, the famous "*Bao Ba*" or safeguarding 8 percent. In explaining the necessity of this objective, former Premier Wen Jiabao who succeeded Premier Zhu clearly indicated that this objective had been established with employment as the foremost consideration.

Promotion of economic growth as a means to expand urban and rural employment has always been a top priority in the economic work of the Chinese government. After the Sixteenth Congress of the CPC Central Committee, the CPC Central Committee and the State Council gave more and more prominence in their policy-making to the promotion of employment in China's socioeconomic development and adopted a pro-employment strategy. By combining job creation with economic development, the Chinese government developed a contemporary Chinese version of classical dual economy development.

In any stage of economic development, these two policy concepts will never become obsolete and should undoubtedly be adhered to at all times. However, once the nature of employment issues evolves, the responses must also be updated in order to achieve specific targets and effects. In the new normal of China's industrial restructuring and upgrading, natural unemployment caused by frictional and structural factors and resulting employment challenges will persist and remain both at present and over a relatively long period to come as the primary issues of China's labor market.

The large-scale labor migration from agricultural to non-agricultural sectors over the past three decades is usually expressed as the reallocation of labor resources. Achieving efficiency of resource reallocation became the primary source of TFP improvement. As a matter of fact, this may also be expressed as creative destruction of jobs. The reducing share of agricultural labor from 70 percent in 1978 to less than 20 percent in 2014 means the destruction of almost 130 million agricultural jobs and the creation of about 500 million non-agricultural jobs. In the future development stage, such storming industrial and employment restructuring will inevitably slow, yet the process of creative destruction of jobs will intensify between secondary and tertiary industries, among various sectors of one industry, and among firms of a sector.

According to economists, in advanced economies like the United States, the reallocation of resources reflected in the creation and bankruptcy, entry and exit, and expansion and downsizing of firms results in the success of more productive firms and the elimination of less productive ones, which accounts for one third to half of productivity improvements (Foster et al., 2008). Economists also found that the large-scale and frequent creation and destruction of jobs and associated job reallocation can explain 35 to 56 percent of labor flow in the labor market. In addition, job reallocation is even more frequent for newly emerging firms and small businesses and is not directly correlated with the macroeconomic cycle (Davis and Haltiwanger, 1991).

In the new normal, maintaining moderately high growth rates requires the survival of the fittest firms, and upgrading of industrial structure will always lead to creative destruction. Hence, the following can be expected: the creation and destruction of jobs will take place simultaneously at an accelerated speed. Employment variations in China's current labor market are just an expression of such creative destruction. For a rather long period of time to come, employment variations can be identified as three scenarios of reallocation with associated challenges.

(1) As less productive and competitive firms give way to more productive and competitive ones, workers will also experience a process of reallocation by changing their jobs. Even if such a change of job does not involve any change or improvement of skills, it still takes time for them to find new jobs after leaving old ones. The implication is that these workers will encounter frictional unemployment in the process of job change.
(2) Reallocation from old jobs to new jobs generally results from the upgrade and optimization of the industrial structure and thus involves greater requirements of skills on the part of workers. As it may take more or less time to complete training and learning of these new skills depending on the human capital endowment and other demographic attributes of workers, workers may remain structurally unemployed while developing skills.
(3) In addition to the disappearance of old jobs, the upgrade of the industrial structure is accompanied by diminishing demand for the skills of the relevant positions. Examples of this phenomenon are numerous throughout economic history. In today's world of ever-changing new technology, this phenomenon finds expression in more extensive instances. As telephones replaced telegrams, operators replaced telegraphers; when emails challenged traditional postal services, software engineers and network administrators replaced mail sorters; as e-commerce challenged

brick-and-mortar stores, network administrators and online shop owners replaced brick-and-mortar shop owners and attendants.[1] In these situations, frictional and structural unemployment become inevitable.

In view of the above analysis, it becomes all the more urgent to understand the new nature of employment issues and to update the policy approach accordingly. If traditional policies of stimulating growth and expanding aggregate employment in disregard of frictional and structural attributes of the labor market continue to be followed, not only will employment problems remain but new potential labor market problems may arise. For instance, in stimulating growth for job creation, investments are often overconcentrated in construction areas where demand for non-skilled workers is high, giving rise to the following negative effects:

(1) It will further exacerbate the shortage of labor and worsen the decline of the potential GDP growth rate. Shortage of labor is the most decisive factor in the reduction of the potential growth rate as a result of diminishing demographic dividends, given that this factor affects not only labor supply and wage cost but human capital improvement, return to capital, and productivity improvement as well. In this sense, growing demand for labor in the construction sector under the effect of stimulative policy will take a toll on the potential growth rate, which not only hampers growth sustainability but exacerbates the contradictions of structural unemployment as well.
(2) Great demand for and rapidly increasing wages of non-skilled workers tend to narrow the wage premium between skilled and non-skilled workers, which discourages the accumulation of human capital. Whether or not workers can adapt to the demand for new skills boils down to education and training, and the development of education and training is not only determined by their supply but also by demand for them. Shortage of labor and particularly of non-skilled labor results in the excessive increase of wages for non-skilled labor, raising the opportunity cost for human capital improvement. In the short run, average workers may benefit from rising wages. Yet delayed human capital accumulation will lead to worsening mismatch of skills and thus employment difficulties, which eventually have to be borne by the workers themselves.
(3) Although economic growth under stimulative policy will increase demand for labor, it will also cause the over-concentration of non-skilled labor in sectors of overcapacity and bubbles. Judging by international experience, overcapacity of the real economy and excessive development of the virtual economy never fail to see their bubbles burst, followed by severe cyclical unemployment. Artificially magnified shortage of labor leads to premature replacement of workers by robots. As a result of this and delayed human capital accumulation, cyclical unemployment will convert into long-term structural unemployment.

10.5 Conclusions and policy recommendations

Giving priority to employment in socioeconomic policies proved important in China's experience and should continue to be followed in the future. In the context of internal and external fluctuations of economic activity, macroeconomic policy-making must follow employment variations in a more timely and sensitive manner. Given the negative growth of China's labor supply and the non-existence of a growth gap, the emphasis and means of China's employment policy need to be shifted to tackle structural employment issues. Hence, the author would like to propose the following policy recommendations.

(1) Further fostering the labor market and promoting market-based allocation of labor resources. According to the experiences of Japan and South Korea, after the economy crossed the Lewis turning point and demonstrated labor shortages, the share of agricultural labor continued to decline, at least to less than 10 percent. If the same applies to China, great potential still exists in the migration of agricultural labor as China evolves into a high-income country. In the decade between 2004 and 2014, the migration of farmers-turned-workers for job and business opportunities in cities contributed to a quarter of the increase of urbanization. As the growth of new entrants in the countryside diminishes, the number of migrant workers will not continue to increase as fast as before. For instance, between 2005 and 2010, the number of migrant workers increased by 4 percent on an annual basis, while this figure dropped to only 1.3 percent in 2014 and only 0.1 percent in the first half of 2015. Reform of the household registration system that aims to provide urban citizenship to migrant workers will further smooth the labor market and prevent the backflow of labor from cities to the countryside in order to maintain a normal process of urbanization and stabilize labor supply for non-agricultural industries.

(2) Structural problems of the labor market should be resolved through education, training, and other types of human capital accumulation. Judging by the education and skills level, the human capital of China's workforce is yet to be compatible with the demand of rapid industrial restructuring. Therefore, human capital accumulation should be not only a long-term vision but also a pressing priority in the short term. Currently, migrant workers account for more than two thirds of the increment in urban employment, while their average education is 9.6 years, which is only suitable for labor-intensive positions in secondary industry (requiring an average education of 9.1 years) and labor-intensive positions in tertiary industry (requiring an average education of 9.6 years). However, according to current human capital requirements of job positions, the years of schooling required should be 10.4 years for capital-intensive positions in secondary industry and 13.3 years for technology-intensive

positions in tertiary industry. If we acknowledge that capital-deepening and technology intensification will significantly increase in the future, the education level of migrant workers will be insufficient to support their transition toward new jobs.

(3) In line with the creative destruction of jobs, labor employment statistics should reflect both the creation of new jobs and the destruction of old ones. According to data released by the Ministry of Human Resources and Social Security (2015), urban employment grew by 13.22 million in 2014. Yet the size of the economically active population in China's rural and urban areas only increased by 3.8 million in the same year. Obviously, rural-to-urban migrant workers who were previously excluded from the scope of urban employment data have been included in urban employment statistics. Further, the increase in employment is not a net increase and only includes entries into job positions without including exits from jobs. On the other hand, in emphasizing job pressures, the media and some scholars often point to job destruction in sectors with overcapacity or resource depletion and inefficient firms without shedding light on job creation in emerging industries and firms. Fragmentation of information does not help reveal the real picture of the labor market and the "new normal".

Lastly, basic public services should be provided more equally and social protection policy should be used to support a flexible and efficient labor market. In the new development stage, efforts must be made to increase the efficiency of resource allocation and thus improve TFP in order to maintain moderately rapid growth rates. This requires a well-functioning mechanism of creative destruction. Protection of existing jobs under the excuse of preventing unemployment is tantamount to preserving the old economic structure and traditional development pattern and will inhibit the fostering of growth momentum for China's economy. Nevertheless, as a unique production factor, labor is embodied in humans. It is true that industries, capacities, firms, and even job positions need creative destruction to complete upgrading and optimization, but workers cannot be simply left to market competition without affording them any assistance. As industrial restructuring accelerates, it becomes more urgent to establish a social safety net and enhance the level of public employment services to help laid-off workers and migrant workers acquire new skills and adapt to new jobs. This should be the key government function and policy focus to address the new features of employment issues in China.

Note

1 Some researchers developed a rather long list to show the substitution between old and new jobs and shift between new skills and old skills resulting from changes of technology. In the history of economic theories, this phenomenon has been discussed in conjunction with the problem of "technological unemployment". See Cox and Alm (2015).

References

Alm, R., and Cox, W. M. (2015). Creative Destruction, in *The Concise Encyclopedia of Economics*, www.econlib.org/library/Enc/CreativeDestruction.html.

Brandt, L., and Zhu, X. (2010). Accounting for China's Growth. Working Paper No. 395, Toronto: Department of Economics. University of Toronto.

Cai, F., and Lu, Y. (2013). The End of China's Demographic Dividend: The Perspective of Potential GDP Growth, in R. Garnaut, F. Cai, and L. Song (eds.), *China: A New Model for Growth and Development*, Canberra: ANU Press, pp. 55–74.

Cai, F. (2015). *Demystifying China's Economy Development*. Beijing: China Social Sciences Press; Berlin: Springer.

Cai, F. (2016). *China's Economic Growth Prospects: From Demographic Dividend to Reform Dividend.* Cheltenham and Northampton, MA: Edward Elgar.

Carter, C., Zhong, F., and Cai, F. (1996). *China's Ongoing Reform of Agriculture*, San Francisco, CA: 1990 Institute.

Davis, S. J., and Haltiwanger, J. (1991). Gross Job Creation, Gross Job Destruction and Employment Reallocation. NBER Working Paper *No. 3728*, Cambridge, MA: National Bureau of Economic Research.

Du, Y., and Lu, Y. (2011). China's Natural Unemployment Level and Connotations, *Journal of World Economy*, 4.

Du, Y., and Meiyan, W. (2010). Discussions on Potential Bias and Implications of Lewis Turning Point. *China Economic Journal*, 3 (2), 121–136.

Foster, L., Haltiwanger J., and Syverson, C. (2008). Reallocation, Firm Turnover, and Efficiency: Selection on Productivity or Profitability? *American Economic Review*, 98 (1), pp. 394–425.

Ministry of Human Resources and Social Security (2015). Statistical Communiqué on the Development of Human Resources and Social Security Undertakings in 2014, Beijing: Ministry of Human Resources and Social Security.

NBS (National Bureau of Statistics) (2015). Report on the Monitoring and Survey of Rural Migrant Workers in China 2014, official website of the NBS, www.stats.gov.cn/tjsj/zxfb/201504/t20150429_797821.html.

Zhang, X. (2008). *Reform and Development of China's Employment*, Beijing: China Labor and Social Security Publishing House.

11 China's demand for human capital and education reform

11.1 Introduction

The important judgment of China's economic development entering a new normal state is based on three features of the specific development stage—that which has already presented itself and those which are yet to do so. Firstly, structural slowdown of China's economic growth. With a fundamental change in the demographics—that is, after rapid growth and slow growth, the working-age population aged between 15 and 59 years reached its peak in 2010, then entered negative growth—the demographic dividends that supported China's high-speed economic growth for more than three decades started to disappear. China's potential growth rate estimated according to the changes of labor supply, capital accumulation, human capital improvement, and increase in productivity decreased from an average of roughly 10 percent during the period since the reform and opening-up until 2010 to an average of 7.6 percent in the Twelfth Five-Year Plan period, and will further decrease to an average of 6.2 percent in the Thirteenth Five-year Plan period (Cai and Lu, 2013). This means that the growth rate of GDP is far lower than the average level since the reform and opening-up, and tends to decrease year after year; this is an existing feature of the new normal state.

Next, during economic slowdown, industrial restructuring, upgrading, and optimization will quicken gradually. Structural slowdown refers to the decline of factors traditionally supporting economic growth, some of which have even disappeared or will disappear gradually. Now that economic growth is an endless dynamic process, both industry structure and technology structure have to be adjusted to adapt to the new situation, and at last only those enterprises, industries, and technologies that retain growth from new sources can win, otherwise they will be eliminated in the competitive environment of creative destruction. The source of China's economic growth in the future will eventually come from the survival of the fittest. Key factors supporting this structural upgrading and optimization are labor creativity and skills related directly to human capital accumulation.

Thirdly, China's long-term sustainable economic growth requires transition of the drivers of economic growth through the above-mentioned industrial structure adjustment and simultaneous transition of economic development mode. This transition means a change from being driven by capital, labor, and land input to being driven by innovation and increase in total factor productivity. Admittedly, in traditional development mode, the quality of labor is of great importance and the contribution of human capital is also significant, yet in the new development mode, human capital will not only become more and more the most important source of growth, but also the prerequisite to promote innovation and increase in productivity.

Economic growth is ultimately driven by creative ideas by the laborers, while increasingly popularized or deepened education becomes a prerequisite for creative ideas, a source of innovation, and a guarantee of productivity in a modern society. Educational development will play a critical and irreplaceable role in the fast adjustment of economic structure, transformation of development mode, and transition of growth driver in China. In addition, education also enhances social mobility, and prevents a yawning income gap and intergenerational transmission of poverty. Therefore, the development of education is not only the forerunner of sustainable economic growth, but also the key to sharing economic development.

Economists have discussed the formation of human capital and its measurement for a long time. So far, enrollment rate of the right-age population, proportion of adult population with a specific educational background, average years of education of adult population (or workforce), etc., are used to measure educational outcomes; they have been proven to be the most observable and collectable human capital proxy indicators with full information. This means that, on the one hand, economists often use similar education indicators as human capital proxy variables in analysis; on the other hand, in the practice of improving human capital, policy-makers and implementers generally start from the development of education to implement human capital accumulation strategy. Hence, as China's economic development enters its new normal state, human capital challenges become new demands for educational development, and there should be new opportunities for educational development.

Human capital accumulation relies on individual, household, social, and governmental inputs, and requires correct signals to motivate human capital investment from the market. At China's current development stage, various structural and institutional obstacles exist, suppressing education demand and supply, thus reform should be deepened in relevant fields to emancipate the productivity of human capital accumulation, especially the reform of the education system, so as to avoid the middle-income trap in China. This paper discusses the new sources of growth required as China's economic development enters its new normal state, reveals the serious challenges of human capital accumulation and the new features of human capital in the new normal state, then puts forward policy suggestions for educational development and reform.

11.2 Sources of growth in the new normal of economic development

Many economists believe that, if average growth rate of the world economy is "mean value", any GDP growth rate significantly above this level will eventually decrease, that is, the so-called "regression toward the mean" (for instance, Pritchett and Summers, 2014). Some scholars also find through statistical analysis that, as far as the mean is concerned, when per capita income of an economy reaches a specific level, for example, when GDP per capita reaches 17,000 dollars as calculated according to the international dollar in 2005, a very high probability of economic slowdown exists (Eichengreen et al., 2012). Although such "statistical regularity" collapses the growth practices of numerous countries over a long development period into a group of panel data, it especially neglects the catch-up feature of developing countries, and fails to answer how the previous catch-up economies such as Japan and the Four Asian Tigers, and China's economy in the past 30 years, have realized high-speed economic growth. Thus it does not demonstrate a convincing basis for slowdown, yet such research reveals, at least on a large number of phenomenon, the transition of economic growth of a country from one normal state to another normal state for specific reasons.

Currently, not only China's economy, but even the global economy faces a downward trend. Correct recognition of the reasons of economic slowdown is critical to cope with growth slowdown and keep long-term sustainable growth. A viewpoint exists, on both the world economic slowdown and China's economic slowdown, that lack of demand after the global financial crisis from 2008 to 2009 led to a downward cycle of sluggish economic growth. However, looking at a longer period, since potential economic growth is ultimately supported by the supply of factors of production and increase in productivity, whereas global productivity slowdown occurred before the financial crisis, so the demand factor is at least insufficient to explain the sluggish growth in all countries.

With respect to China's economy, an important turning point of development—the Lewis turning point—occurred in 2004 well before the outbreak of the financial crisis. Henceforth, just as forecast by this concept, shortage of unskilled labor and a rise in wages has lasted for over a decade. For example, between 2004 and 2014, the annual growth rate of the actual average wage level of rural migrant workers as the representative of unskilled labor reached 11 percent. In addition, wages for workers grew fast in the manufacturing industry and construction industry where an intensive degree of common labor was relatively high, and in several agricultural fields (Figure 11.1). At present, the wage levels of ordinary workers in China are generally higher than in the developing countries in Asia; wage levels in Beijing, Shanghai, and Guangzhou are lower only than Japan, the Four Asian Tigers, and other developed economies in Asia (Bank of Tokyo-Mitsubishi UFJ (China), 2015). What is more, due to demographic change, labor shortage and rises in wages will continue. If the working-age population, which decreased

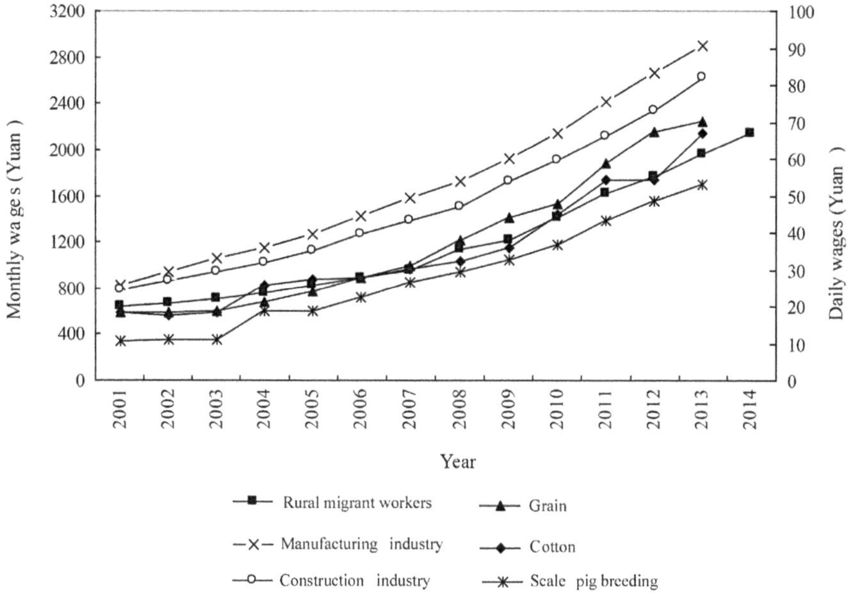

Figure 11.1 Trend of rise in wages of rural migrant workers and some industries.

Note: All wages are based on the constant price in 1998.

Sources: Daily wages for grain, cotton, and scale pig breeding come from *National Agricultural Product Cost-Benefit Data Compilation*; monthly wages for manufacturing and construction industries come from *China Labor Statistical Yearbook*; monthly wages of rural migrant workers come from *China Yearbook of Rural Household Survey*.

absolutely from 2010, cannot represent labor supply, the economically active population that will decrease absolutely from 2017 will undoubtedly become an indicator of labor supply. That is to say, labor shortage will become more serious at that time.

The change from unlimited labor supply as the basic property of dual economy, and the gradual disappearance of demographic dividends that were fully enjoyed in China's economic development during the reform and opening-up, period not only exert a negative impact on the economic growth rate in the sense of labor supply constraints, but are also manifested as slowdown in labor quality (human capital) improvement, decrease of return on capital, and slowdown in total factor productivity growth, which decreases the potential growth rate. In fact, the increase in wage levels does not inevitably mean the decrease of comparative advantage and thus competitiveness. The factor that influences comparative advantage and competitiveness is unit labor cost, that is, the ratio of wages to productivity. A direct relationship is that restriction of GDP growth by the growth of labor quantity actually depends on the growth rate of labor productivity. In other words, even if growth of labor quantity stops, if growth rate of labor productivity can offset the cost increase caused by labor shortage, comparative advantage may still be kept, and economic growth could still maintain the expected rate.

Labor productivity may be increased by three main sources. First, the increase of the capital–labor ratio. With the increase of labor cost, capital–labor substitution (the substitution of workers by machines, i.e., robots) will certainly happen. However, restricted by the law of diminishing returns on capital, such substitution could hardly be accomplished at one stroke. If quality of labor cannot meet the requirement for controlling the machines, the cost of capital–labor substitution outweighs the gain. Second, improvement of human capital. The improvement of operator quality and increase in the proportion of engineering and technical personnel are prerequisites for allowing fewer workers to operate more machines; therefore, if there is a lack of high-quality workers with higher skills, skill updating, and creativity, then the capital–labor substitution process could hardly achieve the desired effect. Third, increase of total factor productivity. The increase of total factor productivity by using new technologies, promoting innovations, and improving resource allocation is the most fundamental, sustainable source of labor productivity. This involves system reform, for example, creating a competitive environment.

We find in the decomposition of the factors influencing China's GDP growth between 1978 and 2010 that physical capital accumulation contributed 73.7 percent, labor quantity contributed 7.1 percent, educational level of the workers (human capital) contributed 4.2 percent, the dependency ratio 6.7 percent, and total factor productivity 15 percent (Cai and Zhao, 2012). From this result, the contribution of human capital does not seem to be as large as imagined. In fact, other researches on the interpretation of China's economic growth factors also show similar results. Two points should be noted for this specifically.

First, education quality is not considered in the estimation above, hence the contribution rate of education to economic growth is underestimated. The latest research of the economist Manuelli shows that, once education quality is considered, human capital may become a more complete and sufficient explanatory variable, its effect of promoting economic growth is enhanced significantly in statistical results, and it even contributes more than the increase in productivity (Manuelli and Seshadri, 2005).

Second, the contribution of human capital to economic growth will become more and more important. In the above decomposition of economic growth factors, with the decrease of the savings rate and the decrease of marginal return to capital caused by the aging of population, the contribution of physical capital accumulation will increasingly decline, while the trend of demographic transition will inevitably change the contributions of labor quantity and dependency ratio to negative numbers; the only sustainable sources of growth that can be relied on are increase of human capital accumulation and total factor productivity.

For example, the contribution rate of human capital estimated by Whalley and Zhao (2010) is much higher. Their estimated results using a neoclassical growth accounting method show that, among the factors such as physical capital stock, workforce, stock of human capital measured by years of education, and total factor productivity between 1978 and 2008, the contribution rate of human capital was 11.7 percent; after different productivity corresponding to different educational level was considered, their estimated contribution rate of human capital increased to 38 percent. The research of John Whalley and other scholars also pointed out that human capital accumulation could not only play an important role in the economic growth of China, but also offset poor performance of total factor productivity.

A neglected consequence of the disappearing demographic dividends is evident slowdown of human capital improvement. In China, which is a country that has made extraordinary leaps in demographic transition and the economic and social development process, the stock of human capital is improved mainly by relying on continuous new addition to the workforce. After extraordinary educational development in the reform and opening-up period—for example, nine-year compulsory education was made universal and enrollment in colleges and universities was expanded—new generations entering the workforce improved its overall human capital based on significantly higher education levels. However, with the quantity of new workforce entering negative growth, human capital improvement thus slows down.

The total number of dropout and graduated students without further studies at all levels and all education stages is actually the so-called new workforce. According to the population forecasts, this population group started negative growth from 2014; if there is no significant change in education development status, according to the trend the growth rate of average years of education of the new workforce will also stagnate, and will even show negative growth after 2019. Accordingly, new total human capital per year (new labor quantity multiplied by average years of education of this group) will present a negative growth trend, and the total scale will decline rapidly (Figure 11.2).

China's economy did not slow down immediately in 2004 due to labor shortage and the Lewis turning point. There were two main reasons. First, after labor shortage occurred, especially after negative growth of working-age population aged between 15 and 59 years appeared in 2010, since the labor participation rate increased slightly, the economically active population still retained a certain amount of growth. Population forecasts show that economically active population will peak in 2017, and enter negative growth thereafter. Next, within a period, increase in labor productivity is still faster than the rise in wages, and the latter has the nature of compensating historical debt, so unit labor cost is not increased significantly.

However, after entering the second decade of the twenty-first century, increase in labor productivity slows down obviously. According to the latest

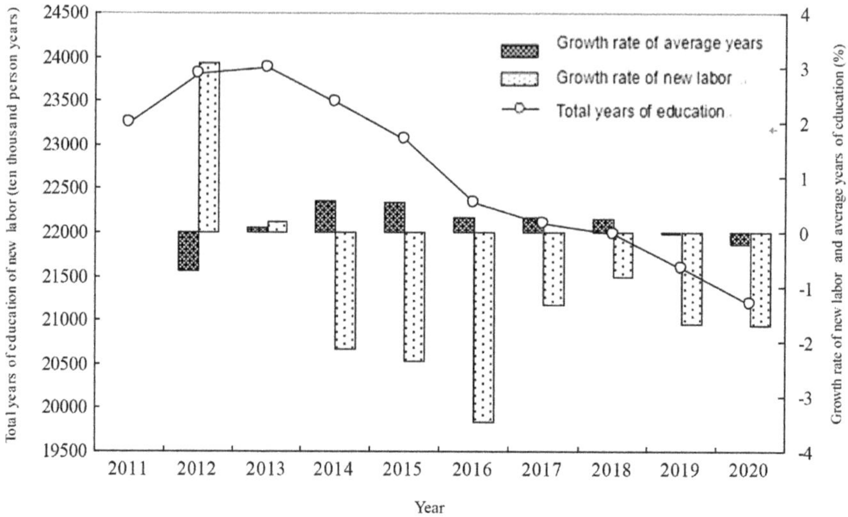

Figure 11.2 New workforce and human capital increment.

Source: Calculation by the author according to Guo Zhenwei's forecast of China's population age structure.

data of the Conference Board (2015), the average growth rate of labor productivity in China decreased from 9.5 percent between 2007 and 2012 to 7.3 percent in 2012 and 2013 and to 7 percent in 2014. The new trend of increase in labor productivity lagged behind the rise in wages, leading to the rise of unit labor cost. The estimates of Du (2014) show that, since the rise in wages is faster than the increase in labor productivity, unit labor cost in China's manufacturing industry has increased since 2004, and increased by 40 percent between 2004 and 2012.

Although I don't think that China's economic slowdown is caused by the demand factor in the "new mediocrity" of the global economy after the financial crisis, yet weak external demand in a specific period imposes real urgency, given the inevitability of slowdown caused by the change of development stage. Consider the change in comparative advantage for labor-intensive products. Although labor shortage and thus spiking wage cost decrease the comparative advantage and thus international competitiveness of such an industry, yet potential international competitors (for example, developing countries with an advantage in population age structure) cannot match the quality of Chinese workers in the short term, nor develop sufficient supply scale to substitute "Made in China", so comparative advantage of Chinese products could be kept for a certain period, and slowdown may occur gradually. Yet financial crisis and sluggish recovery from it shorten this "grace period" greatly, and the fact of accelerated slowdown makes structural adjustment more urgent.

11.3 The race between human capital accumulation and robotics

Britain's *Financial Times* recorded the experience of an American factory owner (Fleming and Giles, 2015). This entrepreneur pointed to his factory workshops and said, this manufacturing previously took place in China, but with the use of robots we stole it from China, and changed it to "Made in USA." This is consistent with the overall recovery of the US economy and employment. Nobel Prize-winning economist Michael Spence once discovered that almost all US employment increments between 1990 and 2008 came from the non-tradable sector, while medium and low-end jobs in the tradable sector flowed to emerging economies; thus he drew the conclusion that it was outsourcing that was destroying the US economy (Spence and Hlatshwayo, 2011). But, due to rapid development of automation and robots on the one hand, and due to the rise of China's labor cost on the other hand, some manufacturing industries have undoubtedly returned to the US. Although this process does not bring the expected jobs back to the US, yet will reduce jobs for Chinese workers substantially.

The other side of this picture is the challenge of substitution of workers by machines (robots) that Chinese unskilled workers have to face. Seemingly, substitution of workers by machines is a natural process and will not impact China's labor market. Then, where is the challenge? Two changes related to human resources will inevitably occur in the process of China entering and adapting to the new normal of economic development: first, continual increase of labor cost will induce the tendency of capital–labor substitution, reducing low-end jobs; second, the urgent shift toward innovation-driven growth imposes a higher requirement for human capital, increasing high-end jobs. Under the current technology development trend in the world, the above-mentioned changes bring special challenges to China. The traditional process of capital–labor substitution—substitution of workers by machines and substitution of workers by old-generation robots—is generally slow and progressive under the law of diminishing returns on capital, allowing adaptation to the need for improvement of labor quality. However, new-generation robots blend physical capital and human capital together, integrate operational skills with cognitive ability, and will inevitably substitute for front-line labor-intensive workers, and will substitute knowledge-intensive workers gradually, and hence break up the law of diminishing returns on capital. Because update speed of the chips commanding robot work is much faster than the transition of workers' skills, so the future substitution and implementation speed will be much faster than ever before.

In 2014, China superseded Japan to become the largest market for robots in the world; the growth of import volume and production output are in the ascendant. According to media reports, Guangdong Provincial Government declared the disbursement of 943 billion yuan to promote technical retrofits, including "substitution of workers by machines (robots)", in the three years to come (see Guangdong Provincial People's Government, 2015). Assume that the annual wage of a front-line worker in the Pearl River Delta is 50,000 yuan; the fund to be invested by the government is sufficient to employ 18.86 million workers, which would solve the labor shortage in three years to come even according to maximum labor shortage of 600,000 workers after the Spring Festival. This ambitious investment plan must be strongly motivated by longer-term expectations of unignorable bottleneck restrictions.

First, puzzles of recruitment difficulties and increase of labor cost have existed for many years. The earliest migrant worker shortage appeared in the Pearl River Delta region of China in 2004; it was also the export-oriented manufacturing enterprises in this region that suffered the most serious labor shortage and rising wage costs thereafter. It was reported that the labor cost in Dongguan City was 10 times higher than in Southeast Asia (Sohu.com, 2015). A survey by the Chartered Bank shows that nine cities of Guangdong Province in the Pearl River Delta region created 27 percent of export, attracted 20 percent of direct investment from foreign merchants and Hong Kong, Macao, and Taiwan, based on 0.6 percent of national area and 4.2 percent of population (Lau et al., 2015), so the situation in this region can fully represent the dilemma of export-oriented manufacturing enterprises in China.

Second, incentive for robotics development has increased by leaps and bounds. Traditional robots were substantively machines, but new-generation robots have learning ability and have made, are making, and will continue to make more and faster progress in intelligence. At present, the foreseeable applications are far beyond previous imagination, ranging from common operations to complicated operation of various machines: home delivery and crop management by unmanned aerial vehicles, self-driving cars and tractors, medical care (including complicated surgery)—the new generation of robots is almost almighty. What is more important, while upgrading and transformation of workers' skills is required by generational change of products and industry upgrading, the reprogramming of robots is far faster and more efficient than personnel training (Reference News, 2015); therefore, substitution of workers by robots might be earlier than anyone expects. In fact, this is merely our observable experience. In succession to Moore's Law and Cooper's Law, Kurzweil's Law, linked with artificial intelligence, points out that technological change has the nature of exponential growth (Kurzweil, 2001). The development of new-generation robotics is the perfect embodiment of this law.

Finally, there is growing international competitive pressure in the manufacturing industries. During the period of accelerated aging and loss of demographic dividends in China, for several decades many developing countries will still enjoy demographic dividends brought by increase of working-age population and decrease of dependency ratio. This is why many international economists predict that the economic growth rate of India will exceed China's, and India will become the most populous country with the fastest growth rate. However, while we must acknowledge the competitive pressure, we should also see that the issue is not so simple. Although population factors affect economic growth rate, a huge gap still exists between the countries with young demographic structure (such as India and Africa) and China in regard to educational level of workers; they cannot catch up with and surpass China in the short term. For example, average years of education of the Indian population aged 35 (5.4 years) is 38.7 percent lower than in China (8.8 years). According to the rules of education development, this gap cannot be closed in the short term.

Real competition comes from the developed countries at the leading edge of technical innovation, with manifest human capital advantages. According to expectations, the development of robots and reduction of costs will rapidly eliminate the advantage of any country in unit labor cost and narrow the gap between countries in this respect. In other words, it is technological innovation capacity and labor quality, rather than labor quantity and wage levels, that will determine the manufacturing configuration map in the future. At age 35, the gap between US and China in regard to average years of education (14.2 years), just the same as that China higher than India. Therefore, the challenge for China is not competition from those developing countries with cheap labor costs, but the race between human capital accumulation and robotics. Winning this race depends on the speed of human capital improvement.

In addition, the experience and lessons of developed countries such as the United States show that failure in the race of human capital accumulation will also lead to social risks. In a new era of globalization plus Internet and robots, on the one hand new technology raises the demand for creativity and skills of workers, and income of the workers with high educational attainment increases significantly, on the other hand jobs of low-end workers are reduced, thus their household income decreases, and the result is just what has been seen in the United States in the past two or three decades: poor families cannot get benefits from globalization and the new technology revolution, and income distribution has accordingly worsened, as shown by a rising Gini coefficient. China's social income distribution has improved gradually, with both the urban–rural income gap and the Gini coefficient decreasing since 2009. However, the trend of a few years is not enough to prove that China is already at the Kuznets turning point of income distribution improvement, therefore, the risk of enlarged income gap will still exist in the future if a necessary and solid foundation is not laid in the field of education.

11.4 Human capital required for "mass entrepreneurship and innovation"

Direction of the brewing (if not occurring) new technological revolution is not the nightmare of unskilled workers and skilled workers as worried by new and old Luddites, that is to say, the combination of new technology and new employment pattern does not substantively enable the labor group to become victim without exception. The development of the Internet, especially mobile Internet, with its nature of zero marginal cost (Rifkin, 2014), helps thousands and thousands of workers to get on-demand jobs, so they become sharers in the new technological revolution. Accordingly, the economic pattern increasingly has a sharing feature, bringing a ray of hope for income inequality reduction. More specifically, whether technological change helps to share economic development depends on the response of the labor market and ultimately the response of government policy. Human capital accumulation linked with education, training, and learning by doing is the key field in which to make the correct response.

To comply with new technology and the new economic model created by it, the Chinese government vigorously advocates a "mass entrepreneurship and innovation" strategy, erecting a stage for all the people to share the results of the new technological revolution, and putting forward higher requirements for human capital of the participants. We will start from human capital theory and practice, and illustrate the human capital features required for this "mass entrepreneurship and innovation" strategy according to the features of new technology, the new business mode, and the new employment pattern, and the need to explore a new reverse in education.

One of the educational objectives is undoubtedly the training of workers' skills. Skill-training forms include basic education aimed at cognitive ability and professional education and training, so years of education may serve as a proxy indicator of skills to a certain degree. With the upgrading and optimization of industry structure, new requirements for workers' skills mean higher requirements for educational level of the working-age population. The demand for unskilled workers is currently strong in the labor market, and this signal does not encourage households and individuals to invest in education, applying negative incentives to human capital accumulation. Such a situation restricts current development of skills, and does not highlight potential human capital crisis in the future.

With respect to educational level of the transferred rural labor force, according to the survey data, the current average years of education of rural migrant workers is 9.6 years. This human capital status just enables them to adapt to labor-intensive jobs in secondary industry (9.1 years of education are required for workers), and labor-intensive jobs in tertiary industry (9.6 years of education are required). But China's economic trend in the future is economic slowdown and quick industrial structure adjustment. According to current requirements of jobs for human capital, 10.4 years of education are required for capital-intensive jobs in secondary industry, and 13.3 years are required for technology-intensive jobs in tertiary industry. If the future industry trend is a notable enhancement of capital-intensive and technology-intensive jobs, predictably, educational attainment of rural migrant workers is insufficient for them to transfer to these new jobs.

With respect to human capital matching of university graduates, an important source of employment difficulty for university graduates is very narrow employment fields for this labor group. Comparing the industrial distribution of workers with educational background above junior college in China and the United States, we find that workers with educational background above junior college in China are excessively concentrated in finance, information, education, health, and public administration; the proportion of university graduates in these industries is even higher than in the United States, while the proportion of university graduates employed in directly productive industries is much lower in China than in the United States. For instance, the employment proportion of university graduates in agriculture is 0.6 percent in China, yet up to 24.6 percent in the United States; the proportion of university graduates in manufacturing industry is 10.3 percent in China and 30.0 percent in the United States; the proportion of university graduates in the transportation industry is 10.8 percent in China and 27.1 percent in the United States; the proportion of university graduates in business, trade, catering and tourist industries is 11 percent in China and 28.6 percent in the United States (Hu et al., 2013).

This is not to say we can encourage university graduates to enter these sectors and get the expected results. In fact, the employment proportion of well-educated workers in the above-mentioned industries is low because these industries are at the low end of the value chain, so demand for university graduates is not high. However, a country may overcome the "Solow Paradox"[1] and embrace extensive applications of new technology as early as possible if it is well prepared for human capital conditions, and thus may drive a new round of economic growth. It may be fully anticipated that industry upgrading of these sectors in the future will inevitably require higher human capital. Whether China's higher educational development could meet such demand depends on whether our choice today is prescient.

Besides skills, a more important function of education is to cultivate the cognitive ability of people. As creators or creative workers, people should have an ability to process, store, and extract the information acquired through brain thinking, so as to grasp composition, performance, and mutual relationships of things and related rules. Therefore, education not only imparts knowledge, but also cultivates the insight, memory, imagination, and attention of the educatees, so that they may grasp new knowledge consciously in the future, and be adept in transferring the knowledge into creativity and skills. Apparently, an educational model that aims to impart knowledge and skills and is oriented to examination often has many difficulties coping with the cultivation of cognitive ability. This means that professional education should without doubt be developed, but should not supersede general education.

In an era of knowledge economy, industry structure changes very rapidly, hence specific special skills will rapidly become obsolete. The experience of many developed countries shows that currently popular jobs and skills did not exist 20 to 30 years ago, so could not be learned in vocational schools. But workers with cognitive ability are more adept in learning new skills and will not be eliminated from the labor market. Therefore, although the signal in the current labor market is unfavorable for encouraging households to increase investment in extending the years of their children's common education, from the perspective of longer-term development, those individuals and households that receive more education, especially higher education, will eventually win out. For example, although employment difficulty and a high unemployment rate of young people are worldwide phenomena, yet the situations in different countries show that workers with an educational background of university and above have lower unemployment rates and their wages rise more quickly in the long term, so they may become members of the middle-income group more easily.

In addition, education increasingly cultivates people's non-cognitive ability, mainly at the early childhood development stage. Non-cognitive ability includes emotional health, social adaptability, and interpersonal skills, etc. Simply speaking, if cognitive ability is reflected by "intelligence quotient", non-cognitive ability belongs more to "emotional quotient." Professor James Heckman studied early childhood education for a long time, with a view to children's mental health, willpower, focusing attention, and confidence, etc., which are thought of as important "soft skills" that could help children to get better results in school and help adults to achieve success in society (Liu, 2012). What is more important, a new generation of robots could substitute not only skills, but also cognitive ability; at least in the current view, non-cognitive ability is one of the unique advantages of human beings, inaccessible to robots in the foreseeable future.

To realize "mass entrepreneurship and innovation" under the new normal of economic development, educational development is required to cultivate human capital comprehensively in the above-mentioned three aspects, hence respective education rules and economic meanings should be understood. Numerous recognized findings show that, among three abilities that must be cultivated by education, skill training provided by professional education and vocational training has the features of highest private rate of return, relatively low social rate of return, and relatively small market externality; by contrast, the cognitive ability cultivated by general school education has higher social rate of return, larger externality, and lower private rate of return; while non-cognitive ability, cultivated mainly by early childhood development and pre-school education, has the highest social rate of return, the most significant externality, and relatively small private rate of return (Carneiro and Heckman, 2003). Therefore, economists obtain the sequence "preschool education–compulsory education–higher education–vocational training" according to the arrangement of social rate of return, (Figure 11.3). Beyond all doubt, priority of government investment should also be arranged on these grounds.

With respect to the recognition of rate of return on human capital, a misunderstanding has existed for a long time: private rate of return on education is regarded as an income indicator of investment, and the incentive system for education is established on this basis. In fact, social rate of return on education is a more fundamental, participatory return, but due to the externality feature of education, labor market signals tend to neglect and

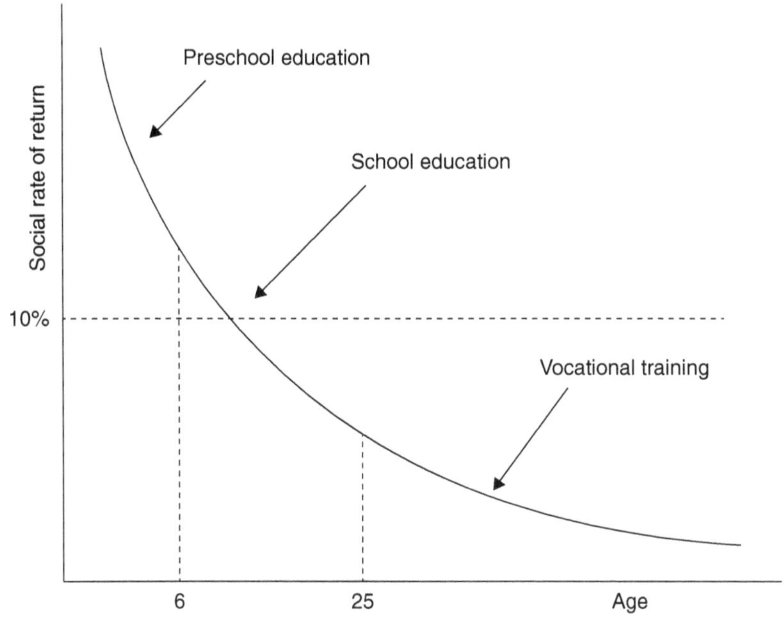

Figure 11.3 Sequence of social rate of return provided by various educations at all levels.

Source: Data from Carneiro and Heckman, 2003.

even conceal this nature, and usually cannot convert social rate of return into education incentive. The latest research has proved how misleading the above-mentioned misunderstanding is. At the beginning of the 1990s, economist James Heckman, who later won the Nobel Prize, lobbied the assistant finance minister at that time, Lawrence Summers, appealing for the government to ensure education opportunity for children aged 3–4 in poor families. He pointed out that this policy suggestion was not kind-hearted, but an investment seeking actual benefits: would bring about substantive return in the form of reducing social welfare expenditure, reducing the crime rate, and increasing tax revenue.

11.5 Sustainability and the reform direction of educational development

Aoki (2012) discovered from the economic development experience of East Asia that any country or region would inevitably enter a human-capital-driven economic development stage after it experienced a government-dominated economic development stage with Kuznets structural adjustment features. This periodic shift mentioned by him is just what we call the Lewis turning point. In the industrial structure adjustment process, the role of human capital is of great importance, even indispensable; and human capital will still be an important source of sustained economic growth in the future.

We estimate through an econometric model that feasible development of education and training could improve overall human capital level, contributing additional potential growth rate of approximately 0.1 percentage points to China in the future (Lu and Cai, 2014). This contribution margin seems to be negligible for an economy that could realize a growth of two digits, but it is a non-negligible figure for China's new normal of economic development where high-speed growth must be maintained to avoid being prematurely trapped in medium-speed or even low-speed growth. And what is under discussion here is merely the quantity of human capital. According to research referenced above, after education quality is added, the role of human capital in economic growth increases notably, becoming more prominent than the contribution of productivity (Manuelli and Seshadri, 2005).

It may be seen that an urgent task for China is to increase education quantity and quality significantly, relying on human capital accumulation to maintain long-term sustainable economic growth. The key to quantitative increase of educational level is to increase years of education for a new generation of workers. Generally speaking, if enrollment rate for compulsory education is very high, it is obviously more difficult to further greatly increase the years of education. The attainment rate of preschool, high school, and higher education must therefore be improved significantly. The key to increasing education quality lies in choosing which knowledge and abilities to be imparted to students in which educational model. Educational development requires reform, no matter whether in respect to quantity or quality.

To improve the attainment rate of preschool, high school, and higher education, some manifest cognitive barriers and policy barriers have to be removed. The dilemma of quantitative development of education thus appears. We may start from here to look for answers and policy responses. One such barrier is the great gap in income level and education supply between urban and rural areas, between districts and between residents. Absolute level and proportion of direct expenditures to be assumed by families are still high after the compulsory education stage, and so insufficiently affordable for low-income families. What is more, a rising trend in the wages of rural migrant workers leads to continuously rising opportunity cost to receiving education; household cost-benefit accounting of children's schooling is unfavorable to expanding education. In case of labor market failure or paradox of return on education, it is a good solution to increase the years of compulsory education, for example, extending three years to the current compulsory education of nine years, both backward (preschool education) and forward (senior high school) respectively, to expand the scope of what is paid for by the government. However, government decision-making might be irresolute. In particular, a question will be raised: is China entering a development stage that requires inclusion of preschool and senior high school in free compulsory education?

Indeed, many developed countries have not extended compulsory education to such a degree. But, considering the features of China's economic development, we understand the necessity to surpass developed countries on education. First, unlike the developed countries with neoclassical growth, China's economic development catches up with and surpasses in dual economy, may realize growth rate faster than the former (the developed countries with neoclassical growth), but may slow down significantly after Lewis Turning Point appears and before entering neoclassical growth (thus high income stage). In order to prevent continuous backsliding of the economic growth rate, and even a middle-income trap, China must keep education development as fast as possible. Second, China's demographic characteristic of getting old before getting rich shows more intense negative incentives for education when reflected in the labor market; to break up such market failure, the only way out is government intervention, that is, increasing the scale and proportion of public input to take a leading role in the development of education.

The next difficulty is where does additional government investment come from? Since 2012, the Chinese government has invested more than 4 percent of GDP in education; this is a relatively high level even by international standards. With the increase of per capita income level, although further increase of this proportion is required, the more feasible and more reasonable way is to reform the input mechanism, adjust the input structure, and increase input–output benefits. It is perceptible that the distribution of government investment in education is non-uniform between urban and rural areas, between districts, and between various levels of education, which is often criticized from a fairness perspective. However, such unbalanced resource allocation is also a lack of efficiency (Heckman, 2005). Therefore, on the one hand, public educational resources should be prioritized for poverty-stricken areas, rural areas, and poor families, and on the other hand, policy priority should be redetermined according to the social rate of return of "preschool education–compulsory education–higher education–vocational training" as a configuration principle of public educational resources, so as to narrow the capacity and thus income difference, prevent intergenerational transmission of poverty, and increase resource efficiency greatly, solving the problem of inadequate investment.

If education is regarded as a production process to cultivate human capital, education quality may be improved in different ways according to external features of different stages and different categories. For more equal resource allocation at the compulsory education stage, bottleneck constraints caused by insufficient resources may be eliminated, and resources may be reallocated to improve overall education efficiency and increase human capital output. At the compulsory education stage, a solid foundation is laid for lifelong learning, and it is critical to develop the same starting line for children in urban and rural areas, and in families of different income. Government should reduce the proportion of household expenditure at compulsory education stage practically, and consolidate and increase the completion rate of compulsory education, while the inclusion of preschool education in compulsory education protects rural and poor children against losing at the starting line, and also helps them to increase their completion rate at primary school and junior high school stages, increasing equal opportunity of further education greatly.

Increasing the rate of senior high school entry significantly promotes a higher education attainment rate. Enrollment rates of senior high school and university promote each other and interact both as cause and effect. If attainment rate of senior high school is high, the number of students who wish to go to university will become larger; more opportunities to go to university will also motivate enrollment at senior high school. The disbursement proportion of the government budget fund is low at senior high school stage; for rural areas, especially poor one, this education stage becomes a bottleneck for educational development in the future because of a too heavy expenditure burden on families at senior high school stage, plus high opportunity cost and low success rate of university entrance. Therefore, for further quick popularization of higher education, government should promote free education at senior high school stage as soon as possible (even if not compulsory education). Relatively speaking, higher education should further bring the initiative of non-government schools and family investment into full play.

Just as in a fully competitive market quality guarantee eventually relies on competition, quality of higher education should also be improved through competition. This requires a series of education system reforms to create a full and fair competitive environment. The colleges and universities in developed countries became able to cultivate talents adaptive to the knowledge-based economy after experiencing long-term exploration and tough reforms. For instance, compared with the universities in the United States, the universities in most European countries lacked competitiveness, so they reformed the university system, mainly focusing on enhancing competition, reducing regulation, empowering stakeholders, and listening more to the opinions of stakeholders (Kim, 2015). China has problems similar to other countries, as well as problems specific to the national circumstances in China's education system, so specific policy suggestions may be achieved only by analyzing both the commonalities and the individual characteristics.

"Why can't our universities cultivate exceptional talents?" The reason for this famous "Question of Qian Xuesen" is not abstruse as a matter of fact. Each university president could enumerate some phenomena, put forward reform proposals on aspects of curriculum, scientific the research system, teaching quality, connection with labor markets, and so on. However, any good intentions and perfect designs should eventually be compatible with an incentive system, and may be turned into actual performance only by a driving mechanism of competitive pressure. The special system factor that hinders university competition in China is administrative university management. For example, universities rely too much on financial investment, and are divided into various grades and ranks, as well as administrative ranks and their administrators within the universities. Such orientation grants administrative monopoly to some universities: they may get abundant financial funds from the state and recruit outstanding students relying on administrative ranking and the status of key schools, without competing for students and social resources based on the improvement of teaching quality. On the other hand, those universities that are divided into lower levels and grades are marketized too much: pursuing market demands blindly regardless of the conditions, they have no enthusiasm for raising teaching standards.

It is thus clear that, for the expansion of education and the improvement of quality, education system reform should be carried out under different policies according to the features of different stages and different categories, especially bearing in mind the relative importance of social rate of return and private rate of return. For those education fields with a relatively high social rate of return, fairness of public resource allocation could exactly guarantee the efficiency of resource utilization. As it is helpful to increase quantity and improve quality of human capital, these fields may be managed as fields of public goods production. And for the education fields with a relatively high private rate of return, market signals should be corrected through reform, an incentive system should be implemented to increase the proportion of market financing, and competitive mechanisms should be improved to promote both education quantity and quality.

Note

1 Economists once observed that the development of information technology did not bring about corresponding timely increase of productivity (see Brynjolfsson, 1993). This paradox may also be broadly understood in the follwing terms: there is no naturally promotional causality between the development of new technology and the expected economic growth, or a certain time lag exists in such a relationship, therefore, necessary conditions should be created to realize the relationship.

References

Aoki, M. (2012). Five Phases of Economic Development and Institutional Evolution in China, Japan and Korea, in M., Aoki, T. Kuran, and G. R. Roland, (eds.), *Institutions and Comparative Economic Development*, Basingstoke: Palgrave Macmillan.

Bank of Tokyo-Mitsubishi UFJ (China) (2015). Foreign Investment Trends of Japanese Enterprises—Is It Possible that All Japanese Enterprises Exit from China? *Outlook for Japanese Economy*, 42.

Brynjolfsson, E. (1993). The Productivity Paradox of Information Technology: Review and Assessment, *Communications of the ACM*, 36 (12), pp. 66–77.

Cai, F., and Lu, Y. (2013). The End of China's Demographic Dividend: The Perspective of Potential GDP Growth, in R. Garnaut, F. Cai, and L. Song (eds.), *China: A New Model for Growth and Development*, Canberra: ANU Press, pp. 55–74.

Cai, F., and Zhao, W. (2012). When Demographic Dividend Disappears: Growth Sustainability of China, in M. Aoki and J. Wu (eds.), *The Chinese Economy: A New Transition*, Basingstoke: Palgrave Macmillan, pp 75–90.

Carneiro, P., and Heckman, J. (2003). Human Capital Policy, in J. Heckman, A. Krueger, and B. Friedman (eds.), *Inequality in America: What Role for Human Capital Policies?* Cambridge, MA: MIT Press, pp. 77–139.

Conference Board (2015). *Productivity Brief 2015*, www.conference-board.org/data/economydatabase.

Du, Y. (2014). The Changes in Labor Market and New Sources of Economic Growth, *China Opening Journal*, 3.

Eichengreen, B, Park, D., and Shin, K. (2012). When Fast Growing Economies Slow Down: International Evidence and Implications for China, *Asian Economic Papers*, 11, pp. 42–87.

Fleming, S., and Giles, C. (2015). The Waiting Game, *Financial Times*, 26 May.

Guangdong Provincial People's Government (2015). Notification of Guangdong Provincial People's Government Concerning the Issuance of Three-Year Action Plan (2015–2017) for Industrial Transformation and Upgrading Battle in Guangdong Province, official website of Guangdong Provincial Science and Technology Department.

Heckman, J. (2005), China's Human Capital Investment, *China Economic Review*, 16(1), pp. 50–70.

Hu, R., et al. (2013). *China's Education Structure: Supply and Demand of Talents*, Subject Report.

Kim, J. (2015). Regulation of University Admission Quotas in Metropolitan Areas and the Competition between Universities, *KDI Focus*, 60.

Kurzweil, R. (2001). The Law of Accelerating Returns, Kurzweil Accelerating Intelligence, 7 March, www.kurzweilai.net/the-law-of-accelerating-returns.

Lau, K., et al. (2015). PRD's pain, China and ASEAN's gain, Global Research Special Report, London: Standard Chartered.

Liu, L. (2012). The Speech of Nobel Prize-winning Economist Heckman on Investing in Disadvantaged Young Children, China Philanthropy Times, 7 November.

Lu, Y., and Cai, F. (2014). China's Shift from the Demographic Dividend to the Reform Dividend, in L. Song, R. Garnaut, and F. Cai (eds.), *Deepening Reform for China's Long Term Growth and Development*, Canberra: ANU Press, pp 27–50.

Manuelli, R. E., and Seshadri, A. (2005). Human Capital and the Wealth of Nations, American Economic Review, 104(9), pp. 2736–2762.

Pritchett, L., and Summers, L. H. (2014). Asiaphoria Meets Regression to the Mean, NBER Working Paper *No. 20573*, Cambridge, MA: National Bureau of Economic Research.

Reference News (2015). Substitution of Workers by Robots Is Becoming a Global Trend, 12 February.

Rifkin, J. (2014). *The Zero Marginal Cost Society*, Beijing: CITIC.

Sohu.com (2015). Difficulties in Dongguan Manufacturing Industry Even after the Powerful "Substitution of Workers by Machines (Robots)", http://mt.sohu.com/20150607/n414565573.html.

Spence, M., and Hlatshwayo, S. (2011). The Evolving Structure of the American Economy and the Employment Challenge, Maurice R. Greeberg Center for Geoeconomic Studies Working Paper, New York: Council on Foreign Relations.

Whalley, J. and Zhao, X. (2010). The Contribution of Human Capital to China's Economic Growth, NBER Working Paper *No. 16592*, Cambridge, MA: National Bureau of Economic Research.

12 China's agricultural modernization and economies of scale

Barriers and solutions*

Correctly identifying the problem is the first step in developing an appropriate theory to guide policy-making. Misled by American scholar Lester Russell Brown, discussions on China's agricultural prospects over the years have been focused on "who will feed China" (Brown, 1995) while neglecting another more important question of "how should China feed its own population"? While the former explores whether China has the ability to achieve self-sufficiency of food and its significance to the rest of the world, the latter is more concerned with the path of China's agricultural development and mode of production. It is fair to say that obsession with the first problem has derailed the answer of academia and the policy research community to the second question.

Since reform and opening-up in 1978, China's agriculture has been developing along a correct path. It delivered food security, enhanced production, released agricultural surplus labor, and raised the income of farmers. However, the shift of development stage entails different objectives and requirements. Previously effective strategies may not work with the change of times. Sparing no effort in "feeding" itself, China finds the cost of the previous approach to be increasingly unsustainable. Hence, it is imperative for China to transform the pattern of its agricultural development in this new stage by shifting priorities.

This paper divides agricultural development into three stages with the following priorities: (1) solving the food shortage problem, (2) increasing farmers' income, and (3) transforming modes of agricultural production. These three stages and priorities are common to all countries and have been experienced or are ongoing for China. Based on empirical analysis, this paper reveals that the primary challenge facing China's agriculture is agricultural efficiency or the mode of production, and that economies of scale must be increased to mitigate diminishing return to capital. On the basis of such analysis, this paper proposes policy recommendations for creating an efficient mode of agricultural production.

12.1 Development stage of China's agriculture

Agricultural development is an important element of economic development and largely determines the latter's success. In economic history, different paths of agricultural development have determined whether a country's agricultural sector is viable and competitive or fragile and reliant on protection. In addition to differences in resource endowments that determine agricultural comparative advantage, policy-making deduced from specific theories is also an influencing factor behind the determinations of countries to follow different paths of agricultural development. To reveal the challenges, we have divided China's agricultural development into the following stages since reform and opening up in 1978.

12.1.1 Stage 1: tackling food security (1978–1984)

This stage of China's agricultural development was characterized by lopsided proportions of labor and output, that is, the former dwarfed the latter, leading to extremely low marginal productivity of agricultural labor, and meager supply of agricultural product. We define the implementation of the household responsibility system as the beginning of this stage and the holistic emergence of the effect of enhanced productivity as its end, that is, 1978–1984.

This early stage of agricultural development struggled to produce primary food supply. This stage can be characterized as traditional agriculture, as defined by Theodore W. Schultz, corresponding to the Malthusian trap commonly understood by development economists. As the stage of agricultural development where subsistence is the first and foremost priority, surplus labor begins to emerge, giving rise to the formation of a dual economy. In describing the relationship between agriculture and economic development in less developed countries, early literature identified the significant share of agriculture as an important characteristic (meaning that more people must engage in agriculture in order to provide a subsistence level of food supply), as well as the asymmetry between agricultural output and labor, that is, the share of agricultural labor dwarfs that of agricultural output (e.g. Johnston and Mellor, 1961). For this reason, the migration of agricultural labor to non-agricultural sectors can increase the comparative labor productivity of agriculture and realize the reallocation of resources, that is, the so-called "Kuznets effect[1]". The lopsided proportion of agricultural labor is caused by the involution process of agriculture during the subsistence stage (see Cai, 2015).

In 1978, the eve of reform and opening-up policy, China's agricultural output accounted for 28.2 percent of the economy yet agricultural labor represented 70.5 percent of the total workforce. The comparative labor productivity of agriculture (the ratio between the share of agricultural output and the share of labor) was estimated to be 0.40, which was only 14.4 percent that of the secondary sector (2.77) and 20.4 percent that of the tertiary sector (1.96). That is to say, laborers in agriculture generated disproportionately less value-added than did their counterparts in non-agricultural sectors. Given the disproportionately smaller share of agricultural products relative to its utilization of labor force, China's per capita possession of agricultural output in 1978 was only 316.6 kilograms of grain, 2.3 kilograms of cotton, 5.4 kilograms of oil crops, and 11.0 kilograms of meat. As a result, food had to be rationed for urban residents with various coupons and 250 million people in the countryside were below subsistence level.

Although essentially caused by the lack of incentives for People's Communes (numerator effect), at least from a statistical point of view, the low agricultural labor productivity also directly had to do with the high share of agricultural labor caused by barriers of the household registration system to the intersectoral flow of labor (denominator effect). Prior to agricultural reforms, the lack of incentives to work concealed the problem of agricultural surplus labor because more people than necessary were involved in agricultural production. Yet in reality, the degree of involution or surplus labor in China's agriculture was already very serious.

12.1.2 Stage 2: raising farmers' income (mid-1980s to 2004)

This stage was defined by the employment of new technology to enhance agricultural supply, the transfer of labor from agriculture to non-agricultural sectors, a declining and more proportionate share of agricultural workforce relative to output, as well as marginal productivity of agricultural labor converging with non-agricultural sectors. The result was an increase in the off-farming income of farmers and narrowing urban–rural income gaps. From the mid-1980s, the household responsibility system was universally implemented in agriculture to create better incentives for farmers. In addition to boosting agricultural production and productivity, this reform also made surplus labor an explicit issue. As reforms have eliminated institutional barriers deterring labor mobility between rural and urban sectors, the degree of labor surplus in agriculture has been significantly eased and eventually the Lewis turning point arrived around 2004, which marked an end to this stage (see Cai, 2016).

In the previous stage, the share of agricultural labor dwarfed the share of agricultural output. As a result, agricultural productivity was significantly below the productivity of non-agricultural sectors. As pointed out by Arthur Lewis in defining the concept of dual economy, the marginal productivity of agricultural labor is so low that it becomes zero or negative, which determines the low income of farmers. As surplus agricultural labor transfers to secondary and tertiary sectors, the marginal productivity of agricultural labor stays on the rise. Along with the mitigation of labor surplus in the sector, advances in agricultural biotechnology in the first place and then rising levels of mechanization (induced by the relative scarcity of labor) have simultaneously enhanced labor productivity in agriculture and food security. By 2014, the share of China's agriculture in gross domestic product dropped to 9.2 percent while the share of agricultural labor fell to 19.1 percent.[2] On the other hand, agricultural productivity jumped to 0.48 and per capita possession of agricultural output reached 443.8 kilograms for grain, 4.5 kilograms for cotton, 25.6 kilograms for oil crops, 97.7 kilograms for sugar crops, and 63.7 kilograms for meat. On the average of labor force actually engaged in agriculture, grain output per unit of labor input increased by 2.8 times over the level of 1978.

According to the theory of induced technological change, the adoption of agricultural technology is induced by the relative scarcity of production factors and their relative prices. That is to say, agricultural technology adoption tends to save scarce production factors and make more intensive use of abundant ones (Hayami and Ruttan, 1980). This hypothesis implies that agricultural development and technological progress can be observed in light of the share of agricultural labor as the defining feature of certain development stages. For instance, as explained in the following paragraph, agricultural mechanization reflects the active response of technological change to the change of production factor endowment in a certain stage of China's agricultural development.

According to the characteristics of agricultural machinery, we roughly define large and medium-sized tractors and their auxiliary implements as labor-saving technology and small tractors and their auxiliary implements as labor-consuming technology. We have observed that during 1979–1995, the total power of large and medium-sized tractors grew by 0.84 percent on an annual average basis and the growth rate for their auxiliary implements was –1.7 percent. During the same period of time, the total power of small tractors increased by 11.2 percent and the growth rate for their auxiliary implements was 10.5 percent. Later, with the massive transfer of agricultural labor into non-agricultural sectors, the relative scarcity of production factor changed, that is, the shortage of agricultural labor emerged, reversing the direction of technological change. During 1996–2012, the total power of large and medium-sized tractors grew by 11.8 percent on an annual average basis and the growth rate for their auxiliary implements was 13.2 percent, while the annual average growth rate of total power of small tractors dropped to 4.7 percent and the growth rate for their auxiliary agricultural implements was 6.7 percent.

12.1.3 Stage 3: transforming the mode of production (2004 to present)

This stage is characterized by labor as a relatively scarce production factor, increasing advancement in labor-saving agricultural technology, and the replacement of labor by capital. Substitution of production factors requires an expansion in the scale of agricultural operation to prevent diminishing return to capital. In this stage, China is confronted with two correlated institutional constraints. Under China's household registration (*hukou*) system, rural migrant workers are not entitled to urban citizenship. They find odd jobs in cities but return to the countryside when farm work is busy to assist their aging parents and other family members. In addition, impediments to land transfer discourage the concentration of farmland essential to achieving economies of scale. It is fair to say that China's agriculture entered into this stage when the Lewis turning point was reached in 2004.

The first two stages have laid the foundation for agricultural modernization and resulted in the growth of capital input outpacing that of labor input and thus significant improvements of labor productivity. According to survey data, we may discern this change from the capital input and labor input for paddy rice, corn, and wheat, which account for 81 percent of grain-sowing area. As Figure 12.1 reveals, the actual material and service costs for paddy rice, corn, and wheat have been on a steep rise since 2004, yet unit-area labor input dropped sharply. During 2003–2013, the actual material and service costs for the three crops increased by 1.9, 3.2, and 2.6 percent on an annual average basis, while labor inputs fell by 4.4, 3.9, and 5.0 percent respectively.

Meanwhile, income growth of farmers and narrowing urban–rural income gaps are increasingly less dependent on agricultural profits. In the context of massive labor transfer and the arrival of the Lewis turning point, incomes from non-agricultural business and wages have become the lion's share in the household income of farmers. In 2014, non-agricultural income accounted for 63 percent of disposable cash income of farmers and constituted 75 percent of their income growth. This reality points to two important issues in agricultural development.

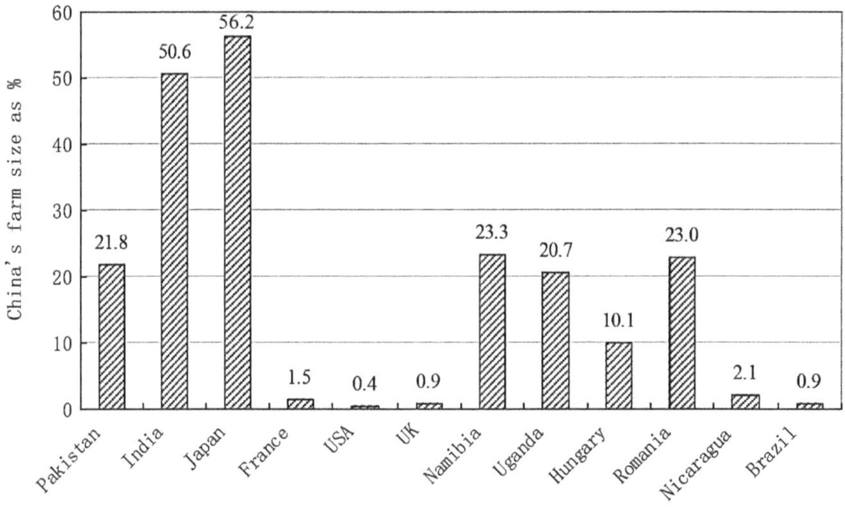

Figure 12.1 International comparison of farmland size in China.
Source: FAO, 2010.

First, with the change in stages of economic development, the previous sources of income growth for farmers became exhausted. According to demographic data, after China's working-age population (16–59 years of age) began to experience negative growth in 2011 for the first time, the potential migrant worker population aged between 16 and 19 also started to decline in 2015. The growth of the migrant worker population will inevitably decelerate. In fact, it has already dropped from 4 percent during 2005–2010 to 1.3 percent in 2014 and further down to 0.4 percent in 2015. This change implies that wage increase as a major contributor to rural households' income can no longer sustain the previous growth momentum.

Second, the same approach used by China to succeed in raising farmers' income may not work in raising agricultural efficiency and thus strengthening capacity of agricultural production. The insignificance of income from farming operations in rural households' income provides neither incentives for laborers to engage in agriculture nor impetus to build a solid foundation of modernized modes of agricultural production. In turn an inefficient mode of production cannot guarantee reasonable return to agriculture to support farmers' income growth. This vicious cycle has become a barrier to China's agricultural modernization.

In addition to ensuring food supply and raising farmers' income, we believe that the more urgent task of China's agricultural development in the current stage is to modernize agricultural production, featuring economies of scale, efficiency of production, external provision of services, commodity competitiveness, and sectoral viability.

12.2 Conventional wisdom on agriculture as an industry

Two theoretical traditions feature prominently in discussions on China's agricultural economics. First, according to Theodore W. Schultz, an American economist very influential in China, the uniqueness of agriculture as an industry excepts it from being characteristic of economies of scale. Second, Chinese scholars and policy researchers widely accept the view that agriculture is congenitally an unviable industry. More or less, those views have become conventional wisdom influencing scholarly debates on, and misleading policy-making for, China's agricultural development. This section tries to break those myths so as to reveal an alternative direction for China's agricultural development.

12.2.1 "Pseudo-indivisibilities" of production factors in agriculture

Theodore W. Schultz (1983) demonstrated that there does not exist an indivisibility of production factor in agriculture as a source of economies of scale—what he terms as "pseudo-indivisibility". Taking tractors as an example, he noted that tractors can be manufactured by different specifications and models according to the size of farmland. Further, he applied "pseudo-indivisibility" derived from tractors to other production factors. For instance, he considered that labor is divisible because farmers can work in cities on a seasonable basis when farming is not intensive. Indeed, he was correct in arguing that the size of farmland is not a decisive feature distinguishing traditional and modern agriculture. He also admitted that small or large tractors are appropriate when labor is relatively cheap or expensive respectively. Yet on the whole, his conclusion—a generalized uniqueness of utilization of production factors in agriculture—should not serve as the reasoning for agriculture as an exception to economies of scale.

In debating the legitimacy of introduction of the household responsibility system—namely, breaking down large production teams into individual households—in the early 1980s, this theory that downplays economies of scale was used to justify reform. However, as the problems of food supply and farmers' income have been primarily resolved, the small size of agricultural operation has become an impediment to the use of agricultural machinery and other new technologies. Although superficially it seems that contracted agricultural machinery services may exempt farmers from purchasing agricultural machinery, thus maintaining the "indivisibility" hypothesis for agricultural machinery, the fact of Chinese farmers' increasing demand for machinery services demonstrates that large tractors and auxiliary implements are no longer unimportant and have become essential inputs in agricultural production today. Furthermore, if production and transaction costs are examined in combination, as shown in real cases, we will discover that the size of agricultural operation has more and more become a real barrier to agricultural efficiency.

First, one view about the pseudo-indivisibility of agricultural production factor is that instead of maintaining their own machinery, small farming households should purchase agricultural machinery services. However, small and scattered farmlands have restricted the use of large agricultural machinery. Theoretically speaking, adjacent farmers may share machinery services. Yet individual households may grow very different varieties of crops. Besides, bargaining with adjacent farmers is also difficult and will raise the transaction cost of hiring agent services for agricultural machinery.

Second, in addition to the process of farm production, economies of scale also exist in the processes of purchasing the means of production and relevant services and selling agricultural products. It takes certain capabilities and incentives to leverage such economies of scale in order to negotiate deals, collect information, evaluate results, and pay the relevant transaction costs. Small farm operations will inevitably increase the unit costs of transaction and reduce incentives to devote efforts to those processes. For instance, farmers often face multiple options in the seed market. Potentially faced with inferior and even fake seeds, farmers may not have the time and knowledge to effectively screen and select the best seeds.

Last, the small scale of agricultural operation impedes the adoption of new technology. The relative scarcity of production factors can change at any time, and so can market demand. Under large-scale operation, such changes in relative prices of production factors and operation costs that serve as market signals will induce technological progress in the direction of saving scarce factors and meeting market demand. However, as the size of farm operation is small, it leaves no capacities for farmers to respond to such market signals. For instance, while raising tax may reduce pesticide consumption, it will also increase the cost of agricultural production, especially in the case of small-sized farming. Large farms have the resources to kill pests by luring them with killer lamps. However, no small farmer would agree to lure pests to his own field parcel.

12.2.2 "Weak nature" of agriculture as industry

Over the years, most Chinese agricultural economists have used the "vulnerabilities" of agriculture as a self-evident justification for the protection of agriculture without conducting empirical tests. In general, the following justifications are offered (e.g., Gao, 2006). First, agriculture is a process of intertwined natural and economic reproduction and labor cannot be fully utilized during production. Second, agriculture is more strongly affected by natural factors, causing uncertainties in the result of production. Thirdly, while agricultural supply is subject to the "cobweb effect" to some extent and the income elasticity of demand for agricultural products is smaller than 1 after entering a certain stage, the income of producers cannot be assured in both short and long run. Obviously, the above justifications are both theoretically and practically outdated. With modern financial and insurance systems, a more sophisticated product market, and necessary government regulations, these justifications for the "vulnerabilities" of agriculture cannot hold.

Shifting focus away from the above outdated discussions that focus on justifying the universality of agricultural "vulnerabilities", a more convincing argument compares economies characterized by high labor–land ratio with those characterized by superior arable land endowment, leading to a static justification, that is, the theory of agricultural comparative advantage, as well as a dynamic justification, that is, the share of agricultural labor. Combining these justifications can seem to conclude the uniqueness of China's agriculture (e.g., Chen, 2015). Based on that view, first, China can never compete with countries like the United States and Australia given the substantial difference in endowments of agricultural resources. Second, it is hard to reemploy labor force released by expanding farm size. Hence, simply expanding the scale of operation does not seem to be a plausible option for China and subsidies and protection for agriculture based on international rules are still necessary.

International empirical studies offered mixed conclusions on the arguments of uniqueness of agriculture. For instance, according to an econometric analysis (Anderson and Hayami, 1986, Chapter 4), economies holding less comparative advantage in agriculture tend to implement policies protecting their agriculture more intensely. Meanwhile, as a declined share of agricultural labor or output means that the non-agricultural populations are more capable and willing to subsidize agriculture, the level of protection naturally increases as the process moves forward. However, since implementing agricultural protection policies undeniably causes inefficiencies, the level of protection cannot be increased forever. International experiences show that protection will cease to rise when the share of agricultural labor falls to around 6–8 percent or the share of agricultural output declines to around 4 percent. That implies that agricultural subsidy is in essence a transitory phenomenon of a certain development stage. While the argument of "agriculture as a vulnerable industry" is reasonable justification for shifting policy orientation away from taxing agriculture, taking it as a law of development and making subsidy or protection permanent policies should be avoided.

According to Hayami (1988), Japan's agriculture experienced stages of solving the food shortage problem and the poverty problem successively. Instead of moving to strengthen the mode of agricultural production, Japan turned to strongly implementing an agricultural protection policy, which persisted even after crossing the critical point of a declining share of agriculture. Having empirically demonstrated the significant loss in efficiency and welfare by implementing protection policies, Anderson and Hayami (1986) and Hayami (1988) suggest that economies like Japan should strive to strengthen the mode of agricultural production instead of offering protection. Studies also offer some lessons in which a handful of economies that were once considered to lack comparative advantage in agriculture have eventually built an efficient and competitive agricultural production mode.

Admittedly, how to develop agriculture in countries lacking comparative advantage is not simply a question concerned with industrial policy, but also involves social, livelihood, and food security issues. However, creating a modern mode of agricultural production lays the foundation for resolving all the above problems. In particular, whether agriculture can be protected as a vulnerable industry is not solely determined by farmers' expectations and government preferences but constrained by a host of objective factors including international price as a ceiling, domestic production cost as a floor, World Trade Organization rules as amber box policy limit, and arable land resources as red line. In exploring all possible solutions, China must expand the scale of agricultural operation and mitigate diminishing return to capital.

12.3 Breaking the constraints on farm size in China's agriculture

With China's introduction of the household responsibility system in the early 1980s, individual farming households replaced production teams to become the basic unit of agricultural operation. A mixture of arable land plots of different quality was allocated to each and every household according to the number of family members. To make the reform permanent and legitimate, the Chinese government identified household-based agricultural operation as a basic system and guaranteed a long-standing period for the land contract. Under this system, farmland was segmented into narrow plots and scattered across individual households. Numerous roads, ridges, and ditches compromised the utilization of arable land as well. Under the current household registration system, although many farmers migrated to find jobs in cities, because it was difficult for migrant workers to change their permanent residency, their land could not be transferred and was thus left uncultivated or inefficiently cultivated. Land could not be concentrated despite growing demand for concentration.

American writer Henry David Thoreau described a self-sufficient mode of agricultural production in *Walden*:

> I learned that [...] if one would live simply and eat only the crop which he raised, and raise no more than he ate, and not exchange it for an insufficient quantity of more luxurious and expensive things, he would need to cultivate only a few rods of ground [a rod squared is equivalent to 25.3 meters squared, and that it would be cheaper to spade up that than to use oxen to plough it.

As shown in Figure 12.1, the average size of land for each farming household in China is much smaller compared with the developed and developing countries in various regions of the world. In addition to the small size of land, on average each farming household is allocated more than five arable land plots scattered across different locations (Gao et al., 2012). Such a pattern of farm size indeed is not much different from what Thoreau described.

According to Chen (2015), policy countermeasures that allow farmers to subcontract their contracted land to other households, large-sized farms, and agribusiness corporations have promoted land concentration. However, only 26 percent of farming households have completely or partially transferred their farmland, involving 28 percent of 92 million hectares of total contracted farmland in China being transferred (Yao and Han, 2015). According to a sample survey, the ratio between the original contract land and transferred land cultivated by farming households changed from 97:3 in 1996 to 81:19 in 2008 (Gao et al., 2012). While land transfer increased its concentration, the size of China's agricultural operation is still very small by international standards. The World Bank defines farms with arable land of less than 2 hectares as small landowners; the average size of Chinese farms—0.6 hectares— can therefore be identified as subminiature type.

This situation has impeded China's agricultural efficiency and modernization. Based on their estimate of agricultural production function, the authors arrived at the following stylized facts on China's agricultural development stages and challenges (Cai and Wang, 2016).

First, until the agricultural system reforms produced their desired results in the mid-1980s, China had been preoccupied with tackling food shortage. This stage was characterized by a mass pool of surplus labor and thus very low marginal labor productivity in agriculture. Our estimates show that marginal labor product in the period 1978 to 1984 was negative for paddy rice and wheat production and zero for corn production. This situation was consistent with the doctrine of agricultural labor of zero-value, which was asserted by Arthur Lewis and denied by Theodore Schultz. Due to the lack of modern production factors in this stage, as can be expected by theory, the marginal product of capital in agriculture was high.

Second, trends of diminishing marginal product of capital and increasing marginal product of labor for those grain crops were both very significant. Compared to the average level of 1978–1990, the average marginal product of capital dropped by 27 percent for paddy rice production, 29 percent for corn production, and 19 percent for wheat production in 2007–2013. On the other hand, marginal product of labor jumped by 50 times for paddy rice, seven times for corn and 55 times for wheat. It is worth noticing that for all three grain crops, the margins of increase in marginal product of labor were far greater than the margins of reduction in marginal product of capital.

Lastly, we have observed that after the arrival of the Lewis turning point, marginal product of capital for China's agriculture stayed on the decline. With labor becoming a relatively scarce factor and capital becoming a relatively abundant factor as the result of rapid substitution of capital for labor, the small scale of agricultural operation has led to diminishing return to capital, making agriculture even less profitable. According to the Schultz theory and its policy implication, the key in transforming traditional agriculture is to introduce modern production factors, which require a critical minimum operation scale to achieve efficiency.

Since the reform initiated in the late 1970s, China's agriculture has experienced a remarkable journey. In addition to resolving the problem of food shortage and raising farmers' income, agriculture has supported China's spectacular economic growth and received generous support from industrial and urban sectors afterwards. After crossing the Lewis turning point, as China's resource endowments change, labor is increasingly replaced by machines in agriculture and the capital-to-labor ratio has significantly increased. However, due to the limitation of small-sized farmland and agricultural operations, return to capital began to diminish, which prevents further improvement of efficiency and market competitiveness. Ultimately, subsidy and protection are not capable of supporting the modernization of the mode of production.

With right incentives and market signals, Chinese farmers, who have been proven to be creative entrepreneurs in both institutional and technological innovation, are poised to choose the appropriate technology and factors input to maximize production and minimize cost. The problem is that institutional factors such as the land system and the household registration system continue to impede the expansion of farmland operation and the modernization of agricultural production mode. Institutional reform and policy adjustments therefore will not only enhance potential growth rates of the macro economy (see Cai and Lu, 2013), they will also unfetter the achievement of agricultural development objectives in the next stage. As part of supply-side structural reforms, China must eliminate all institutional barriers deterring enlargement of farmland side so as to modernize its agricultural production.

Notes

* Coauthored with Wang Meiyan.

1 In 1971, Nobel Prize laureate Simon Kuznets noted that the key in changes in industrial structure is to transfer resources from less productive sectors to more productive ones and thus increase the overall resource allocation efficiency of the economy. This pattern can be regarded as a "Kuznets-type" evolution of industrial structure.

2 This figure is an estimate based on reasonable assumptions, and is obviously below official statistics. See Cai et al., 2016.

References

Anderson, K., and Hayami, Y. (1986). *The Political Economy of Agricultural Protection*, Sydney: Allen & Unwin.

Brown, L. R. (1995). *Who Will Feed China? Wake-Up Call for a Small Planet*, New York: W. W. Norton.

Cai, F. (2015). The Making of Dual Economy as a Stage of Economic Development. *Economic Research Journal*, 7, pp. 4–15.

Cai, F. (2016). *China's Economic Growth Prospects: From Demographic Dividend to Reform Dividend*. Cheltenham, UK • Northampton, MA, USA: Edward Elgar Publishing Limited.

Cai, F., Guo, Z., and Wang, M. (2016). New Urbanisation as a Driver of China's Growth. In L. Song, R. Garnaut, F. Cai, and L. Johnston (eds.), *China's New Sources of Economic Growth, Vol. 1: Reform, Resources, and Climate Changes*, Canberra: ANU Press.

Cai, F., and Lu, Y. (2013). The End of China's Demographic Dividend: The Perspective of Potential GDP Growth. In R. Garnaut, F. Cai, and L. Song (eds.), *China: A New Model for Growth and Development*. Canberra: ANU Press, pp. 55–74.

Cai, F., and Wang, M. (2016). From Economy of the Poor to the Economy of Scale: Challenges of Shifting Development Stage to China's Agriculture, *Economic Research Journal*, 5, pp. 14–26.

Chen, X. (2015). Focal Issues of China's Agricultural Development, *Agriculture Machinery Technology Extension*, 7, pp. 4–7.

FAO (Food and Agriculture Organization of the United Nations) (2010). *2000 World Census of Agriculture: Main Results and Metadata by Country (1996–2005)*, Rome: Food and Agriculture Organization of the United Nations.

Gao, F. (2006). China's Agricultural Vulnerabilities and Pathway of Change. *Yunnan Social Sciences*, 3, pp. 49–53.

Gao, L., Huang, J., and Rozelle, S. (2012). Rental Markets for Cultivated Land and Agricultural Investments in China, *Agricultural Economics*, 43, pp. 391–403.

Hansen, G. D., and Prescott, E. C. (2002). Malthus to Solow. *American Economic Review*, 92(4), pp. 1205–1217.

Hayami, Y. (1988). *Japanese Agriculture under Siege: The Political Economy of Agricultural Policies*, New York: St. Martin's Press.

Johnston, B. F., and Mellor, J. W. (1961). The Role of Agriculture in Economic Development, *American Economic Review*, 51(4), pp. 566–593.

Yao, Y., and Han, M. (2015). Chen Xiwen on Land Transfer: Farmers' Choice Must Be Respected, Xinhua.com, http://news.xinhuanet.com/fortune/2015-03/06/c_1114552132.htm.

13 How can Chinese economic growth be transformed to a total-factor-productivity-driven pattern?

After passing the Lewis turning point, and facing the disappearance of demographic dividend, the resource reallocation effect obtained from workforce transfer among sectors and the effect of stable return on capital from unlimited labor supply will disappear gradually in China. According to the theoretical expectation, an inevitable way out is to transfer the economic growth of China to rely on total factor productivity, especially to the productivity basis related to technological advance. However, just as appeared in the corresponding development phase of other countries, in cases of deep intervention of government in economic activities, when government faces changes of comparative advantage, the easiest response to increase labor productivity is to increase the capital–labor ratio. However, such efforts often encounter reprisals of the law of diminishing returns on capital, and lead to other policy failures.

This paper discusses approaches to preventing diminishing returns on capital after the demographic dividend disappears. It puts forward the task of transition to a neoclassical growth phase based on analysis of China's challenges and with reference to international experience, i.e., developing a domestic Flying Geese Model and creative destruction policy environment through policy adjustment to improve resource reallocation efficiency, and gain higher efficiency from technological advance and system improvement, so as to realize the transition of China's economic growth to a total-factor-productivity-supported model, and avoid the fate of the middle-income trap.

13.1 Law of diminishing returns on capital

Hansen and Prescott (2002) united Malthus growth and neoclassical growth in one model, this united model broke up single economic model and the hypothesis of neoclassical growth theory, and admitted that land factor played an important role in Malthus growth model, while neoclassical model might not recognize this factor. However, analysis of these two growth models, which are successive in time and coexist in space, is difficult when it comes to explaining the typical dual economy development model of China, because it does not include the intermediate development phase summarized by Aoki

(2012), and it neglects the special role of the demographic dividend in the economic development model of East Asia. Argument among economists on the East Asia model is a case in point.

After the World Bank described an "East Asian Miracle" in the East Asia Regional Report for the first time in 1993, economists discussed the economic growth model of East Asia represented by the Four Asian Tigers. The empirical evidence on which different viewpoints are based is mainly the estimated result of total factor productivity of the East Asian economies. For example, based on the quantitative research of Liu and Yang et al., Krugman (1994) thought that the economic growth of East Asian countries and regions was not different from the growth model of the Soviet Union in the planned economy period, mainly relying on capital accumulation and labor input, yet with lack of productivity improvement. A specific manifestation was that, when total factor productivity increased slowly, it would eventually encounter diminishing returns and become unsustainable.

Not all empirical results support the viewpoint represented by Krugman. In the research in the mid-1990s, the estimated total factor productivity in the Four Asian Tigers and other countries in East Asia varied greatly. For example, according to the estimates of Young (1994), annual average growth rate of total factor productivity from 1970 to 1985 was 0.1 percent in Singapore, yet according to the estimates of Marti (1996), annual average growth rate of total factor productivity was 1.45 percent in this country from 1970 to 1990. Therefore, policy conclusions drawn from this empirical research are so different that some researchers (Felipe, 1997) cast doubt on such research approaches that evaluate success or failure of the East Asian growth model based on the calculated total factor productivity, arguing that some mistaken starting points for interpretation of real economic growth need to be changed.

Krugman's prediction of an unsustainable East Asian model did not come true after all. On the contrary, all of the Four Asian Tigers became high-income economies, crossing over the middle-income phase successfully. One of the reasons for such theoretical prediction error is that Krugman and other scholars did not notice the role of demographic dividend; they made judgment only according to the hypotheses of Western countries such as labor shortage and diminishing returns on capital. In fact, since rapid population change of these economies led to increase of the working-age population ratio and decrease of the dependency ratio, a demographic dividend of economic growth was generated, on the one hand, while resource reallocation efficiency was obtained from workforce transfer between sectors; on the other hand, diminishing returns on capital did not occur due to unlimited labor supply before a large contribution from technological advance was obtained, so high-speed economic growth could last for a long time.

The research on the contribution of the demographic dividend to economic growth in East Asia (Bloom and Williamson, 1997; Williamson, 1997) is a useful extension to traditional neoclassical growth theory and provides a more persuasive interpretation. In addition, with the improvement of measurement techniques and data, researchers find that there is not only high investment but also technological advance in East Asian countries and regions; what is more, through export-oriented economic development, they gain more efficient technology and management from imported equipment and introduced foreign funds, the growth rate of total factor productivity quickens perceivably, and its contribution to economic growth increases gradually (Bhagwati, 1996).

According to the same logic, after the demographic dividend disappears, labor shortage and rising wages will become increasingly common. In this circumstance, not only is economic growth driven by further reliance on capital and labor factors unsustainable, but labor productivity improved by blind increase of the capital–labor ratio will also be thwarted by diminishing returns on capital. Thus, if economic growth does not become total-factor-productivity-driven, it will slow down and even stagnate, and thus falling into the middle-income trap or high-income trap (as in Japan) will be inevitable.

For economists in different periods, a perennial subject is exploring sustainable source of economic growth. If only Malthus and Solow growth models are concerned, transition of economic development model from the former to the latter is mainly manifested, in a neoclassical growth situation, by the land factor ceasing to be important. If a dual economy development period is added, the strongest characteristic of this period is the role of the demographic dividend. However, though there is no doubt that unlimited labor supply may postpone diminishing returns on capital, yet such demographic dividend is limited and eventually will disappear inevitably with the change of demographic phase. Continual increase in labor productivity remains an unfailing source of sustainable economic growth.

Increase of the capital–labor ratio is one of the ways to increase labor productivity. The input of physical capital is faster than the input of workforce, thus the increase of capital composition in enterprises and industries is generally helpful to increase labor productivity. In reality, with the increase of labor cost, enterprises purchase more machines to substitute labor. Yet, the increase of the capital–labor ratio is limited: it will be thwarted by diminishing returns on capital. Diminishing returns on capital refers to the decrease of efficiency in the production process due to a lower degree of coordination between man and machine in cases where equipment is added yet the quality of labor remains unchanged. Although new machines and equipment also contain new technology, yet the critical factor is still the increase of capital intensity, rather than technological advance.

In recent years, the factors that promote labor productivity in China have evidently changed. According to the estimates of World Bank economists (Kuijs, 2009), the contribution of total factor productivity to the increase in labor productivity declined significantly from 46.9 percent in the period 1978–1994 to 31.8 percent in the period 2005–2009, and would further decline to 28.0 percent in the period 2010–2015. In the meantime, increase in labor productivity relied more on the increase of the capital–labor ratio caused by investment. In the above-mentioned three periods, the contribution of the capital–labor ratio to the increase in labor productivity rose from 45.3 percent to 64.7 percent, and would rise further to 65.9 percent. Relying only on the investment of physical capital as an economic growth source on the supply side is evidently unsustainable.

Increase in total factor productivity is a more fundamental way to increase labor productivity. Total factor productivity refers to additional production efficiency at fixed input level of various factors. This additional source of labor productivity may offset the adverse impact of diminishing returns on capital, and is a long-term, sustainable, unfailing engine of economic growth. As a residual error, total factor productivity comprises resource reallocation efficiency and micro production efficiency. In fact, the secret to improving total factor productivity in China is to understand how to keep continuous improvement of these two efficiencies, and increase their contribution rate to economic growth. Generally speaking, the main component of total factor productivity in China's economic growth thus far has been resource reallocation efficiency created by workforce transferred from agriculture to non-agricultural industries. From the perspective of special national circumstances in China, economic growth in future not only requires development of new total factor productivity sources, but also needs continuous exploitation of the traditional potential of total factor productivity.

13.2 Domestic Flying Geese Model

Resource reallocation efficiency is obtained from industrial restructuring, upgrading, or supererogation. For example, transfer of workforce and other factors from industries with low productivity to industries with high productivity is a typical form of resource reallocation between sectors. In addition, resource reallocation efficiency may also be developed within sectors, mainly manifested as expansion of the enterprise with the highest productivity, hence the scale of the high-efficiency enterprise becomes larger, and the enterprise may grow more rapidly.

In China's high-speed economic growth period, the contribution of resource reallocation to economic growth is very significant. In fact, the so-called demographic dividend is partially embodied in this contribution. Therefore, it is self-evident that, when the dependency ratio hits bottom and the demographic dividend disappears, labor transfer will also slow down significantly, and the relative contribution rate of this total factor productivity will decrease. Accordingly, the relative contribution rate of micro production efficiency should be increased, otherwise it is difficult to keep continuous economic growth. However, this is not to say that resource reallocation efficiency has no potential to further promote increase in total factor productivity.

Seemingly, "migrant worker shortage" related to the Lewis turning point, disappearance of the demographic dividend, and a rapid rise in the wages of unskilled workers portend the end of comparative advantage in the labor-intensive industries of China. An inevitable result seems to be, first, following the Flying Geese Model, labor-intensive industries will transfer to other developing countries where labor cost is cheaper. Second, the degree of labor surplus decreases, hence labor transfer slows down, meaning the source of resource reallocation efficiency is exhausted gradually. Such a conclusion is drawn due to lack of sufficient understanding of the particularities in China, so it will not become reality at least for a considerably long period.

The theoretical basis of the expected transfer of China's labor-intensive industries to other countries is the so-called Flying Geese Model. Development and improvement of this model experienced several phases, mainly contributed by Akamatsu, Okita, Vernon, Kojima, et al., and a relatively complete theoretical explanation of industry transfer between countries has been developed. This model was originally used to describe how Japan completed a whole catch-up process of "import–import substitution–export" in virtue of dynamic change of comparative advantage as an up-and-coming economy. Later, it was used extensively to explain and understand the economic development model of East Asia, i.e., Japan was the lead goose in that V-formation: labor-intensive industries were successively transferred to the Four Asian Tigers, ASEAN countries, and subsequently maritime provinces in China, according to the dynamic change of comparative advantage.

In the extended version of this model, it still retains the core original idea of industry transfer between countries and regions with relative change of comparative advantage. Second, industrial transfer in the Flying Geese Model is determined by characteristics related to the life cycle of products, thus implying correlation with dynamic change of comparative advantage. Third, the scope of interpretation is expanded to foreign direct investment mode, i.e., investing activity also follows the same logic between countries. Finally, huge differences between countries or regions in terms of development phase, resource endowment, and historical heritage are deemed critical to the various relationships in the Flying Geese Model.

From this theory and experience, transfer of China's labor-intensive industries to other countries is seemingly logical if labor cost increases continuously, and this has really occurred. However, considering the huge economic scale and territorial area of China, and the huge difference between domestic regions with respect to development level and resource endowment, we can expect that room for outward transfer of agricultural labor force still exists to generate resource reallocation efficiency and promote economic growth before the marginal productivity of agricultural and non-agricultural labor become equal, i.e. before the commercialization point comes (Ranis and Fei, 1961). Therefore, transfer of labor-intensive industries between regions occurs more between domestic regions, i.e., transfer from the eastern region to the midwest region. It may be seen that, at least in the next one to two decades, even the first demographic dividend still has potential.

Despite the huge development differences between the regions in China, only the difference in demographic transition may provide powerful grounds of argument for the above-mentioned assertion. Since fertility decline is the result of economic and social development, difference between China's regions in development phase also causes the midwest region to be in a relatively lagged phase in the demographic transition process. For example, the sixth population census data in 2010 showed that the average natural population growth rate (birth rate minus mortality rate) was 5.05 percent nationally, 4.68 percent in the eastern region, 4.73 percent in the central region, and 6.78 percent in the western region.

But, due to the factor of population movement, such difference of demographic transition could not be seen in the age structure of these three regions. For example, among all 153 million rural migrant workers who left their own townships for 6 months or more in 2010, those from the midwest region accounted for 68.2 percent, of whom the proportion of interprovincial floating rural migrant workers was 69.1 percent in the central region and 56.9 percent in the western region, of whom a large number flew to the eastern region. According to the definition of resident population, external population who live in cities for 6 months or more are generally counted as resident population in the place of workforce inflow. Since 95.3 percent of outgoing rural migrant workers are aged below 50 years old, therefore, such population mechanical dynamics increase working-age population ratio in the eastern region, decreasing this proportion in the midwest region. So population statistics in recent years cannot show the advantage of the midwest region in dependency ratio.

However, definition of resident population in the fifth population census in 2000, i.e., only population resident for over one year may be counted as resident population in the place of inflow, was closer to the registered residence principle of population; and scale of rural migrant worker movement at that time was small. We may find from the census data in different regions that the old age dependency ratio is lower in the midwest region than in the eastern region. The census shows that the average old age dependency ratio (i.e., the ratio of population aged 65 and above to the population aged between 15 and 64) is 10.15 percent nationally, 10.9 percent in the eastern region, 9.76 percent in the central region, and 9.53 percent in the western region. In Figure 13.1, we present the old age dependency ratio of the provinces, municipalities, and autonomous regions in three regions to illustrate significant regional disparity.

Rural migrant workers work in the eastern region, yet their registered permanent residence is still in the midwest region—what does such a situation mean? First, according to the existing institutional arrangement of registered permanent residence, they still cannot expect long-term stable lives and old-age care in their working region, so they generally return to farming when they grow older. Therefore, current labor engaged in farming or rural surplus labor in China mainly comprises peasants above 40 years old. Next, according to the reform of the household registration system in some regions, even if permanent residency conditions are relaxed for migrants in cities, this is limited

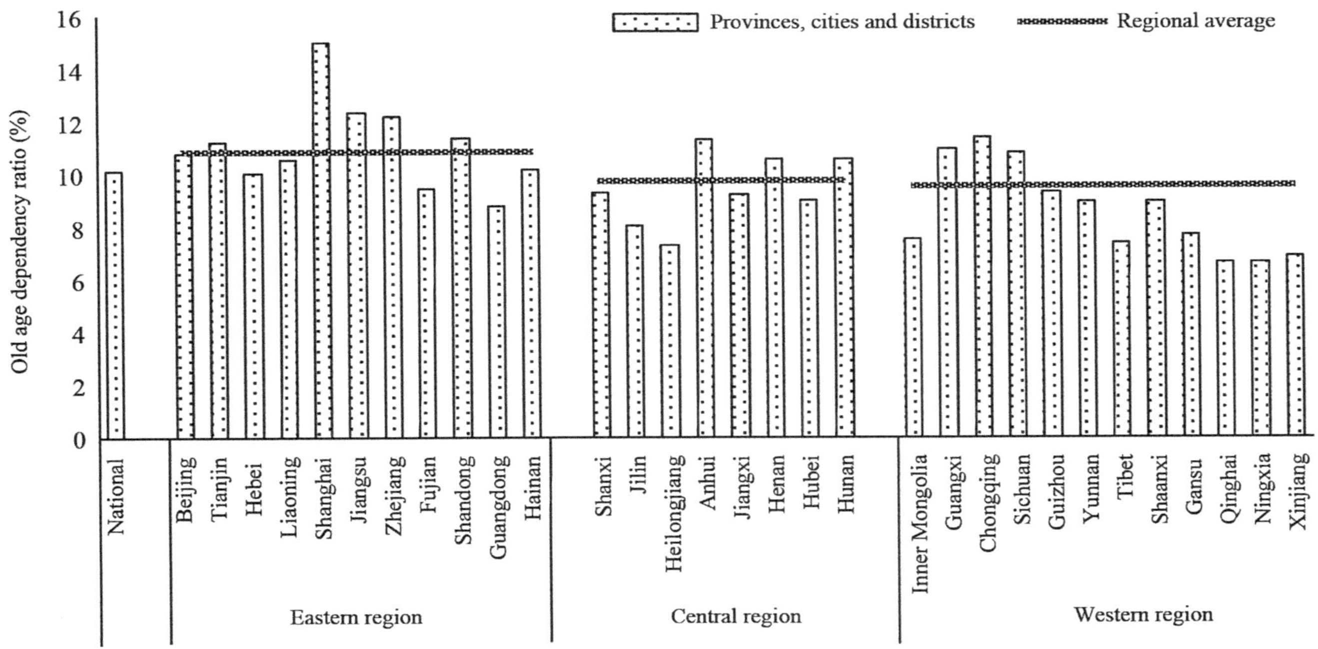

Figure 13.1 Old age dependency ratio in three regions.

Source: Fifth Population Census Data in 2000, www.stats.gov.cn/tjsj/ndsj/renkoupucha/2000pucha/pucha.htm.

to rural registered population in this province, so most rural migrant workers in the midwest region generally could not benefit from reform of the household registration system in coastal areas. We may see that, despite a great number of rural migrant workers flowing into the eastern region, those older rural laborers who find it difficult to overcome obstacles to interprovincial transfer, and who thus return to their registered residence, will be the labor supply base for industrial undertakings in the midwest region.

In 2010, China's GDP per capita reached 4,300 USD. Based on the growth rate over more than 30 years since the reform and opening-up, a constant RMB exchange rate, and other factors, at the end of the Twelfth Five-year Plan GDP per capita should exceed 6,000 USD, and be up to 12,000 USD by 2022 when a moderately prosperous society will be comprehensively established.[1] Industrial restructuring will further speed up to gain resource reallocation efficiency, supporting the increase in total factor productivity as per the same income composition, while per capita income increases continuously and China gradually becomes a high-income country. This means further decrease of the proportion of agricultural labor force.

Compared with middle-income countries whose GDP per capita is 6,000–12,000 USD, the transfer potential of China's agricultural labor force is still huge. We may find from the statistical data of some countries in this phase in 2007 that the average proportion of agricultural labor force was 14.8 percent, approximately 10 percentage points lower than China. This means that, in the next ten years, we could deduct nearly 2 million people per year from the existing agricultural labor force of 192 million , i.e., reduce it by 1 percentage point. Thus, we could keep a continuous increase of resource reallocation efficiency, and support sustainable economic growth in China.

Regional industrial allocation is not only determined by cost factor, but is also closely related to the clustering effect that influences the production cost and transaction cost of enterprises. Research (Qu, Cai, and Zhang, 2012) using manufacturing data for enterprises above a designated size (i.e., income from main business above 5 million yuan) and financial and tax data of the counties in China from 1998 to 2008 reveals that an industrial clustering effect dominated regional allocation of labor-intensive industries before 2004; the result was more concentrated in the eastern region. After that, this effect decreased gradually, and the rise of comprehensive operating cost and increase of factor cost in enterprises became important factors gradually influencing industrial allocation, which was manifested as transfer of manufacturing industry, especially labor-intensive industry, to the midwest inland region.

After China's economy passed through the Lewis turning point in 2004, such transfer of labor-intensive industry from the eastern region to the midwest region (mainly the central region) started. For example, the output value proportion of the eastern region in national labor-intensive manufacturing industry decreased from the highest point of 88.9 percent in 2004 to 84.7 percent in 2008, a yearly decrease exceeding 1 percentage point (Figure 13.2).

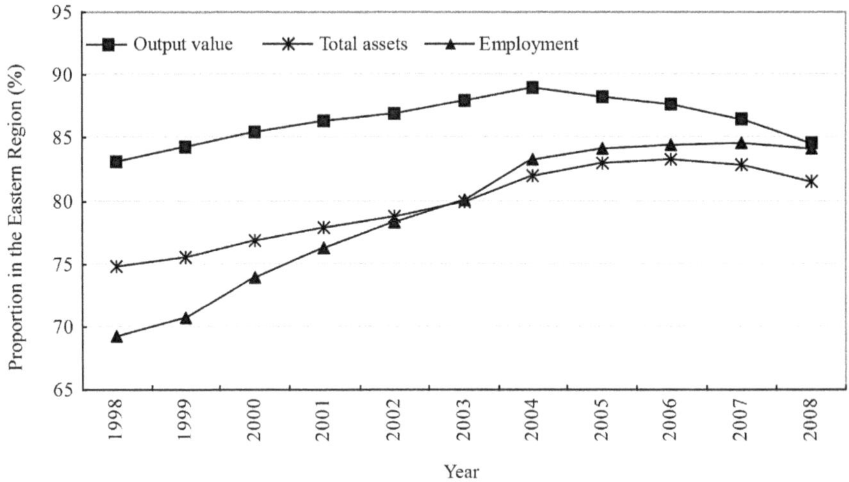

Figure 13.2 Proportion of labor-intensive manufacturing industry in the eastern region.

Source: Author's calculations according to survey data of national manufacturing enterprises.

Restricted by data availability, we may only see the changes over a mere 4 years since the Lewis turning point; nevertheless, it may be anticipated that, after 2008, this industrial transfer will not only continue, but also might speed up greatly.

13.3 Creative destruction mechanism

Total factor productivity appears as a residual error in the production function, of which the part left after separating resource reallocation efficiency is the micro production efficiency of total factor productivity. Numerous factors may increase the micro production efficiency of enterprises, for example, many factors related to systems, management, and technical innovation; in a word, all efficiency improvements brought by creative ideas and innovation are generally embodied in this part of total factor productivity. From the perspective of econometrics, if upgrading through change of industry structure is the only measurement index of resource reallocation efficiency, resource reallocation in the industry, based on which the most efficient enterprise could survive, develop, and become large-scale, may often be included in micro production efficiency. This efficiency source is very important: research on the United States (Foster et al. 2008; Foster et al., 2001) shows that resource reallocation that appears as enterprise entry, exit, expansion, and contraction in manufacturing industry contributes from one-third to half of the increase in productivity.

For already industrialized developed countries, micro production efficiency, especially the efficiency improvement brought by technological advance, is the main form of total factor productivity. Because in these countries regimes are relatively stable and mature, it may even be theorized as a given. Meanwhile, such countries have no significant technology gap with other countries as a whole, so have no late-mover advantage. Therefore, for most developed countries, since their steady economic growth rate is low, economic growth is difficult and slow, depending on the speed of technological advance. Any country that could not rely on technological innovation to realize external expansion of the production possibility frontier could not maintain an appropriate growth rate.

Japan is a classic example of unsuccessful transformation. Japan became a high-income country in the 1990s when the demographic dividend disappeared and economic growth could no longer rely on the late-mover advantage of closing the technology gap. However, to meet this change of development phase and subsequent change of production factor endowment structure, the response of Japan's economy was to input more physical capital, i.e., capital-deepening; in the meantime, performance of total factor productivity was unsatisfactory. The final result: in the average labor productivity of Japan's economy, the contribution rate of capital-deepening increased significantly from 51 percent in the period 1985–1991 to 94 percent in the period 1991–2000, while contribution rate of total factor productivity in the same period decreased from 37 percent to –15 percent (Figure 13.3).

The research of Japanese economist Fumio Hayashi and American economist Edward C. Prescott showed that the reason for economic slowdown in Japan since the 1990s was not the failure of capital market to help enterprises get the funds required for profitable investment, but the poor performance of total factor productivity. The reason for poor performance of total factor productivity lay in government subsidies for low-efficiency enterprises and declining industries. This led to a too high output fraction of low-efficiency enterprises and even "zombie firms," yet investment favorable to increasing productivity decreased correspondingly (Hayashi and Prescott, 2002).

Just as mentioned in ancient Chinese philosophy, there is no making without breaking, no flowing without damming, no motion without rest. If there is no creative destruction environment to let inefficient enterprises go extinct and let efficient enterprises survive and be developed, total factor productivity, especially micro production efficiency, cannot be dominant in economic growth, so in an environment closer to neoclassical growth, sustainable economic growth is impossible.

The author has discussed extensively the special challenges in the transition of China's economic growth model brought by the characteristic of "getting old before getting rich" (Cai, 2012). However, it is worth pointing out that this characteristic also buys time for the transition of China's economic growth model. That is to say, a huge gap exists in technological development level between China and developed countries; the market regime and system of

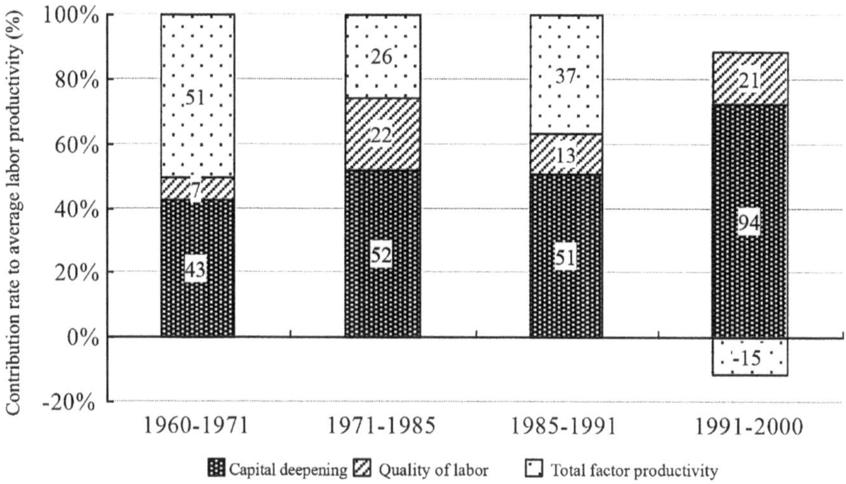

Figure 13.3 Japan's labor productivity sources in different periods.
Source: APO, 2008, p. 23.

resource allocation are not mature, and are twisted in many aspects. All this mean that China still has late-mover advantage in economic development, and may harvest abundant low-hanging fruit in the fields of system reform, management efficiency increase, application of new technology, etc., to improve micro production efficiency notably. In the period of high-speed economic growth, the main source of China's total factor productivity was the resource reallocation efficiency obtained from transfer of workforce between sectors and regions; micro production efficiency should become the more important source of total factor productivity in the new economic development phase.

To maintain sustainable growth, this efficiency source relies on innovative behaviors of enterprises. Management modes and technology should be selected to maximize efficiency, while the government should not exceed its duties and meddle in any microeconomic activity. The government should create an equal competitive environment, let inefficient enterprises exit business, and let efficient enterprises survive, develop, and expand in scale, and eliminate the institutional barriers unfavorable to using new technology.

13.4 Beware of policy distortions

If maintaining the growth of total factor productivity is the only way for any country to enter a high-income phase through continuous economic growth, this task is the most challenging for all countries, and very difficult in practice. In some countries, it is even an "impossible task" to increase the growth of total factor productivity. In fact, adverse policy inclinations seem to appear most likely when the task of increasing total factor productivity becomes more urgent. This may explain puzzles, for example, why the economic growth of numerous countries declines in advance, why countries at middle-income level cannot break away from the middle-income trap for a long time, or why Japan runs into economic stagnation at high-income level.

Increase in total factor productivity is more challenging for China. After the Lewis turning point comes, and when the demographic dividend disappears, potential tendencies unfavorable to increase in total factor productivity appear, regardless of people's recognition of the need for further development, or policy inclination to embrace new challenges, or the practice of economic development. For example, correlational research, by estimating production function, divides China's economic growth in the reform and opening-up period into five contributions, namely, capital, labor, human capital, dependency ratio (demographic dividend), and total factor productivity (Figure 13.4). It may be seen that the contribution rate of total factor productivity tends to decrease. Here we may infer the potential danger for two sources of total factor productivity, i.e. resource reallocation efficiency and micro production efficiency, as well as construction of the policy environment required to increase total factor productivity.

In recent years, industrialization has accelerated in the midwest region. Since the beginning of this century, the central government has implemented various strategies to promote rapid development in the midwest region, for example, the western development strategy, the strategy of revitalizing the old industrial base in the northeast, and the Rise of Central China strategy. In

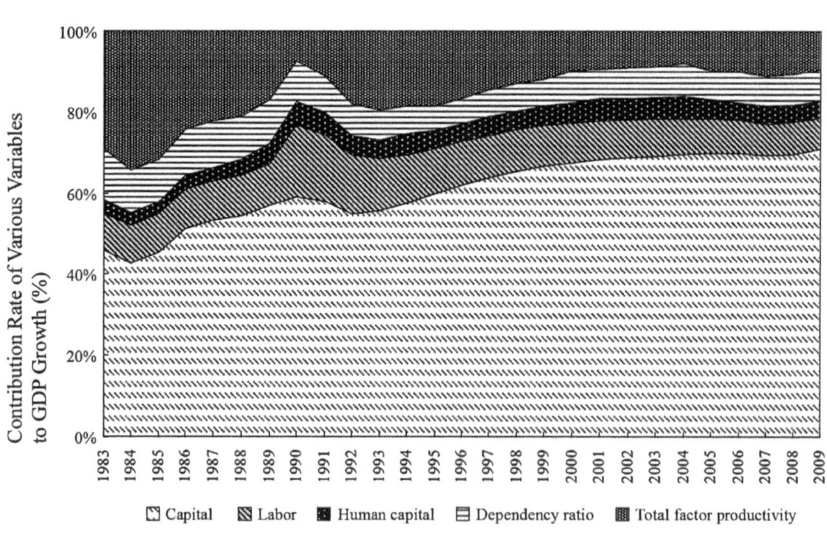

Figure 13.4 Contribution rate of various sources to China's economic growth.
Source: Cai and Zhao, 2012.

the implementation of these strategies, the central government has provided large-scale investment, transfer payments, and other financial support in the form of subsidies for various projects, including infrastructure construction, production capacity-building investment, social security, and public services projects, changing the regional allocation pattern of resource investment significantly in the midwest region. For example, proportion of total social investment in fixed assets of the midwest region increased from 41.2 percent in 2000 to 48.1 percent in 2008, wherein the proportion of state-owned economy increased from 47.0 percent to 58.2 percent in national total investment.

Such an investment structure further enhances the status of state-owned economy. This may be verified indirectly from a statement of a government official. In January 2006, the Deputy Director of the Revitalizing Northeast China Office of the State Council at that time, Song Xiaowu, delivered a speech at the "International Workshop on Improving the Investment Environment for Revitalizing Northeast China." He said that in the two years since the strategy of revitalizing old industrial bases in northeast China was implemented, the state-owned economy in three provinces of northeast China had been centralized to lifeblood industries of national economy. State control and influence had evidently been enhanced (Hu and Sun, 2006).

Government efforts to close the regional development gap are necessary, and industrial policy to promote the catch-up of backward regions should also be properly implemented. In the end, however, such regional development strategy cannot deviate from regional comparative advantage. We describe this principle in Figure 13.5. As shown in the figure, industry layout in compliance with regional comparative advantage should theoretically be represented by the straight line YX, i.e., regions where the economy is relatively backward generally have the resource advantage of relatively abundant

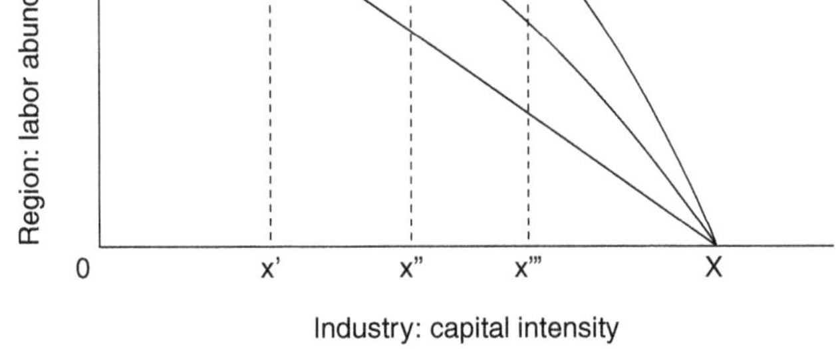

Figure 13.5 Regional comparative advantage and industry selection.

labor, so industry is generally more labor-intensive, in other words capital intensity is relatively low. To the contrary, in developed regions, where labor cost is relatively high and capital is relatively abundant, industry structure should have high capital intensity and technology intensity. For example, in a region with labor abundance y', the industry corresponding to its resource endowment should be x'.

However, in the implementation of regional development strategy, on the one hand industrial policy should foresee the dynamic change of comparative advantage, hence may properly guide industry selection; on the other hand, investment for improving infrastructure in backward regions inevitably has higher capital intensity, therefore resource endowment vs. industry structure shown as YDX shape is also appropriate. For example, in case labor abundance is still y', the matched industry may be x''. However, it is very difficult to strike a balance of moderate guidance: exceeding the necessary and reasonable amplitude, for example industrial allocation in curve YFX position, means deviation from the regional comparative advantage. The shown industry capital intensity x''' corresponding to y' in the same region is undoubtedly too high, if comparing the industry type with resource endowment in this region. In that case, resource reallocation efficiency is unavailable.

The development gap measured by per capita income implies a difference in resource endowment structure, i.e., developed regions have a relatively abundant capital factor, so have comparative advantage in capital-intensive industry, while the relatively undeveloped regions have comparative advantage of abundant labor at low cost. The difference in resource endowment structure between eastern and midwest regions may undoubtedly become an economic catch-up opportunity for the midwest region. However, since the Lewis turning point, the industrialized catch-up trend in the midwest region of China is unsustainable due to its inconsistency with the generally accepted comparative advantage of the midwest region.

The specific index of capital intensity in manufacturing industry of the midwest region is capital–labor ratio. It rose rapidly after 2000, much faster than coastal areas, and after rising fast in 2003 and 2004, the absolute level of capital intensity was higher than in coastal areas. For example, in 2007 the capital–labor ratio of manufacturing industry was 20.1 percent and 25.9 percent higher respectively in the central region and western region than in the eastern region. That is to say, manufacturing industry in the midwest region became more capital-intensive, and the degree of heavy industrialization became higher. Since new investment in the midwest region adopted relatively advanced technology and processes, favorable to the increase in total factor productivity and labor productivity within a certain period and certain limits, and faster than the rise of wage levels, this was therefore favorable to decreasing the unit labor cost over a certain period.[2] However, with the disappearance of the demographic dividend, further increase of capital intensity would encounter diminishing returns.

The continuation of the government-led economic growth model is unfavorable to the development of a creative destruction mechanism, hindering increase in total factor productivity. At present, government-led economic growth is mainly embodied in a too high proportion of government investment. The state-owned economy still has a monopoly, and accordingly, small and medium-sized enterprises encounter entry barriers and other discrimination in development conditions, for instance, financing. In 2010, state-owned and state-holding enterprises accounted for 42.3 percent of total urban investment in fixed assets. Among industrial enterprises above a designated size, total assets of state-owned and state-holding enterprises accounted for 41.8 percent, gross output value accounted for 26.6 percent, profit accounted for 27.8 percent, main business tax and extra charges accounted for 71.7 percent, and employment accounted for 19.2 percent.

This too high proportion of state-owned economy hinders the increase of enterprise efficiency and thus overall economic health. If a state-owned economy is more protected, and relatively inhibits non-public economy accordingly, the creative destruction mechanism becomes ineffective. In China's orientation of industrial policies and industrial organizations, some industries and sectors are granted a strategic position, so entry of non-public economy is strictly restricted in those sectors where state-owned economy must keep "absolute control," for example, military industry, the electric power grid, petroleum and petrochemicals, telecommunication, coal, air transport, and the shipping industry. And the state-owned economy must keep "strong control" in some basic and pillar sectors, including equipment manufacturing, automobiles, electronic information, building, iron and steel, non-ferrous metals, chemicals. Here, the expressions of "control" to different degrees require state-owned capital to keep sole proprietorship, absolute holding, or conditional relative holding (Ren and Liu, 2006).

Monopoly in these sectors not only appears as various barriers against free entry, but also no exit of inefficient enterprises. In addition, the government is reluctant to let any low-efficiency, large-scale, state-owned enterprise exit operation in consideration of output value, tax, employment stability, and thus social stability. What is more, in case of monopolistic operation, low-efficiency state-owned enterprises make profits due to their monopoly position.

Such monopoly position of state-owned economy inevitably hinders the application of new technologies by its very nature. In China's current development phase, sustainability urges technological advance, the transfer of enterprise development, and economic growth along efficiency-driven tracks such as technological advance, as soon as possible. No matter what China's overall economy level or enterprise level, new technology is not a restrictive factor; the most important thing is incentive for new technologies and applicability of selected technologies. As economists have pointed out (Parent and Prescott, 2010), existing expertise, creative ideas, and scientific knowledge

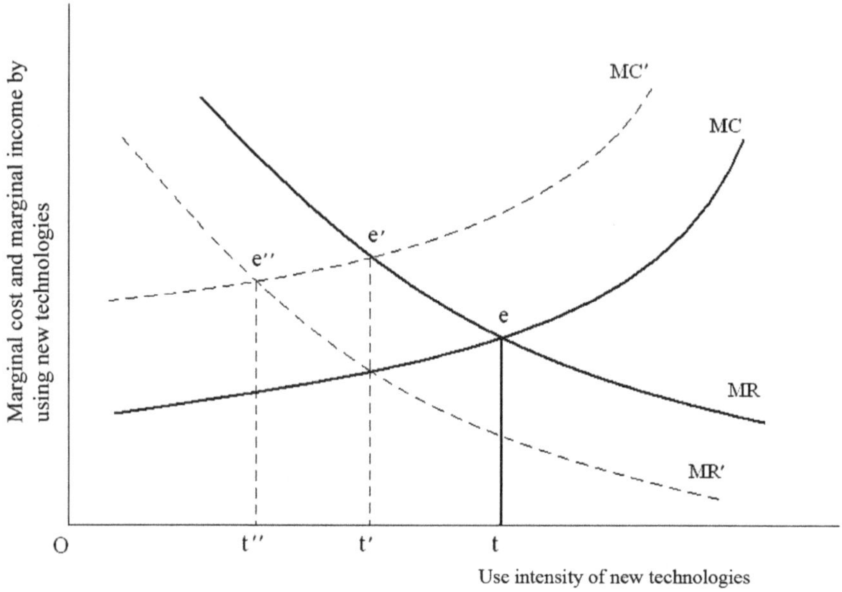

Figure 13.6 How monopoly hinders the use of applicable technologies.

may be obtained by each country and each enterprise; therefore, this does not cause difference of total factor productivity. However, if monopoly and protection exist, problems such as insufficient incentive for technology application and improper choice of technology will appear. These two problems are interrelated, because lack of incentive for technology application also means lack of incentive for reasonable selection of applicable technologies.

We use Figure 13.6 for illustration. If various technologies already exist, application of technologies is not exploration on the forefront of innovation, but only search, purchase, reference, and adaptive innovation issues. However, whether enterprises use new technologies or not, and to what degree, depends on the comparison of marginal cost and marginal income from using new technologies. That is to say, enterprises make decisions to use new technologies on the principle of maximum gross income. As shown in the figure, marginal income represented by MR has a degressive nature, while marginal cost represented by MC has an incremental nature; balanced choice of technology is generally located on the intersection point of two curves; for example, at point e in the figure, enterprises will make a choice of technology t.

Relying on cheap and readily available funds, land, and natural resources, as well as operation under restricted competition, state-owned enterprises tend not to use more efficient new technologies, or they twist the decision-making principles for use of new technologies and select inappropriate technologies for use, and thus develop enterprise technology composition of low efficiency. This means movement of the marginal cost curve to the top left, or movement of the marginal income curve to the bottom left, or both occurring simultaneously; then the use of new technologies cannot reach optimal level. As shown in the figure, choice of technology is not at level t, but at level t' or even t'.

The inevitable result is that, after rejecting the profit-making factors due to monopoly position, the efficiency of state-owned economy will be significantly lower than non-state-owned enterprises that account for a larger proportion in more competitive sectors. Such judgment of lower efficiency of state-owned economy than non-public economy has been verified by numerous researchers. For example, Dollar and Wei (2007) showed that average return on capital of private enterprises was 50 percent higher than wholly state-owned enterprises. Brandt and Zhu (2010, Table A1) showed that the average annual growth rate of total factor productivity in state-owned sectors calculated using official data in the period 1978–2007 was 1.36 percent, while the growth rate in non-state-owned sectors was 4.74 percent; the former was equivalent to only 28.7 percent of the latter.

The existence of state-owned enterprises hinders the formation of survival of the fittest through enterprise entry and exit. Poor performance of total factor productivity in the overall economy is inevitable if resource reallocation efficiency is unavailable in industry. For example, econometric research reveals that resource reallocation barriers lead to resource misallocation in Chinese industrial enterprises, and great differences exist in marginal productivity of capital and labor between enterprises in the sectors. Simulation of such research shows that, if difference of marginal productivity factor between Chinese industrial enterprises were narrowed to the level of the United States, the total factor productivity of China's industry would increase 30 to 50 percent (Hsieh and Klenow, 2009).

13.5 Conclusion

Ever since Solow laid the cornerstone of neoclassical growth theory, the decisive role of total factor productivity for breaking up diminishing returns on capital, and thus keeping sustainable economic growth, has been widely accepted, and supported by more and more empirical research. For example, this type of research conducted by economists has proved that total factor productivity may explain the difference of per capita income level between countries, the collapse of planned economy in the former USSR, Japan's "lost decade," and the slowdown in many high-growth countries.[3] Beyond all doubt, total factor productivity is an important factor, and may be used to explain why some countries fall into the middle-income trap, some countries face the challenge of the middle-income trap, while other countries may avoid or break away from the middle-income trap.

When providing suggestions for China to formulate and implement the Twelfth Five-year Plan, American economist Paul Romer (2011) proposed pertinently that the central government should change the practice of evaluating political achievements of local government in promoting economic development according to GDP, and should carry out corresponding evaluation and assessment according to the improvement of total factor productivity; he particularly advised breaking down the entire economy into a number of parts for statistics and accounting of total factor productivity. Theoretically speaking, now that China's local government not only has strong motivation to promote local economic development, but also has considerable power and satisfactory effect in execution of central economic and social development goals, then this proposal is undoubtedly of great significance for incentive and guidance from local government in pursuit of a more sustainable economic growth model.

Historically, the experience of Singapore also proves that whether or not the government recognizes the importance of improving total factor productivity is not insignificant for the transition of economic growth model. After the questioning and criticizing of Young and Krugman on Singapore's growth miracle, and the great debate among economists concerning the economic growth model of East Asia and the performance of total factor productivity, although the Singapore government did not concede to economists' criticism of its growth model and "preferred to believe," it especially recognized the importance of total factor productivity for sustainable economic growth, and set the goal of increasing total factor productivity 2 percent per year (Felipe, 1997). Perhaps that is why Singapore's economic development ultimately did not let the predictions of those economists come true.

Huge space still exists to increase total factor productivity in China regardless of the resource reallocation efficiency between agricultural and non-agricultural industries, or micro production efficiency in industrial sectors and enterprises. However, significant increase in total factor productivity really needs a series of human capital conditions and system environment. Evidently, these factors and corresponding reform should be an independent research subject.

Notes

1 Since the economic growth rate might slow down, it might be a little late to reach 12,000 USD, but China's GDP per capita in 2022 will surely fall into the bracket of 6,000–12,000 USD.
2 For two research efforts in this aspect, see Cai et al., 2009a and 2009b.
3 In such research, the most representative important publications include Parent and Prescott, 2010; Krugman, 1994; Hayashi and Prescott, 2002; and Eichengreen et al., 2011.

References

Aoki, M. (2012). The Five-Phases of Economic Development and Institutional Evolution in China and Japan, in M. Aoki and J. Wu (eds.), *The Chinese Economy: A New Transition*, Basingstoke: Palgrave Macmillan.

APO (Asian Productivity Organization) (2008). *APO Productivity Databook 2008*, Tokyo, APO.

Bhagwati, J. N. (1996). The Miracle that Did Happen: Understanding East Asia in Comparative Perspective, Keynote speech, Conference on Government and Market: The Relevance of the Taiwanese Performance to Development Theory and Policy in honor of Professors Liu and Tsiang, Cornell University, 3 May, 1996.

Bloom, D., and Williamson, J. (1997). Demographic Transitions and Economic Miracles in Emerging Asia, *NBER Working Paper No. 6268*, Cambridge, MA: National Bureau of Economic Research.

Brandt, L., and Zhu, X. (2012). Accounting for China's Growth, *Working Paper No. 395*, Toronto: Department of Economics, University of Toronto.

Cai, F. (2012). Getting Old before Getting Rich and Sustainability of China's Economic Growth, *Review of International Economics*, 1.

Cai, F., Wang, D., and Qu, Y. (2009a). Flying Geese within Borders: How Does China Sustain Its Labour-intensive Industries? in R. Garnaut, L. Song, and W. T. Woo (eds.), *China's New Place in a World in Crisis: Economic, Geopolitical and Environmental Dimensions*, Canberra: ANU Press, pp. 209–232.

Cai, F., Wang, M., and Qu, Y. (2009b). China's Industrial Reconfiguration and Labor Mobility Trends, *China Industrial Economics*, 8.

Cai, F., and Zhao, W. (2012). When Demographic Dividend Disappears: Growth Sustainability of China, in M. Aoki and J. Wu (eds.), *The Chinese Economy: A New Transition*, Basingstoke: Palgrave Macmillan.

Dollar, D., and Wei, S. (2007). Das (Wasted) Kapital: Firm Ownership and Investment Efficiency in China, *NBER Working Paper No. 13103*, Cambridge, MA: National Bureau of Economic Research.

Du, Y., and Wang, M. (2011). Aggregate Employment and Employment Structure in China: Reestimation and Discussion, in F. Cai (editor in chief), *Reports on China's Population and Labor (No. 12): Challenges during the 12th Five-Year Plan Period: Population, Employment, and Income Distribution*, Beijing: Social Sciences Academic Press.

Eichengreen, B., Park, D., and Shin, K. (2011). When Fast Growing Economies Slow Down: International Evidence and Implications for China, *NBER Working Paper No. 16919*, Cambridge, MA: National Bureau of Economic Research.

Felipe, J. (1997). Total Factor Productivity Growth in East Asia: A Critical Survey, *EDRC Report Series No. 65,* Manila: Asian Development Bank.

Foster, L., Haltiwanger, J., and Krizan, C. J. (2001). Aggregate Productivity Growth: Lessons from Microeconomic Evidence, in C. R. Hulten, M. J. Harper, and D. Edwin (eds.), *New Developments in Productivity Analysis*, Chicago: University of Chicago Press.

Foster, L., Haltiwanger, J., and Syverson, C. (2008). Reallocation, Firm Turnover, and Efficiency: Selection on Productivity or Profitability? *American Economic Review*, 98, pp. 394–425.

Hansen, G. D., and Prescott, E. (2002). Malthus to Solow, *American Economic Review*, 92, pp. 1205–1217.

Hayashi, F., and Prescott, E. C. (2002). The 1990s in Japan: A Lost Decade, *Review of Economic Dynamics*, 5(1), pp. 206–235.

Hsieh, C.-T., and Klenow, P. J. (2009). Misallocation and Manufacturing TFP in China and India, *Quarterly Journal of Economics*, 124(4), pp. 1403–1448.

Hu, T., and Sun, Y. (2006). Evident Increase of State-Owned Economic Control in Two Years Since the Implementation of Revitalizing Northeast China Strategy, official web portal of the Chinese Central Government, www.gov.cn/jrzg/2006-01/16/content_160944.htm.

Kojima, K. (2000). The "Flying Geese" Model of Asian Economic Development: Origin, Theoretical Extensions, and Regional Policy Implications, *Journal of Asian Economics,* 11, pp. 375–401.

Krugman, P. (1994). The Myth of Asia's Miracle, *Foreign Affairs*, 73(6), pp. 62–78.

Kuijs, L. (2009). China through 2020 – a Macroeconomic Scenario, *World Bank China Research Working Paper No. 9*, Washington, DC: World Bank.

Marti, C. (1996). Is There an East Asian Miracle? *Union Bank of Switzerland Economic Research Working Paper*, Zurich: Union Bank of Switzerland.

Parent, S., and Prescott, E. (2010). *Barriers to Riches*, Beijing: China Renmin University Press.

Qu, Y., Cai, F., and Zhang, X. (2012). Have the "Flying Geese" in Industrial Transformation occurred in China? in H. McKay and L. Song (eds.), *Rebalancing and Sustaining Growth in China*, Canberra: ANU Press.

Ranis, G., and Fei, J. C. H. (1961). A Theory of Economic Development, *American Economic Review*, 51(4), pp. 533–565.

Ren, F., and Liu, B. (2006). SASAC: State-Owned Economy Should Keep Absolute Control over Seven Industries, official web portal of the Chinese Central Government, www.gov.cn/jrzg/2006–12/18/content_472256.htm.

Romer, P. (2011). Analysis of the Optimized New Growth Model of China, in C. Lin and M. Spence (eds.), *The Medium and Long Term Development and Transformation of China's Economy—Thinkings and Suggestions from an International Perspective*, Beijing: CITIC, pp. 572–587.

Williamson, J. (1997). Growth, Distribution and Demography: Some Lessons from History, *NBER Working Paper No. 6244*, Cambridge, MA: National Bureau of Economic Research.

Young, A. (1994). Lessons from the NICs: A Contrarian View, *European Economic Review*, 38, pp. 964–973.

14 The new normal

The macro history and grand logic of China's economic development

In 2014, China's President Xi Jinping remarked for the first time that China's economy had entered into the "new normal". Since then, the concept with Chinese characteristics has been developed and enriched and has become a cornerstone in understanding the Chinese economy. This theory offers important guidance for China to complete its mission of building an overall well-off society by 2020 and realizing further ambitions beyond this timeframe. By providing theoretical insight and empirical evidence on the present stage of China's economic development, this paper intends to shed light on the concept of the new normal.

The new normal of China's economy is not a symptom of mid- and short-term cyclical volatility or any known long-cycle phenomenon. Rather, it marks a new stage in the long course of China's economic development and a new milestone in the renaissance of the Chinese nation. In this historical context, we must identify the factors of economic growth deceleration from the supply-side perspective, capture the new features of structural reforms, and make appropriate choices for advancing reforms to reap reform dividends. By tapping traditional growth potentials and exploring new sources of growth, China's economy will be able to sustain moderate to high growth in the mid- and long-run, thus achieving the first and second "Centennial Goals" by 2020 and 2050 as adopted at the Eighteenth CPC National Congress (to build an overall well-off society by 2020 and to build a modern socialist country by the middle of the twenty-first century).

14.1 New normal of China's economic development

Some problems in economic activities are local and occasional, caused by short-term disruptions, which fall under the study of theory of the business cycle, while others reflect long-term, overall trends that are inevitable. Such problems usually fall under the study of economic growth theory or economic history, requiring researchers and policy-makers to have a historical depth in order to maintain a sober-minded understanding of strategic priorities and take correct countermeasures. President Xi Jinping remarked that China's development must be viewed in the broad perspectives of time and space in order to properly live with and direct the new normal.

The new normal is first characterized by slowdown of economic growth. Economists habitually attempt to explain economic growth deceleration from the perspective of business cycles. For instance, macroeconomists summoned up various manifestations and forms of business cycles and offered all sorts of analytical frameworks for comprehending it. In the policy toolbox, all sorts of weaponry have been made available to implement countercyclical measures.

In economic history, there have appeared short cycles of three to four years known as Kitchin cycles; medium-term cycles lasting nine to ten years known as Juglar cycles; mid- and long-term cycles of 20 to 25 years known as Kuznets cycles; as well as long-term business cycles spanning five to six decades known as Kondratieff cycles (Tvede, 2006). In the process of economic development in the capitalist world, various types of business cycles alternate with economic crises, both of which have proved unavoidable. Business cycles, economic recessions, and financial crises and their resultant problems have become a catalyst of macroeconomics and a long-term issue in the discipline's development.

In most instances, business cycles are caused by demand-side shocks. Once disruptions, whether internal or external, cause the inadequacy of aggregate demand to become so serious that the speed of real growth is significantly below the potential growth rate, negative growth gaps (difference between actual and potential growth rate) will occur and the factors of production will be underutilized, resulting in serious cyclical unemployment. In this situation, most macroeconomists believe that with their countercyclical functions, macroeconomic policies intended to stimulate aggregate demand may be adopted to spur economic growth and iron out growth gaps. These policies range from loose monetary policy and/or expansionary fiscal policy to other policies used in combination such as industrial policy and even regional policy.

During its unprecedentedly robust growth in the period of reform and opening-up, China's economy also experienced a few rounds of cyclical deceleration resulting in growth gaps. According to Cai and Lu (2013), during 1979–1994 and 1995–2010, China's potential growth rates were 9.66 percent and 10.34 percent respectively. By subtracting the actual growth rates from the corresponding potential growth rates, we may arrive at the growth gaps of various years. Such a calculation shows that in the 30-odd years before 2010, China's economic growth experienced three cycles with four troughs, that is, the four biggest growth gaps of –0.42 percent in 1981, –5.82 percent in 1990, –2.72 percent in 1999, and –1.13 percent in 2009 (Cai, 2016). Interestingly, the span between any two adjacent troughs was generally between nine and ten years, which coincided with the features of Juglar cycles (Figure 14.1).

In a retrospect of China's economic development since reform and opening-up in 1978, the few growth decelerations occurred when the factors of production were underutilized, as embodied in severe employment shocks. Similarly,

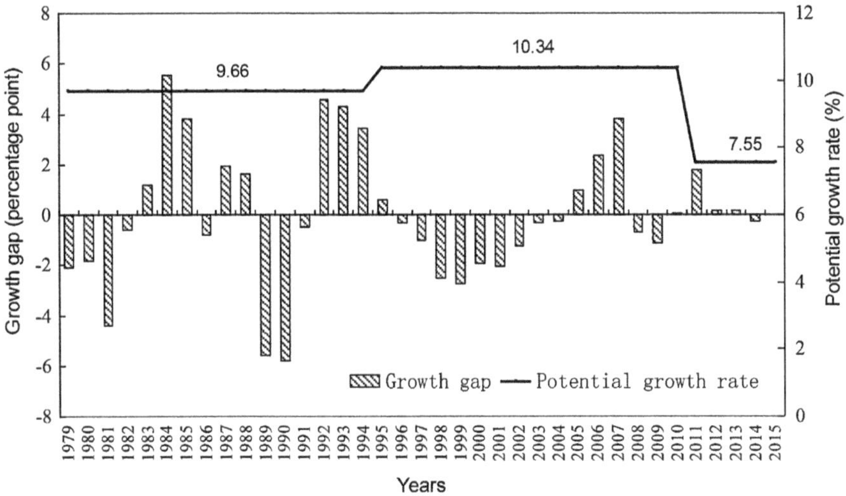

Figure 14.1 Potential growth rates and growth gaps of China's economy.
Source: Cai and Lu (2013); *China Statistics Yearbook* (various years).

despite the different forms and intensities of each slowdown, macroeconomic policies all intervened by spurring economic growth to iron out the cycles and lift actual growth to potential growth rate (Cai, 2015).

Since the deceleration of China's economy in 2012, China's GDP growth rate has been on the decline. Assuming that potential growth rates remained around 10 percent by previous experience, China's annual growth rates registered 7.7, 7.7, 7.3, and 6.9 percent respectively during 2012–2015, which formed widening growth gaps. However, according to the estimation and forecast by Cai and Lu (2013), China's potential growth rate will drop from an average of 7.55 percent during the Twelfth Five-Year Plan period (2011–2015) to 6.20 percent during the Thirteenth Five-Year Plan period (2016–2020). In this case, no growth gaps exist. The question is: why will China's potential growth rate fall so steeply? This question must be addressed at three levels: the historical context of China's renaissance, the transition from the middle-income to the high-income stage, and the changing stage in economic development.

14.2 Understanding characteristics of the Chinese new normal from a historical perspective

According to the World Bank database, China's GDP aggregate in current-price US dollars was 10.35 trillion in 2014, accounting for 13.28 percent of the world total; China's per capita GDP in current-price US dollar was 7,590, or 70.68 percent of the world average. According to the World Bank classification in 2014, countries with per capita gross national income (or per capita GNI, roughly equivalent to per capita GDP) below 1,035 US dollars are low-income countries; countries with per capita GNI between 1,035 and 4,086 US dollars are lower middle-income countries; countries with per capita GNI between 4,086 and 12,616 US dollars are upper middle-income countries; countries with per capita GNI above 12,616 US dollars are high-income countries. Being ranked as an upper middle-income country, China is in a historical position nearer to its great renaissance than ever before.

British scientific historian Joseph Needham devoted his entire life to the study of the development of science and technology in ancient China. He discovered that from the third century BC to the fifteenth century AD, China's scientific inventions and discoveries far outstripped those of Europe and led the world throughout most of the history before being overtaken by the West (Temple, 2007). Economic historians such as Kenneth Pomeranz (2003) demonstrated with extensive historical evidence that the Orient represented by China used to be the center of the world economy, which had been far more advanced than the Occident before the "Great Divergence" occurred 400 years ago, when Western countries gained an upper hand of scientific and technological inventions and championed the Industrial Revolution.

After this turning point, the chasm between developed and developing countries came into existence and widened. The late economic historian Angus Maddison verified the above conclusion with demographic and GDP data of major countries and regions. Based on the historical data compiled by Maddison, we may depict China's journey of transformation from prosperity to decline in the past nearly 200 years and back to prosperity since the initiation of reform and opening-up.

From Angus Maddison's works (Maddison 2003, 2007, 2009), we may collect cross-regional data on GDP and per capita GDP ranging from AD 1 to AD 2003, based on the concept of purchasing power parity and with 1990 as the base year. Furthermore, we updated Maddison's data series to 2014 based on the World Bank dataset in term of purchasing power parity in 2011 international dollars. Using this long-term historical data series, this paper respectively calculated the share of China's GDP in the world economy and the percentage of China's per capita GDP relative to the world average (Figure 14.2). Despite various defects in the data series and different statistical standards as compared with data used for country comparison, these are the only available and extensively recognized data that may help us depict the course of China's development across the longest time span.

As shown in Figure 14.2, China's per capita GDP was no less than the world average level between AD 1000 and 1600. After that, China's relative per capita income began to decline but its economy as a whole still ranked high as a share in the world total. In 1820, China's GDP aggregate accounted for 32.9 percent of the world total. While Western countries embraced the Industrial Revolution, however, China missed the opportunities of technological and industrial revolutions, with the share of its GDP in the world

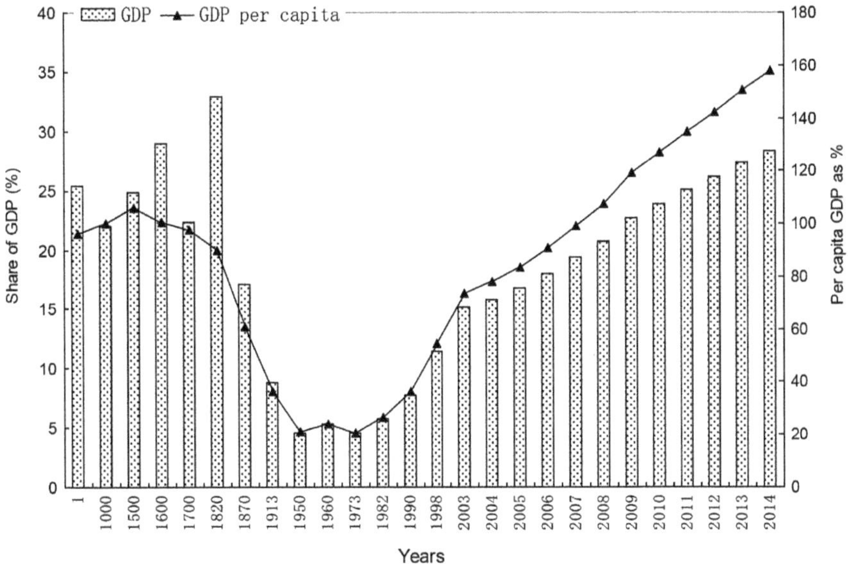

Figure 14.2 Change of China's status in the world economy.

Source: Data of 2003 and before are taken from Maddison, 2003, 2009, and 2007, p. 379, Tables A.4 and A.7; data after 2004 are calculated based on the growth rates of relevant indices recorded in the World Bank database, http://data.worldbank.org.

total and per capita GDP relative to the world average on the decline until the founding of the People's Republic of China in 1949.

In the first 30 years after the founding of the People's Republic of China in 1949, China swiftly recovered from war's devastation, established an independent industrial system, and achieved fairly rapid economic growth. After the 1950s, while the world economy ushered in a period of "great convergence" (Spence, 2011, Part One), China stumbled and failed to realize its vision to catch up with developed countries due to a series of mistakes in its economic developments during this period. According to Maddison's data, China's GDP growth rate (5.0 percent) and per capita GDP growth rate (2.9 percent) on annual average during 1950–1978 were only slightly above world average levels (4.6 and 2.7 percent respectively) and its economic level and living standard remained low.

Since reform and opening-up in 1978, China has achieved the most enduring economic upsurge for any single economy after World War II for over three decades and significantly narrowed its gaps with advanced economies in terms of the level of development and standard of living. This remarkable achievement is clearly manifested in Figure 14.2. It needs to be noted that the horizontal scale of Figure 14.2 is not even. In other words, what is shown in the chart is a V-shaped course of China's development. The first part of this course is characterized by China's economic decline from a superpower to the bottom of the world, which is measured through a long time span, while the latter half of this course shows that in a very short period of time, China's economy was miraculously restored to its historical position and beyond.

It took 58 years for the United Kingdom to double its per capita income from 1780 to 1838, 47 years for the United States from 1839 to 1886, 34 years for Japan from 1885 to 1919, 11 years for South Korea from 1966 to 1977, while only nine years for China from 1978 to 1987. Afterwards, it took eight years and nine years for China to double its per capita income during 1987–1995 and again in 1995–2004 respectively. By 2011, China's income per capita had doubled for the third time, which only took seven years. China's GDP aggregate only ranked tenth in 1990, but overtook Canada, Spain, and Brazil in 1995 to rank seventh. By 2000, China surpassed Italy to become the sixth largest economy in the world. In the first decade of this century, China successively overtook France, the UK, and Germany and surpassed Japan in 2009 to become the world's second largest economy, after only the United States.

China's rise as the world's second largest economy, and its per capita GDP crossing the threshold of the upper middle-income category, coincided with a demographic turning point. That is, according to the Sixth National Census, China's working-age population, between 15 and 59 years, peaked in 2010 before shifting to negative growth thereafter. Prior to this demographic shift, China's rapid economic growth had been largely fueled by a surging working-age population and falling dependency ratio. Unlimited labor supply increased China's savings rate, deferred diminishing return to capital, maintained sufficient supply of labor and human capital, and raised resource allocation efficiency through labor mobility. As the result of such a demographic transition, stage of economic development inevitably changed.

According to econometric analysis, during 1982–2009, capital accumulation contributed 7.1 percentage points to China's average GDP growth rate of 10 percent, labor contributed 0.8 percentage points, education (human capital) 0.4 percentage points, falling dependency ratio 0.7 percentage points, and total factor productivity (TFP) 0.1 percentage point (Cai and Zhao, 2012). Nearly half of the TFP increase derived from resource reallocation efficiency. As such, the shifting stage of development characterized by diminishing demographic dividends indicates the weakening of traditional drivers of economic growth, which led to a falling potential growth rate (Figure 14.1) and actual economic growth rate.

Hence, China's economic growth deceleration must be put into perspective of the following facts. First, in the course of China's renaissance, China has leaped from low-income to middle-income and upper middle-income status within a short time and is striving to join the ranks of high-income countries. The new normal characterized by slowing growth is a result of this historical transition. Second, the rationale of the new normal is to speed up the transition of economic growth pattern, tap new sources of growth, and maintain a more balanced, more inclusive, and more sustainable growth rate. Third, there are challenges facing China in maintaining its growth momentum—namely, (1) institutional barriers deterring sufficient supply and efficient allocation of production factors, (2) the legacy of previously implemented stimulus policies that cause excessive debt, overcapacity, and heavy reliance on investment, and (3) while traditional sources of growth (demographic dividend) are being exhausted, more sustainable sources of growth (TFP and human capital) tend to weaken as well.

Given the urgency and difficulty of tackling the challenges, China must promote supply-side structural reforms that spur a reasonable speed of growth in order to complete its mission of great renaissance.

14.3 Developing the Chinese economy under the new normal through supply-side structural reforms

If economic growth deceleration is caused by demand-side factors, it makes sense to identify policy paths and instruments through the national economy identity—namely, $Y = C + I + G + (E - M)$—or the analytical approach of the demand-side "troika" (export, consumption, and investment). Now that China's economic slowdown is caused by supply-side factors, the answer may no longer be found under such an analytical framework. On the contrary, we must proceed with analysis through the production function $(Y = A * F(K,L) = K^{\alpha} * (AL)^{1-\alpha})$[1]. That is, increasing labor supply, improving return on capital, and enhancing TFP is the only way to maintain a reasonable economic growth rate.

In the discussion on the growth slowdown of the world economy, one argument contends that insufficient effective demand is caused by the lack of willingness of firms and investors to invest. For instance, Reinhart and Rogoff (2010) attributed the growth conundrum of developed countries and the world economy to borrowing sprees and the consequent deleveraging. Koo (2008) echoed this view through his revelation at the micro level that after the burst of asset bubbles, firms changed their operational behavior and instead of continuing to pursue maximal profits, strove to repair their balance sheets and refrained from borrowing as lavishly as before.

In addition, some other views also gained ground in Western countries. For instance, Ben Bernanke blamed the emerging markets for splashing cash and causing a savings glut and Paul R. Krugman offered his explanation of a Keynesian liquidity trap. Lawrence Summers (2016) made a clear-cut remark that the problems facing developed countries were on the demand side rather than supply side. Specifically, he put forward an argument of "secular stagnation", attributing the problems to excessively low "neutral" real interest rates. He pointed to the ineffectiveness of conventional monetary policy as a cure.

Despite the differences in the above views, they have one thing in common: they all resorted to the demand side and cycle theory in explaining why investment was sluggish and the economy stalled. While China's growth deceleration is also manifested in falling willingness to invest, the reason for China's slowing economy has nothing to do with any of the above explanations and must be found in supply-side factors. Supply of production factors and productivity improvement (resource reallocation and technological progress) determine the potential growth rate of an economy from the supply side. Hence, supply-side structural reforms are intended to eliminate institutional barriers to the supply of production factors, the efficiency of their allocation, and the improvement of TFP, to remove unbalanced, uncoordinated, and unsustainable factors, to explore the potentials of traditional growth momentum, and to kick-start new drivers of sustainable growth. Obviously, supply-side structural reforms are an inevitable option under the overarching logic of the new normal.

Falling actual growth rates as a result of diminishing potential growth are manifested in diminishing return to capital investment resulting from labor shortage, which undercuts the willingness of firms and investors to increase their investment in the real economy and thus prevents aggregate output from expanding as rapidly as before. As such, structural reforms must be advanced with targeted reform priorities.

First is to eliminate institutional barriers deterring labor mobility and tap the potentials of labor supply. The core assumption of the neoclassical theory of growth based on Western experience is that the limited supply of labor may cause diminishing return to capital. As shown by China's experience of dual economy development, if labor supply is sufficient, the law of diminishing return to capital will not hold and return to investment will stay high for a certain period of time. Given that China's working-age population between 15 and 59 years has begun to experience negative growth since 2011 and the economically active population of the same age group will also record negative growth in 2018, China must increase effective allocation and labor participation in order to expand labor supply. Following the principle of resource allocation efficiency, the promotion of labor migration from the countryside to cities and the flow of labor across industries and enterprises may all achieve the effect of raising labor participation in high-productivity sectors, increasing labor supply, and improving allocation efficiency to mitigate diminishing return to capital.

Second, insufficient human capital is another important reason for diminishing return to capital. The negative growth of working-age population reduces not only new entrants to the labor market but the entry of human capital as well. By aggregating the numbers of graduates of junior middle school, high school, and college/university who enter into the workforce without pursuing further studies, we may arrive at the number of new workforce entrants, which already peaked in 2012 and diminished thereafter. Consequently, the total amount of human capital, which is calculated by summing up graduates at all levels of education with the weight of their average years of schooling, also peaked in 2013 before diminishing. Slowing human capital improvement in tandem with accelerating substitution of labor by capital inevitably undermined return to capital and TFP growth. Hence, reform of educational and training systems will also contribute to increase potential growth rates and thus the actual growth rate of the Chinese economy.

Third, unbalanced, uncoordinated, and unsustainable factors in economic operation take their toll on return to investment. These persistent ills of economic development are manifested in high leverage ratios, excessive real estate inventory, overcapacity, zombie firms, and areas with apparent weakness. These problems indicate distorted allocation of capital, labor, land, and other factors. The most prominent drawback is the inefficiency of allocation and slowing TFP improvement. To this end, the Chinese government has been correctly committed to addressing overcapacity, reducing inventory, deleveraging, lowering cost, improving weak links, and disposing of zombie firms. To accomplish those tasks, China must create new systems and mechanisms for resource allocation based on the decisive role of market forces, in addition to setting up quantitative objectives.

Finally, the above-mentioned areas of structural reform aim to correct distortions in resource allocation and foster a policy environment and incentive mechanism in favor of innovative development, creating sustained sources of growth—namely, TFP improvement primarily derived from resource reallocation and technological progress. In the context of dwindling potential for labor migration from agriculture to urban sectors, the reallocation of production factors among sub-sectors and among enterprises within subsectors will become the linchpin of resource allocation efficiency. As shown by the experience of advanced market economies, the mechanism of creative destruction characterized by the entry, exit, survival, and death of enterprises contributes one third to one half of TFP improvement (Foster et al., 2008). Hence, the aforementioned reforms with clear objectives must directly or indirectly enhance TFP through the improvement of resource allocation efficiency and the creation of a conducive policy environment and institutional mechanisms.

Notable progress has already been made in economic reform endeavors initiated at the Eighteenth CPC National Congress and particularly the Third and Fifth Plenary Sessions of the Eighteenth CPC Central Committee. Nevertheless, some reform endeavors failed to make good on their targets, stagnated, or encountered some inaction and resistance at the local level. As a result, the progress of reforms falls short of the requirement of "making all systems more sophisticated and established" by the end of the Thirteenth Five-Year Plan period. The question is: why is progress lacking for some prioritized reform areas on which consensus has already been reached? The following observations may shed light on which understandings must be clarified, which barriers must be overcome, and which circumstances must be avoided in order to advance supply-side structural reforms.

First, structural reforms are not a trade-off for economic growth. Rather, they may bring about tangible reform dividends manifested in increase of potential growth. As a result of underappreciated benefits of reform, reform incentives have been insufficient. Over the years, it has been considered both in and outside China that a trade-off exists between reform and growth; at best, the progress of reform may be achieved at a certain sacrifice of speed. For government departments or local governments highly concerned with economic growth rate, specific instruments may be employed to implement demand-side stimulative policies swiftly and promptly. On the contrary, supply-side structural reform endeavors appear to be invisible and intangible and are not clearly correlated with the effects.

Second, reform responsibilities are not properly assigned to governments at various levels. As a result, the costs and dividends of reform are not properly shared and reform incentives are not proportionate. Because reformers who bear the cost of reform may not benefit from the dividends of reform, some departments and local authorities have followed a wait-and-see attitude toward reform. As is universally observed in international experiences, it takes a lot of work to convince reformers and create incentives. Yet it pays to cajole reformers into believing in the existence of reform dividends and foster reasonable expectations on the sharing of reform costs and dividends (Rajan, 2016). This is vital to initiating reforms in certain areas such as reform of the household registration system.

Third, under the above misunderstandings and practical obstacles, the reform blueprint drawn by the central government failed to fully bear fruit and certain areas of reform are shunned, delayed, or even deviated from their original intentions, timetables, and roadmaps, more or less. This is manifested in the following facts: (1) in the choice between supply-side structural reforms and demand-side stimulus plans, there has been a preference for and even reliance on the latter, which delayed the timing of implementing reforms; (2) due to the overemphasis on meeting quantitative targets rather than eliminating defects in institutional mechanisms, the symptoms of problems are addressed without correcting the root causes; (3) reform performers tend to choose light-touch and administrative approaches in promoting reforms, while avoiding shaking up vested interests and transforming institutional mechanisms.

14.4 Triumphing over the "new mediocre" of the world economy through the new normal, Chinese style

China's rapid growth coincided with the golden period of Western countries and emerging economies in a climax of economic globalization and was therefore buoyed by favorable external demand during the reform period prior to the 2008–2009 financial crisis. China's entry to the WTO in particular yielded tremendous dividends. The eruption of the global financial crisis marked the end of the golden period of growth for Western countries and the world economy is falling into what Christine Lagarde, the managing director for the International Monetary Fund, described as the "new mediocre". Economic globalization also suffered setbacks. Against this stark reality, it needs to be recognized that, even though the external shocks of sluggish world economy and trade may not be to blame for China's growth slowdown, the external environment of China's economic development has indeed deteriorated.

Still, China's economic growth deceleration is generally independent from the changing world economy pattern and a sign of its own economic development entering into the new normal. Thus, world economic recovery is helpful but not essential to China's maintenance of economic growth. On the other hand, supply-side structural reforms are expected to kick-start new momentum of economic growth to help China's economy move beyond the "new mediocre" of the world economy through the new normal.

Trying to come to conclusions based on cross-country and time series data, which tend to see the trees but not the forest when they are applied to the present situation of the Chinese economy, some predictions conducted by international scholars underestimate China's future economic growth rate.[2] For example, based on a statistical law called "regression to the mean", Pritchett and Summers (2014) predicted that China's economic growth rate would drop to 5.01 percent during 2013–2023 and 3.38 percent during 2023–2033; based on the assumption that China cannot remain an exception to the "iron rule" of convergence on 2 percent forever, Barro (2016) came out with the prediction that China's economic growth rate would quickly drop to 3–4 percent.

As demonstrated by the author and his coauthor (Cai and Lu, 2013), even without additional stimulus and reform initiatives, China's economy is still able to maintain a growth significantly higher than the world average for a fairly long period of time following the trend of natural decline of potential growth rates. More importantly, structural reforms will unleash extra potentials—that is, a reform dividend—by eliminating barriers to the supply and allocation of production factors and increase of TFP.

A proper understanding of the new normal will help policy-makers to recognize the existence of reform dividends and create a mechanism to reasonably split the reform costs and share the reform benefits among the stakeholders of reforms and different social groups, with a proper balance between short-term and long-term interests. In this manner, reforms will proceed precisely as intended and yield dividends that serve as long-term drivers of China's economy to triumph over the "new mediocre" of the world economy through the new normal.

In view of the new normal of China's economic development, the challenges it faces, and its reform objectives, Cai and Lu (2016) have made assumptions on the effects of reforms of the household registration system and education and training systems, postponement of the retirement age, and reduction of the tax burden for enterprises, that is, the positive effects of such reforms on labor participation rate, human capital, and TFP. In addition, they aligned the above effects with family planning policy adjustments of different levels of intensity (thus corresponding to different fertility scenarios) to simulate the future scenarios of China's potential economic growth rates. The differences of potential growth rates between the scenarios of more reforms and fewer reforms are the dividends of supply-side structural reforms. As revealed by

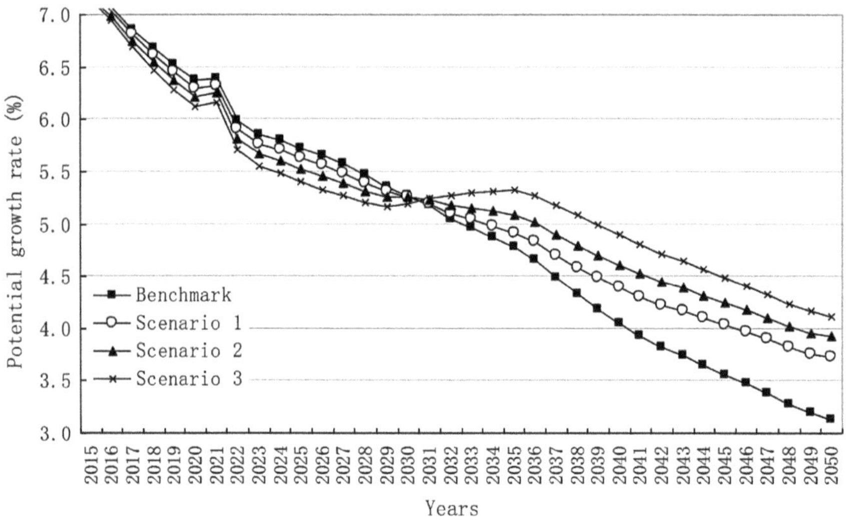

Figure 14.3 Simulation of dividends of supply-side structural reforms.
Source: Based on results from Cai and Lu, 2013.

the simulation results (Figure 14.3), reforms with different levels of intensity may yield reform dividends on different scales (that is, additional potential growth rates).

It is also clearly revealed in Figure 14.3 that the following three conclusions may be drawn from observations on China's long-term economic growth tendency based on the perspectives of supply-side factors and potential reform dividends. First, following the logic of the new normal, that is, the slowdown is not a short-term turbulence but long-term trend, one should not expect a V-shaped rebound through implementing countercyclical policy measures. Second, compared with the "benchmark scenario" without significant reform measures taken, deeper reforms will generate significantly positive effects on labor participation rate, human capital, and TFP, thus bringing the long-term course of potential growth rate closer to an L-shaped pattern. Third, supply-side structural reforms will undoubtedly spur the potential growth rate and make China's economy remain fast-growing for a fairly long period of time.

Figure 14.3 appears to show that under the scenarios of more intense reforms, potential growth rates demonstrate a deeper decline in the short- and mid-run and will rise only in the long-run. In fact, falling potential growth rates in the short- and mid-run are mainly based on the simulation result that assumes a rising dependency ratio caused by a substantially increased fertility rate in the short-run. However, our assumption of population forecast is that total fertility rate would rise under the population policy relaxation, reaching 1.94 in 2017 before falling to a stable level of 1.71 thereafter.

It needs to be noted that despite the necessity for broader policy adjustments, that is, better provision of basic public services should be offered to households as birth incentives, the assumption of a rising fertility rate in Figure 14.3 could be too optimistic. Moreover, this assumption of population growth may generate dual effects, that is, if actual population growth falls short of expectation, the effects of falling short- and mid-run potential growth rates and rising long-term potential growth rates could be less potent; meanwhile, a diminishing population base is conducive to rising per capita GDP.

According to World Bank data and income-grouping criteria, China's per capita GNI was 7,400 US dollars in 2014, according to which it joined the rank of upper middle-income countries. With this base point, we may subtract the simulated potential growth rate of GDP based on "Reform Scenario 3" in Figure 14.3 from the estimated natural population growth rate to forecast the increase of China's per capita GDP (or GNI) and reveal a few important time points.

Based on this forecast and following the constant price of 2014 (thus also the comparable grouping criteria of the World Bank), China's per capita GNI will reach 12,600 US dollars by 2022—reaching the threshold between the upper middle-income group and the high-income group and initially crossing the middle-income stage; 19,007 US dollars by 2030—cementing its status as a high-income country and successfully avoiding the middle-income trap; 32,162 US dollars by 2040—approaching the average income level of high-income countries (37,000 US dollars); and 51,900 US dollars by 2050—securing its status as a high-income country of the high-income group. The implication is that the achievement of the second "Centennial Goal"—to build a modern socialist country by the middle of the twenty-first century—will vastly improve China's national strength and people's livelihood.

Notes

1 In this equation, *Y* is output or GDP and *K* and *L* respectively denote capital and labor (other factors of production such as human capital may also be included), while *A* denotes technological progress or TFP.

2 For critical comments on such studies, see Cai, 2016.

References

Barro, R. J. (2016). Economic Growth and Convergence, Applied Especially to China, NBER Working Paper *No. 21872*, Cambridge, MA: National Bureau of Economic Research.

Cai, F. (2015). The Role of Macro Economic Policy in Promoting More and Better Jobs in China: Issues, Evidence and Policy Options, *Studies in Labor Economics*, 3.

Cai, F. (2016). A Supply-side Perspective on China's Economic Deceleration, *Studies in Labor Economics*, 4.

Cai, F., and Lu, Y. (2013). The End of China's Demographic Dividend: The Perspective of Potential GDP Growth, in R. Garnaut, F. Cai, and L. Song (eds.), *China: A New Model for Growth and Development*, Canberra: ANU Press, pp. 55–74.

Cai, F., and Zhao, W. (2012). When Demographic Dividend Disappears: Growth Sustainability of China, in M. Aoki and Jinglian Wu (eds.), *The Chinese Economy: A New Transition*, Basingstoke: Palgrave Macmillan.

Foster, L., Haltiwanger, J., and Syverson, C. (2008). Reallocation, Firm Turnover, and Efficiency: Selection on Productivity or Profitability? *American Economic Review*, 98(1), pp. 394–425.

Koo, R. C. (2008). *The Holy Grail of Macroeconomics: Lessons from Japan's Great Recession*. New York: John Wiley & Sons.

Maddison, A. (2003). *The World Economy: A Millennial Perspective* (Chinese version). Beijing: Peking University Press.

Maddison, A. (2007). *Contours of the World Economy, 1–2030 AD: Essays in Macro-Economic History*, Oxford: Oxford University Press.

Maddison, A. (2009). *The World Economy: Historical Statistics* (Chinese version), Beijing: Peking University Press.

Pomeranz, K. L. (2003). *The Great Divergence: China, Europe, and the Making of the Modern World Economy* (Chinese version). Nanjing: Jiangsu People's Publishing House.

Pritchett, L., and Summers, L. H. (2014). Asiaphoria Meets Regression to the Mean, NBER Working Paper *No. 20573*, Cambridge, MA: National Bureau of Economic Research.

Rajan, R. (2016). Why Are Structural Reforms So Difficult? *Comparative Studies*, 2.

Reinhart, C., and Rogoff, K. S. (2010). Growth in a Time of Debt, *American Economic Review*, 100(2), pp. 573–578.

Spence, M. (2011). *The Next Convergence: The Future of Economic Growth in a Multispeed World*, New York: Farrar, Straus and Giroux.

Summers, L. H. (2016). The Age of Secular Stagnation: What It Is and What to Do About It, *Foreign Affairs*, 95(2), pp. 2–9.

Temple, R. K. G. (2007). *The Genius of China: 3000 Years of Science, Discovery, and Invention*, London: André Deutsch.

Tvede, L. (2006). *Business Cycles: History, Theory and Investment Reality*. Chichester: John Wiley & Sons.

Index

Note: Page numbers in *italics* indicate figures and in **bold** indicate tables on the corresponding pages.

For Product Safety Concerns and Information please contact our EU
representative GPSR@taylorandfrancis.com
Taylor & Francis Verlag GmbH, Kaufingerstraße 24, 80331 München, Germany

www.ingramcontent.com/pod-product-compliance
Ingram Content Group UK Ltd.
Pitfield, Milton Keynes, MK11 3LW, UK
UKHW010959180926
475701UK00004B/459

* 9 7 8 1 0 3 2 2 3 5 9 0 5 *